ANALYTICAL PHILOSOPHY

SECOND SERIES

ANALYTICAL PHILOSOPHY

SECOND SERIES

Edited by

R. J. BUTLER

Associate Professor of Philosophy, University of Toronto

BARNES & NOBLE INC. · NEW YORK

PUBLISHERS · BOOKSELLERS · SINCE 1873

© *Basil Blackwell & Mott Ltd.*, 1965

PRINTED IN GREAT BRITAIN

CONTENTS

PREFACE

The present years are exciting ones philosophically. Sometimes the climate of opinion evolves more rapidly than the leading players realize and, curiously, their achievement is greater when their manner of achieving is not the subject of scrutiny. Too much philosophy of philosophy gives philosophers the cramp, but this kind of affliction, still rampant in some quarters, is not the disabling disease that it was. There is a return to hard-headed subjects, to problems which would have commanded the attention of Leibniz, Hume, Mill or Peirce. Not infrequently it is a return to *their* problems.

In the First Series I remarked that cross-fertilization of methods and a general broadening of interests defeat the attempt to classify contemporary analytical philosophy into ' schools of thought '. Probably there has never been a period when English-speaking philosophers were so curious to know of philosophical happenings in other parts of their world. Widespread travel between academic centres has done more than anything else to generate the dialogue which has produced this cross-fertilization.

Since I prepared the First Series attention has focussed to quite a remarkable extent upon problems raised by Mr. P. F. Strawson in *Individuals*: upon the problems rather than upon the book. Four papers selected for the Second Series stem from that source.

None of the papers in this volume has previously been published. I wish to thank all who encouraged me by allowing me to read their unpublished writings, and my colleagues at the University of Toronto for their interest and co-operation.

R.J.B.

BRAINS AND BEHAVIOUR[1]

H. Putnam

Once upon a time there was a tough-minded philosopher who said, ' What is all this talk about " minds ", " ideas ", and " sensations "? Really—and I mean *really* in the real world—there is nothing to these so-called " mental " events and entities but certain processes in our all-too-material heads.'

And once upon a time there was a philosopher who retorted, ' What a masterpiece of confusion!' Even if, say, *pain* were perfectly correlated with any particular event in my brain (which I doubt) that event would obviously have certain properties—say, a certain numerical intensity measured in volts—which it would be *senseless* to ascribe to the feeling of pain. Thus, it is *two* things that are correlated, not *one*—and to call *two* things *one* thing is worse than being mistaken; it is utter contradiction.'

For a long time dualism and materialism appeared to exhaust the alternatives. Compromises were attempted (' double aspect ' theories), but they never won many converts and practically no one found them intelligible. Then, in the mid-1930s, a seeming third possibility was discovered. This third possibility has been called *logical behaviourism*. To state the nature of this third possibility briefly, it is necessary to recall the treatment of the natural numbers (*i.e.*, zero, one, two, three . . .) in modern logic. Numbers are identified with *sets*, in various ways, depending on which authority one follows. For instance, Whitehead and Russell identified zero with the set of all empty sets, one with the set of all one-membered sets, two with the set of all two-membered sets, three with the set of all three-membered sets, and so on. (This has the appearance of circularity, but they were able to dispel this appearance by defining ' one-membered set ', ' two-membered set ', ' three-membered set ', &c., without using ' one ', ' two ', ' three ', &c.) In short, numbers are treated as *logical constructions out of sets*. The number theorist is doing set theory without knowing it, according to this interpretation.

[1] This paper was read as a part of the programme of The American Association for the Advancement of Science, Section L (History and Philosophy of Science), December 27th, 1961.

What was novel about this was the idea of getting rid of certain philosophically unwanted or embarrassing entities (numbers) without failing to do justice to the appropriate body of discourse (number theory) by treating the entities in question as logical constructions. Russell was quick to hold up this ' success ' as a model to all future philosophers. And certain of those future philosophers—the Vienna positivists, in their ' physicalist ' phase (about 1930)—took Russell's advice so seriously as to produce the doctrine that we are calling *logical behaviourism*—the doctrine that, just as numbers are (allegedly) logical constructions out of *sets*, so *mental events* are logical constructions out of actual and possible *behaviour events*.

In the set theoretic case, the ' reduction ' of number theory to the appropriate part of set theory was carried out in detail and with indisputable technical success. One may dispute the philosophical significance of the reduction, but one knows exactly what one is talking about when one disputes it. In the mind-body case, the reduction was never carried out in even *one* possible way, so that it is not possible to be clear on just *how* mental entities or events are to be (identified with) logical constructions out of behaviour events. But, broadly speaking, it is clear what the view implies: it implies that all talk about mental events is translatable into talk about actual or potential overt behaviour.

It is easy to see in what way this view differs from both dualism and classical materialism. The logical behaviourist agrees with the dualist that what goes on in our brains has no connection whatsoever with what we *mean* when we say that someone is in pain. He can even take over the dualist's entire stock of arguments against the materialist position. Yet, at the same time, he can be as ' tough-minded ' as the materialist in denying that ordinary talk of ' pains ', ' thoughts ', and ' feelings ' involves reference to ' Mind ' as a Cartesian substance.

Thus it is not surprising that logical behaviourism attracted enormous attention—both pro and con—during the next thirty years. Without doubt, this alternative proved to be a fruitful one to inject into the debate. Here, however, my intention is not to talk about the fruitfulness of the investigations to which logical behaviourism has led, but to see if there was any upshot to those investigations. Can we, after thirty years, say anything about the rightness or wrongness of logical behaviourism? Or must we say that a third alternative has been added to the old two; that we cannot decide between three any more easily than we could decide between two; and that our discussion is thus half as difficult again as it was before?

One conclusion emerged very quickly from the discussion pro and con logical behaviourism: that the extreme thesis of logical behaviourism, as we just stated it (that all talk about ' mental events ' is translatable into talk about overt behaviour) is false. But, in a sense, this is not very interesting. An extreme thesis may be false, although there is ' something to ' the way of thinking that it represents. And the more interesting question is this: what, if anything, can be ' saved ' of the way of thinking that logical behaviourism represents?

In the last thirty years, the original extreme thesis of logical behaviourism has gradually been weakened to something like this:

(1) That there exist entailments between mind-statements and behaviour-statements; entailments that are not, perhaps, analytic in the way in which 'All bachelors are unmarried ' is analytic, but that nevertheless follow (in some sense) from the meanings of mind words. I shall call these *analytic entailments*.

(2) That these entailments may not provide an actual *translation* of ' mind talk ' into ' behaviour talk ' (this ' talk ' talk was introduced by Gilbert Ryle in his *Concept of Mind*), but that this is true for such superficial reasons as the greater ambiguity of mind talk, as compared with the relatively greater specificity of overt behaviour talk.

I believe that, although no philosopher would to-day subscribe to the older version of logical behaviourism, a great many philosophers[1] would accept these two points, while admitting the unsatisfactory imprecision of the present statement of both of them. If these philosophers are right, then there is much work to be done (*e.g.*, the notion of ' analyticity ' has to be made clear), but the direction of work is laid out for us for some time to come.

I wish that I could share this happy point of view—if only for the comforting conclusion that first-rate philosophical research, continued for some time, will eventually lead to a solution to the mind-body problem which is independent of troublesome empirical facts about brains, central causation of behaviour,

---

[1] *E.g.*, these two points are fairly explicitly stated in Strawson's *Individuals*. Strawson has told me that he no longer subscribes to point (1), however.

evidence for and against non-physical causation of at least some behaviour, and the soundness or unsoundness of psychical research and parapsychology. But the fact is that I come to bury logical behaviourism, not to praise it. I feel that the time has come for us to admit that logical behaviourism is a mistake, and that even the weakened forms of the logical behaviourist doctrine are incorrect. I cannot hope to establish this in so short a paper as this one[1]; but I hope to expose for your inspection at least the main lines of my thinking.

Logical Behaviourism

The logical behaviourist usually begins by pointing out what is perfectly true, that such words as ' pain ' (' pain ' will henceforth be our stock example of a mind word) are not taught by reference to standard examples in the way in which such words as ' red ' are. One can point to a standard red thing, but one cannot point to a standard pain (that is, except by pointing to some piece of *behaviour*) and say: ' Compare the feeling you are having with this one (say, Jones's feeling at time t_1). If the two feelings have the identical *quality*, then your feeling is legitimately called a feeling of *pain*.' The difficulty, of course, is that I cannot have Jones's feeling at time t_1—unless I *am* Jones, and the time *is* t_1.

From this simple observation, certain things follow. For example, the account according to which the *intension* of the word ' pain ' is a certain *quality* which ' I know from my own case ' must be wrong. But this is not to refute dualism, since the dualist need not maintain that I know the intension of the English word

---

[1] An attempted fourth alternative—*i.e.*, an alternative to dualism, materialism, *and* behaviourism—is sketched in ' The Mental Life of Some Machines ', which appeared in the Proceedings of the Wayne Symposium on the Philosophy of Mind. This fourth alternative is materialistic in the wide sense of being compatible with the view that organisms, including human beings, are physical systems consisting of elementary particles and obeying the laws of physics, but does not require that such ' states ' as *pain* and *preference* be defined in a way which makes reference to either overt behaviour or physical-chemical constitution. The idea, briefly, is that predicates which apply to a system by virtue of its *functional organization* have just this characteristic: a given functional organization (*e.g.*, a given inductive logic, a given rational preference function) may realize itself in almost any kind of overt behaviour, depending upon the circumstances, and is capable of being ' built into ' structures of many different logically possible physical (or even metaphysical) constitutions. Thus the statement that a creature prefers A to B does not tell us whether the creature has a carbon chemistry, or a silicon chemistry, or is even a disembodied mind, nor does it tell us how the creature would behave under any circumstances specifiable without reference to the creature's other preferences and beliefs, but it does not thereby become something ' mysterious '.

' pain ' from my own case, but only that I experience the referent of the word.

What then is the intension of ' pain '? I am inclined to say that ' pain ' is a cluster-concept. That is, the application of the word ' pain ' is controlled by a whole cluster of criteria, *all of which can be regarded as synthetic.*[1] As a consequence, there is no satisfactory way of answering the question ' What does " pain " mean? ' except by giving an exact synonym (*e.g.*, ' Schmerz '); but there are a million and one different ways of saying what pain *is*. One can, for example, say that pain is that feeling which is normally evinced by saying ' ouch ', or by wincing, or in a variety of other ways (or often not evinced at all).

All this is compatible with logical behaviourism. The logical behaviourist would reply: ' Exactly. " Pain " is a cluster-concept—that is to say, it stands for *a cluster of phenomena.*' But that is not what I mean. Let us look at another kind of cluster-concept (cluster-concepts, of course, are not a homogeneous class): names of diseases.

We observe that, when a virus origin was discovered for polio, doctors said that certain cases in which all the symptoms of polio had been present, but in which the virus had been absent, had turned out not to be cases of polio at all. Similarly, if a virus should be discovered which normally (almost invariably) is the cause of what we presently call ' multiple sclerosis ', the hypothesis that this virus is *the* cause of multiple sclerosis would not be falsified if, in some few exceptional circumstances, it was possible to have all the symptoms of multiple sclerosis for some other combination of reasons, or if this virus caused symptoms not presently recognized as symptoms of multiple sclerosis in some cases. These facts would certainly lead the lexicographer to *reject* the view that ' multiple sclerosis ' means ' the simultaneous presence of such and such symptoms '. Rather he would say that ' multiple sclerosis ' means ' that disease which is normally responsible for some or all of the following symptoms. . . .'

[1] I mean not only that *each* criterion can be regarded as synthetic, but also that the cluster is *collectively* synthetic, in the sense that we are free in certain cases to say (for reason of inductive simplicity and theoretical economy) that the term applies although the whole cluster is missing. This is completely compatible with saying that the cluster serves to fix the meaning of the word. The point is that when we specify something by a cluster of indicators we assume that people will *use their brains*. That criteria may be over-ridden when good sense demands is the sort of thing we may regard as a ' convention associated with discourse ' (Grice) rather than as something to be stipulated in connection with the individual words.

Of course, he does not have to say this. Some philosophers would prefer to say that ' polio ' *used to mean* ' the simultaneous presence of such-and-such symptoms '. And they would say that the *decision* to accept the presence or absence of a virus as a criterion for the presence or absence of polio represented a *change of meaning*. But this runs strongly counter to our common sense. For example, doctors used to say ' I believe polio is caused by a virus '. On the ' change of meaning ' account, those doctors were *wrong*, not *right*. Polio, *as the word was then used*, was not always caused by a virus; it is only what *we* call polio that is always caused by a virus. And if a doctor ever said (and many did) ' I believe this may not be a case of polio ', knowing that all of the text-book symptoms were present, that doctor must have been contradicting himself (even if we, to-day, would say that he was right) or, perhaps, ' making a disguised linguistic proposal '. Also, this account runs counter to good linguistic methodology. The definition we proposed a paragraph back—' multiple sclerosis ' means ' the disease that is normally *responsible* for the following symptoms . . . .'—has an exact analogue in the case of polio. This kind of definition leaves open the question whether there is a single cause or several. It is consonant with such a definition to speak of ' discovering a single origin for polio (or two or three or four) ', to speak of ' discovering X did not have polio ' (although he exhibited all the symptoms of polio), and to speak of ' discovering X did have polio ' (although he exhibited *none* of the ' textbook symptoms '). And, finally, such a definition does not require us to say that any ' change of meaning ' took place. Thus, this is surely the definition that a good lexicographer would adopt. But this entails *rejecting* the ' change of meaning ' account as a philosopher's invention.[1]

Accepting that this is the correct account of the names of diseases, what follows? There *may* be analytic entailments connecting diseases and symptoms (although I shall argue against this). For example, it looks plausible to say that:

' Normally people who have multiple sclerosis have some or all of the following symptoms. . .'

is a necessary (' analytic ') truth. But it does not follow that ' disease talk ' is translatable into ' symptom talk '. Rather the

---

[1] Cf. ' Dreaming and " Depth Grammar ",' *Analytical Philosophy*, First Series.

contrary follows (as is already indicated by the presence of the word
' normally '): statements about multiple sclerosis are not translatable into statements about the symptoms of multiple sclerosis,
not because disease talk is ' systematically ambiguous ' and symptom talk is ' specific ', but because *causes* are not logical constructions out of their *effects*.

In analogy with the foregoing, both the dualist and the materialist would want to argue that, although the meaning of ' pain '
may be *explained* by reference to overt behaviour, what we mean
by ' pain ' is not the presence of a cluster of responses, but rather
the presence of an event or condition that normally causes those
responses. (Of course the pain is not the whole cause of the pain
behaviour, but only a suitably invariant part of that cause;[1] but,
similarly, the virus-caused tissue damage is not the whole cause
of the individual symptoms of polio in some individual case, but
a suitably invariant part of the cause.) And they would want to
argue further, that even if it *were* a necessary truth that
' Normally, when one says " ouch " one has a pain '
or a necessary truth that
' Normally, when one has a pain one says " ouch " '
this would be an interesting observation about what ' pain '
means, but it would shed no metaphysical light on what pain *is*
(or *isn't*). And it certainly would not follow that ' pain talk ' is
translatable into ' response talk ', or that the failure of translat-
ability is only a matter of the ' systematic ambiguity ' of pain talk
as opposed to the ' specificity ' of response talk: quite the contrary.
Just as before, *causes* (pains) are *not* logical constructions out of
their *effects* (behaviour).

The traditional dualist would, however, want to go farther,
and deny the *necessity* of the two propositions just listed. Moreover, the traditional dualist is right: there is nothing self-contra-
dictory, as we shall see below, in talking of hypothetical worlds in
which there are pains but *no* pain behaviour.

The analogy with names of diseases is still preserved at this
point. Suppose I identify multiple sclerosis as the disease that
normally produces certain symptoms. If it later turns out that a
certain virus is the cause of multiple sclerosis, using this newly

---

[1] Of course, ' the cause ' is a highly ambiguous phrase. Even if it is correct
in certain contexts to say that certain events in the brain are ' the cause ' of my
pain behaviour, it does *not* follow (as has sometimes been suggested) that my
pain must be ' identical ' with these neural events.

discovered criterion I may then go on to find out that multiple sclerosis has quite different symptoms when, say, the average temperature is lower. I can then perfectly well talk of a hypothetical world (with lower temperature levels) in which multiple sclerosis does *not* normally produce the usual symptoms. It is true that if the *words* ' multiple sclerosis ' are used in any world in such a way that the above lexical definition is a good one, *then* many victims of the disease must have had some or all of the following symptoms. . . And in the same way it is true that *if* the explanation suggested of the word ' pain ' is a good one (*i.e.*, ' pain is the feeling that is normally being evinced when someone says "ouch", or winces, or screams, &c.'), *then* persons in pain must have at some time winced or screamed or said ' ouch '—but this does *not* imply that ' if someone ever had a pain, then someone must at some time have winced or screamed or said " ouch ".' To conclude this would be to confuse preconditions for *talking* about pain as *we* talk about pain with preconditions for the existence of pain.

The analogy we have been developing is not an identity: linguistically speaking, mind words and names of diseases are different in a great many respects. In particular, *first person uses* are very different: a man may have a severe case of polio and not know it, even if he knows the word ' polio ', but one cannot have a severe pain and not know it. At first blush, this may look like a point in favour of logical behaviourism. The logical behaviourist may say: it is because the premises 'John says he has a pain ', ' John knows English ', and ' John is speaking in all sincerity ',[1] *entail* ' John has a pain ', that pain reports have this sort of special status. But even if this is right, it does not follow that logical behaviourism is correct unless *sincerity* is a ' logical construction out of overt behaviour '! A far more reasonable account is this: one can have a ' pink elephant hallucination ', but one cannot have a ' pain hallucination ', or an ' absence of pain hallucination ', simply because any situation that a person cannot discriminate from a situation in which he himself has a pain *counts* as a situation in which he has a pain, whereas a situation that a person cannot distinguish from one in which a pink elephant is present does not necessarily *count* as the presence of a pink elephant.

To sum up: I believe that pains are not clusters of responses, but that they are (normally, in our experience to date) the causes of

[1] This is suggested in Wittgenstein's *Philosophical Investigations*.

certain clusters of responses. Moreover, although this is an empirical fact, it underlies the possibility of talking about pains in the particular way in which we do. However, it does not rule out in any way the possibility of worlds in which (owing to a difference in the environmental and hereditary conditions) pains are not responsible for the usual responses, or even are not responsible for any responses at all.

Let us now engage in a little science fiction. Let us try to describe some worlds in which pains are related to responses (and also to causes) in quite a different way than they are in our world.

If we confine our attention to non-verbal responses by full grown persons, for a start, then matters are easy. Imagine a community of ' super-spartans ' or ' super-stoics ' —a community in which the adults have the ability to successfully suppress *all* involuntary pain behaviour. They may, on occasion, admit that they feel pain, but always in pleasant well-modulated voices—even if they are undergoing the agonies of the damned. They do *not* wince, scream, flinch, sob, grit their teeth, clench their fists, exhibit beads of sweat, or otherwise act like people in pain or people suppressing the unconditioned responses associated with pain. However, they do feel pain, and they dislike it (just as we do). They even admit that it takes a great effort of will to behave as they do. It is only that they have what they regard as important ideological reasons for behaving as they do, and they have, through years of training, learned to live up to their own exacting standards.

It may be contended that children and not fully mature members of this community will exhibit, to varying degrees, normal unconditioned pain behaviour, and that this is all that is necessary for the ascription of pain. On this view, the *sine qua non* for the significant ascription of pain to a species is that its immature members should exhibit unconditioned pain responses.

One might well stop to ask whether this statement has even a clear meaning. Supposing that there are Martians: do we have any criterion for something being an ' unconditioned pain response ' for a Martian? Other things being equal, one *avoids* things with which one has had painful experiences: this would suggest that *avoidance* behaviour might be looked for as a universal unconditioned pain response. However, even if this were true, it would hardly be specific enough, since avoidance can also be an unconditioned response to many things that we do not associate with pain—to things that disgust us, or frighten us, or even merely bore us.

Let us put these difficulties aside, and see if we can devise an imaginary world in which there are not, even by lenient standards, any unconditioned pain responses. Specifically, let us take our ' super-spartans ', and let us suppose that after millions of years they begin to have children who are born fully acculturated. They are born speaking the adult language, knowing the multiplication table, having opinions on political issues, and *inter alia* sharing the dominant spartan beliefs about the importance of not evincing pain (except by way of a verbal report, and even that in a tone of voice that suggests indifference). Then there would not *be* any ' unconditioned pain responses ' in this community (although there might be unconditioned *desires* to make certain responses—desires which were, however, always suppressed by an effort of will). Yet there is a clear absurdity to the position that one cannot ascribe to these people a capacity for feeling pain.

To make this absurdity evident, let us imagine that we succeed in converting an adult ' super-spartan ' to *our* ideology. Let us suppose that he begins to evince pain in the normal way. Yet he reports that the pains he is feeling are not more *intense* than are the ones he experienced prior to conversion—indeed, he may say that giving expression to them makes them *less* intense. In this case, the logical behaviourist would have to say that, through the medium of this one member, we had demonstrated the existence of unconditioned pain responses in the whole species, and hence that ascription of pain to the species is ' logically proper '. But this is to say that had this one man never lived, and had it been possible to demonstrate only indirectly (via the use of *theories*) that these beings feel pain, then pain ascriptions *would* have been improper.

We have so far been constructing worlds in which the relation of pain to its non-verbal *effects* is altered. What about the relation of pain to *causes*? This is even more easy for the imagination to modify. Can one not imagine a species who feel pain only when a magnetic field is present (although the magnetic field causes no detectable damage to their bodies or nervous systems)? If we now let the members of such a species become converts *to* ' super-spartanism ', we can depict to ourselves a world in which pains, in our sense, are clearly present, but in which they have neither the normal causes nor the normal effects (apart from verbal reports).

What about verbal reports? Some behaviourists have taken these as the characteristic form of pain behaviour. Of course, there is a difficulty here: If ' I am in pain ' means ' I am disposed to utter this kind of verbal report ' (to put matters crudely), then how do we tell that any particular report is ' this kind of verbal report '? The usual answer is in terms of the unconditioned pain responses and their assumed supplantation by the verbal reports in question. However, we have seen that there are no *logical* reasons for the existence of unconditioned pain responses in all species capable of feeling pain (there *may* be logical reasons for the existence of avoidance desires, but avoidance *desires* are not themselves behaviour any more than pains are).

Once again, let us be charitable to the extent of waving the first difficulty that comes to mind, and let us undertake the task of trying to imagine a world in which there are not even pain *reports*. I will call this world the ' X-world '. In the X-world we have to deal with ' super-super-spartans '. These have been super-spartans for so long, that they have begun to suppress even *talk* of pain. Of course, each individual X-worlder may have his private way of thinking about pain. He may even have the *word* ' pain ' (as before, I assume that these beings are born fully acculturated). He may *think* to himself: ' This pain is intolerable. If it goes on one minute longer I shall scream. Oh No! I mustn't do that! That would disgrace my whole family. . .' But X-worlders do not even admit to *having* pains. They pretend not to know either the word or the phenomenon to which it refers. In short, if pains are ' logical constructs out of behaviour ', then our X-worlders behave so as not to have pains!—Only, of course, they do have pains, and they know perfectly well that they have pains.

If this last fantasy is not, in some disguised way, self-contra-dictory, then logical behaviourism is simply a mistake. Not only is the second thesis of logical behaviourism—the existence of a near-translation of pain talk into behaviour talk—false, but so is even the first thesis—the existence of ' analytic entailments '. Pains *are* responsible for certain kinds of behaviour—but only in the context of our beliefs, desires, ideological attitudes, and so forth. From the statement ' X has a pain ' by itself *no* behavioural statement follows—not even a behavioural statement with a ' normally ' or a ' probably ' in it.

In our concluding section we shall consider the logical behaviourist's stock of counter-moves to this sort of argument. If the
logical behaviourist's positive views are inadequate owing to an
oversimplified view of the nature of cluster words—amounting, in
some instances, to an open denial that it is *possible* to have a word
governed by a cluster of indicators, *all* of which are synthetic—
his negative views are inadequate owing to an oversimplified
view of empirical reasoning. It is unfortunately characteristic of
modern philosophy that its problems should overlap three
different areas—to speak roughly, the areas of linguistics, logic,
and 'theory of theories' (scientific methodology)—and that many
of its practitioners should try to get by with an inadequate knowledge of at least two out of the three.

Some behaviourist arguments

We have been talking of 'X-worlders' and 'super-spartans'.
No one denies that, in *some* sense of the term, such fantasies are
'intelligible'. But 'intelligibility' can be a superficial thing. A
fantasy may be 'intelligible', at least at the level of 'surface
grammar', although we may come to see, on thinking about it for
a while, that some absurdity is involved. Consider, for example,
the supposition that last night, just on the stroke of midnight, all
distances were instantaneously doubled. Of course, we did not
notice the change, for *we* ourselves also doubled in size! This
story may seem intelligible to us at first blush, at least as an
amusing possibility. On reflection, however, we come to see
that a logical contradiction is involved. For 'length' means
nothing more nor less than a relation to a standard, and it is a
contradiction to maintain that the length of everything doubled,
while the relations to the standards remained unchanged.

What I have just said (speaking as a logical behaviourist might
speak) is false, but not totally so. It is false (or at least the last
part is false), because 'length' does *not* mean 'relation to a standard'. If it did (assuming a 'standard' has to be a macroscopic
material object, or anyway a material object), it would make no
sense to speak of distances in a world in which there were only
gravitational and electromagnetic fields, but no material objects.
Also, it would make no sense to speak of the *standard* (whatever it
might be) as having changed its length. Consequences so counter-
intuitive have led many physicists (and even a few philosophers of

physics) to view ' length ' not as something operationally defined, but as a theoretical magnitude (like electrical charge), which can be measured in a virtual infinity of ways, but which is not explicitly and exactly definable in terms of any of the ways of measuring it. Some of these physicists—the ' unified field ' theorists—would even say that, far from it being the case that ' length ' (and hence ' space ') depends on the existence of suitably related material bodies, material bodies are best viewed as local variations in the curvature of space—that is to say, local variations in the intensity of a certain magnitude (the tensor g_{ik}), one aspect of which we experience as ' length '.

Again, it is far from true that the hypothesis ' last night, on the stroke of midnight, everything doubled in length ' has no testable consequences. For example, if last night everything did double in length, and the velocity of light did not also double, then this morning we would have experienced an apparent halving of the speed of light. Moreover, if g (the gravitational constant) did not double, then we would have experienced an apparent halving in the intensity of the gravitational field. And if h (Planck's constant) did not change, then. . . . In short, our world would have been bewilderingly different. And if we could survive at all, under so drastically altered conditions, no doubt some clever physicist would figure out what had happened.

I have gone into such detail just to make the point that in philosophy things are rarely so simple as they seem. The ' doubling universe ' is a favourite classroom example of a ' pseudo-hypothesis '—yet it is the worst possible example if a ' clear case ' is desired. In the first place, what is desired is a hypothesis with no testable consequences—yet *this* hypothesis, as it is always stated, *does* have testable consequences (perhaps some more complex hypothesis does not; but then we have to see this more complex hypothesis stated before we can be expected to discuss it). In the second place, the usual argument for the absurdity of this hypothesis rests on a simplistic theory of the meaning of ' length ' —and a full discussion of *that* situation is hardly possible without bringing in considerations from unified field theory and quantum mechanics (the latter comes in in connection with the notion of a ' material standard '). But, the example aside, one can hardly challenge the point that a superficially coherent story may contain a hidden absurdity.

Or can one? Of course, a superficially coherent story may contain a hidden logical contradiction, but the whole point of the logical behaviourist's sneering reference to ' surface grammar ' is that *linguistic coherence, meaningfulness of the individual terms,* and *logical consistency,* do not by themselves guarantee freedom from another kind of absurdity—there are ' depth absurdities ' which can only be detected by more powerful techniques. It is fair to say that to-day, after thirty years of this sort of talk, we lack both a single *convincing* example of such a depth absurdity, and a technique of detection (or alleged technique of detection) which does not reduce to ' untestable, *therefore* nonsense '.

To come to the case at hand: the logical behaviourist is likely to say that our hypothesis about ' X-worlders ' is untestable in principle (if there *were* ' X-worlders ', by hypothesis we couldn't distinguish them from people who really didn't know what pain is); and *therefore* meaningless (apart from a certain ' surface significance ' which is of no real interest). If the logical behaviourist has learned a little from ' ordinary language philosophy ', he is likely to shy away from saying ' untestable, therefore *meaningless* ', but he is still likely to say or at least think: ' untestable, therefore in *some* sense absurd '. I shall try to meet this ' argument ' *not* by challenging the premiss, be it overt or covert, that ' untestable synthetic statement ' is some kind of contradiction in terms (although I believe that premiss to be mistaken), but simply by showing that, on any but the most naive view of testability, our hypothesis *is* testable.

Of course, I could not do this if it were true that ' by hypothesis, we couldn't distinguish X-worlders from people who *really* didn't know what pain is '. But that isn't true—at any rate, it isn't true ' by hypothesis '. What is true by hypothesis is that we couldn't distinguish X-worlders from people who really didn't known what pain is *on the basis of overt behaviour alone.* But that still leaves many other ways in which we might determine what is going on ' inside ' the X-worlders—in both the figurative and literal sense of ' inside '. For example, we might examine their *brains.*

It is a fact that when pain impulses are ' received ' in the brain, suitable electrical detecting instruments record a characteristic ' spike ' pattern. Let us express this briefly (and too simply) by saying that ' brain spikes ' are one-to-one correlated with experiences of pain. If our X-worlders belong to the human species, then we can verify that they do feel pains, notwithstanding their claim that they don't have any idea what pain is, by applying our electrical instruments and detecting the tell-tale ' brain spikes '. This reply to the logical behaviourist is far too simple to be convincing. ' It is true,' the logical behaviourist will object, ' that experiences of pain are one-to-one correlated with " brain spikes " in the case of normal human beings. But you don't know that the X-worlders are normal human beings, in this sense—in fact, you have every reason to suppose that they are *not* normal human beings.' This reply shows that no *mere* correlation, however carefully verified in the case of normal human beings, can be used to verify ascriptions of pain to X-worlders. Fortunately, we do not have to suppose that our knowledge will always be restricted to mere correlations, like the pain-' brain spike ' correlation. At a more advanced level, considerations of simplicity and coherence can begin to play a rôle in a way in which they cannot when only crude observational regularities are available.

Let us suppose that we begin to detect waves of a new kind, emanating from human brains—call them ' V-waves '. Let us suppose we develop a way of ' decoding ' V-waves so as to reveal people's unspoken thoughts. And, finally, let us suppose that our ' decoding ' technique also works in the case of the V-waves emanating from the brains of X-worlders. How does this correlation differ from the pain-' brain spike ' correlation?

Simply in this way: it is reasonable to say that 'spikes'— momentary peaks in the electrical intensity in certain parts of the brain—could have almost any cause. But waves which go over into coherent English (or any other language), under a relatively simple decoding scheme, could not have just any cause. The ' null hypothesis '—that this is just the operation of ' chance '—can be dismissed at once. And if, in the case of human beings, we verify that the decoded waves correspond to what we are in fact thinking, then the hypothesis that this same correlation holds in the case of X-worlders will be assigned an immensely high probability, simply because no other likely explanation readily suggests itself. But ' no other likely explanation readily suggests itself ' isn't verification, the logical behaviourist may say. On the contrary. How, for example, have we verified that cadmium lines in the spectrographic analysis of sunlight indicate the presence of cadmium in the sun? Mimicking the logical behaviourist, we might say: ' We have verified that under normal circumstances, cadmium lines only occur when heated cadmium is present. But we don't know that circumstances on the sun are normal in this sense.' If we took this seriously, we would have to *heat cadmium on the sun* before we could say that the regularity upon which we base our spectrographic analysis of sunlight had been verified. In fact, we have verified the regularity under ' normal ' circumstances, and we can *show* (deductively) that *if* many other laws, that have also been verified under ' normal ' circumstances and *only* under ' normal ' circumstances (*i.e.*, never on the surface of the sun), hold on the sun, *then* this regularity holds also under ' abnormal ' circumstances. And if someone says, ' But perhaps *none* of the usual laws of physics hold on the sun ', we reply that this is like supposing that a random process always produces coherent English. The fact is that the ' signals ' (sunlight, radio waves, &c.) which we receive from the sun cohere with a vast body of theory. Perhaps there is some other explanation than that the sun obeys the usual laws of physics; but *no other likely explanation suggests itself*. This sort of reasoning *is* scientific verification; and if it is not reducible to simple Baconian induction—well, then, philosophers must learn to widen their notions of verification to embrace it.

The logical behaviourist might try to account for the decodability of the X-worlders' ' V-waves ' into coherent English (or the appropriate natural language) without invoking the absurd ' null hypothesis '. He might suggest, for example, that the ' X-worlders ' are having fun at our expense—they are able, say, to produce misleading V-waves at will. If the X-worlders have brains quite unlike ours, this may even have some plausibility. But once again, in an advanced state of knowledge, considerations of coherence and simplicity may quite conceivably ' verify ' that this is false. For example, the X-worlders may have brains quite like ours, rather than unlike ours. And we may have built up enough theory to say how the brain of a human being should ' look ' if that human being were pretending not to be in pain when he was, in fact, in pain. Now consider what the ' misleading V-waves ' story requires: it requires that the X-worlders produce V-waves in quite a different way than we do, without specifying what that different way is. Moreover, it requires that this be the case, although the reverse hypothesis—that X-worlders' brains function

exactly as human brains do—in fact, that they *are* human brains—
fits all the data. Clearly, this story is in serious methodological
difficulties, and any other ' counter-explanation ' that the logical
behaviourist tries to invoke will be in similar difficulties. In short,
the logical behaviourist's argument reduces to this: ' You cannot
verify " psycho-physical " correlations in the case of X-worlders
(or at least, you can't verify ones having to do, directly or indirectly, with *pain*), because, by hypothesis, X-worlders won't tell
you (or indicate behaviourally) when they are in pain. ' Indirect
verification '—verification using theories which have been ' tested '
only in the case of human beings—is not verification at all, because
X-worlders *may* obey different laws than human beings. And it is
not incumbent upon *me* (the logical behaviourist says) to suggest
what those laws might be: it is incumbent upon *you* to rule out
all other explanations.' And this is a silly argument. The scientist
does not have to rule out all the ridiculous theories that someone
might suggest; he only has to show that he has ruled out any
reasonable alternative theories that one might put forward on the
basis of present knowledge.

Granting, then, that we might discover a technique for
' reading ' the unspoken thoughts of X-worlders: we would then
be in the same position with respect to the X-worlders as we were
with respect to the original ' super-spartans '. The super-spartans
were quite willing to tell us (and each other) about their pains; and
we could see that their pain talk was linguistically coherent and
situationally appropriate (*e.g.*, a super-spartan will tell you that
he feels intense pain when you touch him with a red hot poker).
On this basis, we were quite willing to grant that the super-
spartans did, indeed, feel pain—all the more readily, since the
deviancy in their behaviour had a perfectly convincing ideological
explanation. (Note again the rôle played here by considerations
of coherence and simplicity). But the X-worlders also ' tell ' us
(and, perhaps, each other), exactly the same things, albeit *un-*
willingly (by the medium of the involuntarily produced ' V-waves')
Thus we have to say—at least, we have to say as long as the ' V-
wave ' theory has not broken down—that the X-worlders are
what they, in fact, are —just ' super-super-spartans '.

Let us now consider a quite different argument that a logical
behaviourist might use. ' You are assuming,' he might say, ' the
following principle:

' If someone's brain is in the same state as that of a human being in pain (not just at the moment of the pain, but before and after for a sufficient interval), then he is in pain.

' Moreover, this principle is one which it would never be reasonable to give up (on your conception of " methodology "). Thus, you have turned it into a tautology. But observe what turning this principle into a tautology involves: it involves changing the meaning of " pain ". What " pain " means for *you* is: the presence of pain, in the colloquial sense of the term, *or* the presence of a brain state identical with the brain state of someone who feels pain. Of course, in that sense we can verify that your " X-worlders " experience " pain "—but that is not the sense of " pain " at issue.'

The reply to this argument is that the premiss is simply false. It is just not true that, on my conception of verification, it would *never* be reasonable to give up the principle stated. To show this, I have to beg your pardons for engaging in a little more science fiction. Let us suppose that scientists discover yet another kind of waves—call them ' W-waves '. Let us suppose that W-waves do not emanate from human brains, but that they are detected emanating from the brains of X-worlders. And let us suppose that, once again, there exists a simple scheme for decoding W-waves into coherent English (or whatever language X-worlders speak), and that the ' decoded ' waves ' read ' like this: ' Ho, ho! are we fooling those Earthians! They think that the V-waves they detect represent our thoughts! If they only knew that instead of pretending not to have pains when we really have pains, we are really pretending to pretend not to have pains when we really do have pains when we really don't have pains!' Under these circumstances, we would ' doubt ' (to put it mildly) that the same psycho-physical correlations held for normal humans and for X-worlders. Further investigations might lead us to quite a number of different hypotheses. For example, we might decide that X-worlders don't think with their brains at all—that the ' organ ' of thought is not just the brain, in the case of X-worlders, but some larger structure—perhaps even a structure which is not ' physical ' in the sense of consisting of elementary particles. The point is that what is necessarily true is not the principle stated two paragraphs back, but rather the principle:

If someone (some organism) is in the same state as a

human being in pain in all relevant respects, then he (that organism) is in pain.

—And *this* principle *is* a tautology by anybody's lights! The only *a priori* methodological restriction I am imposing here is this one:

If some organism is in the same state as a human being in pain in all respects *known* to be relevant, and there is no reason to suppose that there exist *un*known relevant respects, then don't postulate any.

—But this principle is not a ' tautology '; in fact, it is not a *statement* at all, but a methodological directive. And deciding to conform to this directive is not (as hardly needs to be said) changing the meaning of the word ' pain ', or of *any* word.

There are two things that the logical behaviourist can do: he can claim that ascribing pains to X-worlders, or even super-spartans, involves a ' change of meaning ',[1] or he can claim that ascribing pains to super-spartans, or at least to X-worlders, is ' untestable '. The first thing is a piece of unreasonable linguistics; the second, a piece of unreasonable scientific method. The two are, not surprisingly, mutually supporting: the unreasonable scientific method makes the unreasonable linguistics appear more reasonable. Similarly, the normal ways of thinking and talking are mutually supporting: reasonable linguistic field techniques are, needless to say, in agreement with reasonable conceptions of scientific method. Madmen sometimes have consistent delusional systems; so madness and sanity can both have a ' circular ' aspect. I may not have succeeded, in this paper, in breaking the ' delusional system ' of a committed logical behaviourist; but I hope to have convinced the uncommitted that that system need not be taken seriously. If we have to choose between ' circles ', the circle of reason is to be preferred to any of the many circles of unreason.

[1] This popular philosophical move is discussed in ' Dreaming and " Depth Grammar ", ' *Analytical Philosophy*, First Series.

SOCRATES' LOGIC AND THE UNITY OF WISDOM AND TEMPERANCE

D. SAVAN

IT is not difficult to find fallacies in Socrates' arguments. It is not difficult, either, to find some plausible way to make the fallacy vanish. Plato's charm is such that nearly all of us are tempted to co-operate, as Ryle puts it. It is, therefore, striking to find near unanimity among scholars that the argument at *Protagoras* 332A–333B is fallacious. This is the argument by which Socrates professes to demonstrate the unity of wisdom and *sophrosynē* (to be rendered, in this paper, as ' temperance ').

Professor Gregory Vlastos, in his examination of this argument[1] finds two major logical flaws. First, the conclusion is incomplete. The full and correct conclusion would be an alternation of four propositions: ' Either (*a*) wisdom and temperance are not distinct, or (*b*) some things do not have just one opposite, or (*c*) wisdom and folly are not opposites, or (*d*) temperance and folly are not opposites.' Socrates, however, offers Protagoras a choice only between (*a*) and (*b*). Secondly, Vlastos contends that ' temperance and folly are opposites ' is weak, and is itself supported by fallacious argument.

I shall attempt to show, on the contrary, that Socrates' argument is clear and sound. All his premises are very carefully and explicitly stated, the more important among them being thrice repeated. The reasoning is formally valid. The argument is, in fact, stronger and broader than it need be to establish that wisdom is one with temperance. The same form of argument could be used to establish the unity of *all* the virtues. The reason for the common accusation of fallacy is, I believe, that Socrates does not use a technical vocabulary which could distinguish in every case among incompatibility, contrariety, and contradiction.

Since several distinct forms of opposition are relevant to the argument, let us begin with an agreement on terms. Socrates uses the one word, *enantion*, translated ' opposite ' by Jowett and

[1] *Plato's Protagoras* (New York, 1956), Introduction, pp. xxviii–xxix. Professor Vlastos reviews some of the many scholars who have found fault with the argument.

'contrary' by Guthrie,[1] but it will be seen below that Socrates and Protagoras are quite able to distinguish incompatibility, contrariety, and contradiction. The broad and generic term here is *incompatibility*. If two terms cannot both at once be predicated of the same subject, they may be said to be *incompatible*. The colour red, like any intermediate colour, is incompatible with white and with black, although it is not the contrary of either. Mediocrity, of whatever degree, is incompatible with perfect good and with unadulterated evil. When incompatible terms are at two opposite extremes of a graded scale they may be said to be *contraries*. Between a pair of contraries intermediates must be possible. White and black, hard and soft (331D), are standard examples of contrariety. When two incompatible terms do not permit of intermediates, and everything of a given kind must be one or the other but not both, they may be called *contradictories*. Odd and even, male and female, right and left hand, are contradictories.

Are Socrates and Protagoras able to make these distinctions? They do not, of course, make them generally and formally, but it is apparent that they are capable of drawing the necessary distinction where the particular case seems to them to require it. Twice in this dialogue Protagoras points out that intermediates are distinct from contraries. At 334A he says that between what is beneficial to men and what is harmful there are things which are not beneficial and yet not harmful either. Again, at 351D he says that between pains which are evil and their contraries there lies 'a third class which are neither evil nor good.' It is possible, I suppose, that Protagoras failed to see that such intermediates are incompatible with their contraries, but it is hardly likely.*

The distinction between contraries and contradictories is sharply drawn in one important passage by Protagoras and in another by Socrates. At 346C–D Socrates points to white and black as examples of contraries between which there are inter-

---

[1] *Plato. Protagoras and Meno* (Harmondsworth, 1956). I follow Guthrie's translation.

*Although the Greeks tended to treat all qualities as lying between contraries, Protagoras may well have learned from students of plant and animal life that there are other kinds of incompatibilities. He suggests (320E–321B) that the swift are not strong, animals that dig burrows are not large, etc. Yet strength does not fall between the contraries, speed and slowness, nor does digging fall between largeness and smallness. To show that he recognized true incompatibility here Protagoras would have to say that speed *can not* be joined to strength, and this he does not say.

mediates. On the other hand, he says, anything at all that is not actually foul could be said to be fair. Many degrees of imperfection would then be fair. At various places in his long speech, Protagoras makes a similar distinction. At 327C–D he says, ' The man who in a civilized and humane society appears to you the most wicked must be thought just . . . in comparison with men who have neither education nor courts of justice nor laws nor any constraint compelling them to be continually heedful of virtue— savages in fact '. In other words, while within a civilized society justice and injustice are contraries, savagery is contradictory to civilized behaviour even at its most wicked.

Let me turn now to the argument. The argument leads to two statements which contradict one another. One or the other must be rejected.

A. Whatever admits of a contrary admits of one only (333A).

B. Folly, which is one thing, has two contraries, wisdom and temperance (333B).

Whether *A* is said of contraries or of contradictories it is an analytic statement, true by definition. Socrates' cursory induction at 332C is perhaps intended only as a reminder. *B* is the conjunction of

B(1). Folly is the contrary of wisdom (332A), and

B(2). Folly is the contrary of temperance (332E).

B(1) is accepted without argument, and none is needed. No one would be inclined to question it. Only *B(2)* is likely to be questioned, and for this reason Socrates offers a careful argument in its support.

B(2) follows from three premises, each of them supported by an argument, and each of them thrice affirmed by Protagoras.

C. Foolish acts are done by folly, temperate acts by temperance (332A, B, D, and E).

D. What is done in the same way is done by the same agency, and what is done in contrary ways is done by contrary agencies (332C, D, and E).

E. Foolish acts and temperate acts are contraries (332B, D, and E).

C follows from the analogy between the sense organs and the virtues mentioned by Protagoras a few lines earlier (331D–E), and recalled by Socrates at the conclusion of the argument (333A). Just as each part of a face has a power or function (*dunamis*) through which it acts, so each virtue may be supposed to be a thing with its corresponding power or function of action. In seeing colours, for example, the eye fulfills its function. In analogous fashion, foolish acts and temperate acts fulfill the functions of folly and temperance, respectively.

The extreme care with which Socrates builds his case should be noticed here. Not only does he point out that from the quality of an act we can infer the quality of its agency, but also that the converse holds. From the quality of the agency we can infer the quality of its action. This he does by remarking that what is done with strength is done strongly, and similarly for weakness, speed, and slowness (332B).[1] *D* is the necessary consequence of the reciprocal implication thus established between agencies and actions. If foolish actions are always the outcome of folly, and if folly always, when it acts, issues in foolish actions, we must agree that as actions are to one another so are their agencies.

It is at *E*, however, that the critics balk. Vlastos, for example, says it is ' deduced by the shadiest of logic '. *B(2)*, its counterpart for agencies rather than acts, is ' miserably lame duck '.[2] *E* follows, however, from three conditionals:

F. If an act is right and advantageous, then it is temperate (332A),

G. If an act is wrong, then it is foolish (332B),

H. If an act is foolish, it is not temperate (*ibid.*).

H affirms that temperate and foolish actions are incompatible. By itself it does not establish that they are contraries, much less contradictories. Protagoras might honestly have agreed to

F'. If an act is temperate, then it is right, and

G'. If an act is foolish, then it is wrong.

From *F'* and *G'* Socrates could have inferred only that temperate and foolish acts are incompatible, not that they are contraries or

---

[1] It is possible that this list of agencies and acts is intended to remind us of Protagoras' earlier listing of these same powers at 320E.

[2] *Loc. cit.*

contradictories. Protagoras might have argued that some temperate acts are among the intermediates between the two admitted contraries, foolish acts and wise acts. We have noted above that he clearly recognizes that between contraries there may be intermediates which are neither. Or again he might have argued that temperate acts need not be classed as intermediates. They may simply be incompatible with foolish acts.*

Neither of these possibilities could be plausible to Protagoras and his students. Protagoras teaches men to act temperately and wisely because both are right. He teaches men to avoid foolish and intemperate acts because both are wrong. In his long speech, Protagoras' emphasis is that if a man is to lead a human and civilized life all his actions must display some measure of temperance and justice. There is no doubt that F and G represent Protagoras' position more accurately than do their converses, F' and G'. It may be a debating mistake to admit them, but it is honest and there is no fallacy. In gaining Protagoras' assent to F and G rather than to their converses Socrates displays clarity and logical skill.

From F, G, and H it follows that 'An act is right' and 'An act is temperate' are truth functionally equivalent, as are 'An act is wrong' and 'An act is foolish.'[1] They must be true or false together. Since right and wrong are either contraries or contradictories, temperate and foolish acts must also be either contraries or contradictories. To discover which they are, we must look back to Protagoras' long speech.

Socrates states at the beginning of this argument (332A) that we are discussing what Protagoras has previously said. To what passages are we being referred? Perhaps there is a hint at the close of the argument (333A) when Socrates says, ' The two statements are not very harmonious. They don't chime well together.' In the long speech, at 326A–B, Protagoras describes how the music master instills harmony and, with it, temperance. Rhythm, harmony, and temperance, he says, are ' essential to the whole of human life '. At 327A–C Protagoras draws an analogy between teaching how to play the flute and teaching politically virtuous action. Even the poorest flautist, like the least virtuous citizen, is

* See note p 21.
[1] From G and H we can infer I: If an act is wrong, then it is not temperate. From I and F it follows that 'An act is right' and 'An act is temperate' are formally equivalent.

far better than he who knows neither music nor civilized life. Protagoras hints that perhaps no one in the city is perfectly noble and virtuous. He himself claims to be ' only a little better than the others at advancing us on the road to virtue ' (328A). Still, as we have already seen, compared to the uncivilized acts of a savage, even the most wicked actions of a citizen will appear to be in some measure right. Right and wrong, then, are contradictories, and the citizen whose actions are in no degree right must be killed, or expelled to live out his miserable life among the savages.

It follows that temperate and foolish actions are contradictories, like odd and even, male and female, right hand and left hand. Temperance is then the contradictory of folly. But wisdom is apparently the contrary, and not the contradictory, of folly. It is to be presumed, then, there may be actions which are temperate and hence not foolish, but also not wise. Indeed, this admission can be extracted from Protagoras' words. At 329E he asserts that some men are just but not wise. At 333B–C he says he would be ashamed to admit that an act could be at once temperate and unjust. It would follow that an act could be temperate and just *and* unwise. It is unfair, however, thus to bring together into a single argument remarks made in different contexts.

Socrates may properly conclude that wisdom is a part of temperance and is not distinct from it. By means of the same sort of argument he could conclude that justice, piety, and courage must be parts of temperance and not separable from it. In this sense, his argument is stronger and broader than it need be. But if temperance is the contradictory of folly while wisdom is only its contrary he has *not* proved that temperance is identical with wisdom. He has proved instead that wisdom is some part of temperance. This result is particularly interesting in view of the conclusion of the dialogue. There he will show (356C ff.) that wisdom is an art or science of true measurement. Between it and the folly of savagery lie all the mediocre intermediates of which the average man is the fallible measure.

It remains to consider Vlastos' contention that the formally correct conclusion of Socrates' argument would be an alternation of four (or more) propositions. Now it is certainly true that the *argument* could be converted into the single conditional, ' If H and G and F and D and C and $B(1)$, then B.' The contrapositive is, ' If *not B*, then either *not H* or *not G* or . . .' But surely so long as Socrates is not composing a logic text this can not be required of him. Nor does Vlastos ask it. What Vlastos wishes to argue is that Socrates did not fully understand the rule of conditionalization, and *that* I am not going to dispute. Socrates has done all that can be asked of him in showing that *B*, together with the statement that wisdom and temperance are distinct (333A),[1] contradicts *A*.

Socrates has a positive purpose in constructing so careful an argument. He wishes to show that two major propositions earlier laid down contradict one another. On the one hand, Protagoras has maintained that there is *one* thing in which all citizens must share, each according to his measure, ' and this one essential is . . . justice and moderation (*sophrosynē*) and holiness of life, or to concentrate it into a single whole, manly virtue ' (325A). On the other hand, Protagoras has said that each of the five virtues is different from the others and may exist without them. Socrates has obtained from Protagoras explicit agreement with each step of the argument by which he demonstrates a contradiction between these two propositions.

[1] Notice here again how careful Socrates is to include every premiss a logician could ask for.

MODALITY AND QUANTIFICATION

B. Rundle

THE introduction of modal operators into quantification theory is commonly thought to give rise to considerable difficulties concerning the interpretation and validity of various formulas and rules of inference within the resultant system. Indeed, to some these difficulties appear so formidable as to cast doubt on the very possibility of combining modality and quantification in a satisfactory way. I shall argue, however, that the customary difficulties have been exaggerated, that certain suspect formulas and rules of inference may be reinstated, and that the problem, if any, arises in contexts other than those which are generally taken to generate paradoxes.

First, it is worth mentioning an analogous situation which arises when we attempt to enrich quantification theory by the introduction of tense-operators. In the system devoid of such operators, it is customary to interpret the existential quantifier timelessly, such a reading being best suited to mathematical contexts, and in general desirable if we are to recognize as valid the rule of existential generalization. We cannot, for instance, pass from ' Napoleon was a general ' to ' $\Sigma x(x$ was a general) ', if we read the latter as an assertion of present existence.[1] Accordingly, it is less misleading to interpret the existential quantifier in terms of the neutral ' some ', rather than ' there is ': ' For some x, x was a general ' is less likely to suggest that a general is now in existence than is ' There is an x such that x is a general '. On the other hand, although this interpretation preserves such inferences, it thereby fails to distinguish between statements which are differently tensed. For ' $\Sigma x(x$ was a general) ', so understood, is ambiguous as between (1) ' There was a general ', and (2) ' There is someone who was a general.' Similarly, ' $\Sigma x(x$ will be a general) ' could provide a translation of both (3) ' There will be a general ', and (4) ' There is someone who will be a general '—with, in the former case, the additional problem of knowing what

[1] The notation I shall use is that of Lukasiewicz. For an explanation, see A. N. Prior, *Formal Logic* (Oxford, revised edition, 1962).

to make of values of x which are individuals not yet in existence.
Suppose, then, following Prior,[1] we introduce the operators ' P ',
meaning ' It was the case that ', and ' F ', meaning ' It will be the
case that '. It would then appear that we are now able to differentiate these variously tensed propositions from one another, for,
interpreting ' ϕx ' as ' x is a general,' (3) becomes $F\Sigma x\phi x$, whilst
(4) becomes $\Sigma x F\phi x$. We could then hold that although
$C\Sigma x F\phi x F\Sigma x\phi x$ is valid, $CF\Sigma x\phi x\Sigma x F\phi x$ is not; that is, (3) and
(4) do not collapse into one another, but the original distinction
has been preserved: if there is someone who will be a general,
then there will be someone who is a general, but not conversely,
since the person who will be a general may not as yet exist.
However, a moment's reflection shows this solution to be inadequate. We appear to have devised two forms suited to expressing
the difference between (3) and (4), but this is only because we
have reintroduced a tensed reading of the unqualified quantifier
in the symbolic version of (4). That is, we have interpreted
$\Sigma x F\phi x$ as ' There is (at present) an x such that x will be a general.'
But if we do abide by the timeless interpretation, it is no longer
clear that the distinction between $\Sigma x F\phi x$ and $F\Sigma x\phi x$ will be
maintained, since if it will be the case that for some x, x is a
general, then for some x, timelessly conceived, it will be the case
that x is a general. It is extremely easy to slip from a timeless
interpretation of the quantifier to one in terms of the present
tense, but if we are going to insist on the former as basic, an
operator for ' It is now the case that ' is just as necessary as
operators for past and future. Symbolizing this operator by ' S ',
we should now write (4) as $S\Sigma x F\phi x$. Yet even this refinement
does not rule out the possibility of ambiguity, for we could understand $S\Sigma x F\phi x$ as corresponding to either of (i) ' It is now the case
that for some x, it will be the case that ϕx ', and (ii) ' There is now
some x for which it will be the case that ϕx.' In the former case
we retain the untensed reading of the quantifier when prefaced by ' S ', and so appear obliged to accept the unwanted
$CF\Sigma x\phi x S\Sigma x F\phi x$. That is, if it will be the case that for some x,
ϕx, then surely it is now the case that for some x, timelessly
conceived, it will be the case that ϕx. It would seem, then, that
we should opt for (ii), taking the tense-operators to nullify completely the timelessness of the quantifiers which they govern. In

[1] *Time and Modality* (Oxford, 1957), chapter II.

the case of a quantifier preceded by ' S ', we have the reading ' There is now an x such that . . . ', rather than ' It is now the case that there is (timelessly) an x such that . . . '. In this way the desired distinction may be preserved, though to achieve this we have been obliged to modify considerably the reading of the quantifier when prefaced by a tense-operator.

I shall not pursue this topic any further, but I mention it only as providing an analogy for the case of modal operators. Just as care is called for in interpreting the quantifier when distinctions of tense are important, so we are forced to reconsider its interpretation in contexts where mood is significant. As $CF\Sigma x\phi x\Sigma xF\phi x$ may be troublesome, so it is not clear exactly what one is to make of $C\Sigma xL\phi xL\Sigma x\phi x$, or, even, of $CL\phi aL\Sigma x\phi x$, which can be derived from it.[1] More commonly, it has been denied that the conditional $CL\phi a\Sigma xL\phi x$ is valid; that is, it has been denied that we can quantify into modal contexts. Not only have these inferences been questioned, but it has been doubted whether there can be any true statements of the form $L\phi a$, where the ' a ' is some referring expression—where, that is, the modality is *de re*. Further, the possibility of there being any true statement of the form $L\Sigma x\phi x$ has frequently been rejected, at least implicitly, in accordance with the view that no existential statement can be necessarily true.

Before discussing quantified modal statements, I should like to make a few remarks about certain of the particular statements from which these appear to be derivable, namely statements in which some individual is said to be necessarily so-and-so or possibly such-and-such. In this context, the verbal form of a statement may be misleading, for it may suggest that a *de re* modality is being asserted, when none is in fact intended. Consider

(5) The first man into space might not have been a Russian. We should not generally mean by this that the man who was in fact the first into space might not have been a Russian, *i.e.*, that Gagarin might not have been a Russian. This is a possible interpretation, but (5) is more likely to have the sense of ' It is possible that someone other than a Russian should have been the first man into space.' The distinction is perhaps clearer if we substitute a proper name for ' a Russian ' in (5):

(6) The first man into space might not have been Gagarin. In accordance with the second interpretation, (6) comes to ' It

---

[1] From here on I am using C to symbolize C-strict.

might not have been Gagarin who was the first into space ', or simply ' Gagarin might not have been the first man into space ', and whilst this is true, (6) could hardly be true if ' the first man into space ' were here used to refer to Gagarin himself, *i.e.*, if (6) bore the *de re* interpretation.

There is another ambiguity in this context which is generated by the modal expressions. Consider again

(7) Gagarin might not have been the first man into space.

This might be said in order to throw doubt on his exploit: perhaps Gagarin was not the first man into space. Or it may be assumed that Gagarin was in fact the first into space, but nevertheless it could have been true that he was not. I shall be concerned with this latter style of interpretation, not the former—with ' It is possible that Gagarin should not have been the first man into space ', rather than with ' It is possible that Gagarin was not the first man into space.'

Cases where a *de re* interpretation is even less plausible than with (5) are provided by

(8) The year might not have been 1950,

(9) The cat's name might not have been ' Tabby '.

It would be most odd to construe ' the cat's name ' as referring to the actual name borne by the cat, but (9) simply means that the cat might not have been called ' Tabby '. Similarly, (8) does not mean that 1950 might have been dated differently.

The two sorts of interpretation which I have illustrated do not depend on anything peculiar to modal notions, but the same possibilities may arise in the case of the unmodalized versions of the assertions in question. Consider

(10) The cat's name is ' Tabby '.

One would not in general arrive at (10) by examination of the cat's name with the consequent identification of it as ' Tabby '. Not in general, though if, for instance, (10) were asserted as the result of deciphering a badly written version of ' Tabby ', it could represent a further specification of something less precisely identified as the cat's name. Or take

(11) He was wondering whether the cat's name was ' Tabby '. For all the person concerned may know, the cat may have no name, in which case he would presumably be wondering simply whether the cat was called ' Tabby '. On the other hand, his wondering could be directed at the actual name of the cat if, as

before, he were trying to make out whether an illegible version of this name was ' Tabby '.

Analogous to (10) under its more natural interpretation is

(12) The number of planets is 9.

This is most readily understood as a variant on: ' There are 9 planets.' If I count the planets and come up with ' 9 ' as the answer, this surely does not represent a further identification or characterization of what is referred to by ' the number of planets ', unlike, say, ' The number of planets is an odd number.' Similarly,

(13) The number of planets is greater than 7

is naturally taken not as an assertion about some particular number, other than 7, but simply as equivalent to

(14) There are more than 7 planets.

It is analogous to ' The number of planets has changed ', where there is no question of asserting of some particular number that it has undergone an alteration. On the other hand, it would be possible to think of (13) as equivalent to the result of taking ' The number of planets, namely 9, is greater than 7 ', and removing from this the specification, ' namely 9 ', and in this case, to bring out the fact that we do have in mind some particular number, we might say ' That number which is the number of the planets is greater than 7 ', or some such version which is more emphatic in this respect. Both these possibilities carry over to the modalized version of (13), viz.,

(15) The number of planets is necessarily greater than 7.

If this means that there are necessarily more than 7 planets, it is clearly false. But if ' the number of planets ' is used as a referring expression, and on the strength of (12) is taken to refer to 9, then it is true. That is, granted (12), then that number which is the number of the planets is necessarily greater than 7. What of course is not necessarily true is that the number of planets should be 9, but given that it is, it is true that this number, which just happens to be the number of the planets, is necessarily greater than 7.

These considerations are clearly relevant to Quine's argument for showing the referential opacity of modal contexts. Modal contexts are held to be referentially opaque in that the truth of a modal statement will depend on the precise way in which reference is made to something by a term in that statement. Accordingly, we may test a context for referential opacity by seeing whether the

replacement of some term occurring in it by another expression
having the same reference results in unintended sense or nonsense.
Since, that is, ' whatever can be affirmed about the object remains
true when we refer to the object by any other name ',[1] the failure
of substitutivity indicates that the truth-value of the statement
does depend on the way in which reference is secured, and hence
that the context is referentially opaque. According to this
criterion, we are allegedly obliged to consider modal contexts as
referentially opaque if we are to avoid concluding from

(16) 9 is necessarily greater than 7,
and
(12) The number of planets is 9,
to
(15) The number of planets is necessarily greater than 7.
Now we have seen that (15) is false if it means that there are
necessarily more than 7 planets, but equally clearly, when understood in this way, it cannot be derived from (16) and (12). But
nor does it reveal a failure of the law of substitutivity in this
context, since given this reading, ' the number of planets ' does not
signify some definite number, and so cannot, *a fortiori*, be replaced
by some term signifying the same number. On the other hand,
interpreting ' the number of planets ' in (15) as a referring
expression introduced by means of a substitution in (16) licensed
by (12), we have an interpretation which does not result in falsity.
Incidentally, I am not claiming that (12) is an *identity* licensing
this substitution, since the preceding discussion suggests that it
should be distinguished from statements which are commonly
so characterized. In place of my ' is ' in (12), Quine actually
has ' = ', which, though it may just come to ' is ', could also be
read as ' equals '. It is perhaps a fine point, but I should say that
although the number of planets equals (or is the same as) the
number of Muses, the number of planets simply *is* 9.

The failure of this argument of Quine's results in the failure
of his ensuing argument to show that we cannot quantify into
modal contexts. We cannot, he claims, infer

(17) $\Sigma x(x$ is necessarily greater than 7)
from
(16) 9 is necessarily greater than 7,

---

[1] ' Reference and Modality,' *From a Logical Point of View* (Harvard, 1953),
p. 140. See also *Word and Object* (Cambridge, Mass., 1960), pp. 195–200.

for, ' What is this number which, according to (17), is necessarily greater than 7? According to (16), from which (17) was inferred, it was 9, that is, the number of planets; but to suppose this would conflict with the fact that (15) is false.'[1] The inadmissability of the inference from (16) to (17) would be paradoxical in the extreme, but we have seen that when (15) is understood as involving reference to some particular number, namely 9, it is not false, and hence the alleged conflict does not arise. Moreover, in view of the break-down of Quine's arguments, the remark which he then makes is left without support, the remark that ' In a word, to be necessarily greater than 7 is not a trait of a number, but depends on the manner of referring to the number '.[2] But clearly, the number 9 is necessarily greater than 7, and that no matter how you refer to it. You might even truthfully say ' The number which I just mentioned is necessarily greater than 7.' This would certainly be false if it meant that you necessarily did mention a number greater than 7, but it could be true of the number which you did, as a matter of fact, mention, that it was necessarily greater than 7. If these criticisms are correct, there is at least so far no reason for supposing that we must impose restrictions on substitutivity in modal contexts. We do not, for instance, have to limit ourselves to substitutions based on necessary identities, but it suffices if, as a matter of fact, reference to the same object is preserved by a given substitution.[3]

Quine has another argument designed to show the referential opacity of modal contexts, and hence the impossibility of quantifying into them. Thus, if unrestricted substitutivity were allowed in such contexts, we could pass from the premisses

(18) Necessarily if there is life on the Evening Star then there is life on the Evening Star,
and
(19) The Evening Star is the Morning Star,

---

[1] ' Reference and Modality,' *op. cit.*, p. 148.
[2] *Ibid.*
[3] I have taken Quine to be claiming that the impossibility of quantifying into modal contexts is a *consequence* of their referential opacity, but it may be that he regards the impossibility rather as *proof* of opacity, arguing that since the principles of universal instantiation and existential generalization are simply ' the logical content of the idea that a given occurrence is referential ', the opacity of a context is revealed by the failure of quantification into it. This would be even more dubious, since the failure of quantification would surely mark out those terms which are not referential at all, and not those which fail to be purely referential.

to the false conclusion
>   (20) Necessarily if there is life on the Evening Star
>   then there is life on the Morning Star.

However, given (18) and (19), it is far from clear that (20) *is* false. *If* the Evening Star is in fact the Morning Star then it must be the case that if there is life on the former, there is life on the latter. Similarly, if the milkman and the postman are one and the same person, it is impossible for the milkman to be ill without the postman being ill.

I shall not discuss this example any further, since the relevant points are similar to those already mentioned in the case of (12), (15) and (16). The same holds for the consequent proof that quantification into (18) is impossible, which runs parallel to that given for (16). However, there is a general observation which is worth making on this last topic. Independently of the foregoing criticisms, we might suspect that Quine's arguments were invalid by considering an interpretation of quantified statements which is possible when the relevant universe of discourse is limited to finitely many named objects. Suppose the universe in question contains just the individuals a, b, c, and suppose too that b is necessarily ϕ. Then the disjunctive interpretation of $\Sigma x L \phi x$ yields a formula $A A L \phi a L \phi b L \phi c$ which is clearly a consequence of $L \phi b$. Similarly, with respect to the quantified version of (18), viz., ' Σx (necessarily if there is life on the Evening Star then there is life on x) ', we have for a universe containing just d, e, f, the interpretation $A A C \phi d \phi d C \phi d \phi e C \phi d \phi f$, which is strictly implied by $C \phi d \phi d$. In both cases the inferences are so straightforward, it is difficult to see what could lead to the failure of their generalizations.

Although Quine rejects (21) $C L \phi a \Sigma x L \phi x$, he is perhaps willing to countenance (22) $C L \phi a L \Sigma x \phi x$,[1] and, indeed, it is at first sight difficult to see how this latter could be denied, since it is apparently a straightforward case of the general truth that if q follows from p, and p is necessary, then q is necessary. However, it is just when the quantifier is prefaced by a modal operator that difficulties with respect to its interpretation do arise, and I shall now consider some of the ways in which (22) might be attacked. In the first place, anyone who shares the contemporary misgivings about the possibility of necessarily true existential statements will no doubt

[1] *Ibid.*, p. 148.

wish to question (22) if he is prepared to grant the necessity of such a statement as ' 7 is a prime ', since this in conjunction with (22) yields a consequence which appears to conflict with this view. The conflict is, I believe, more apparent than real, but on the other hand, the view itself has not, despite its currency, been conclusively established.

We are frequently told that the necessity of a statement is merely a reflection of certain arbitrary linguistic conventions, and this is taken to have the consequence that existential statements are invariably contingent. This argument may even be represented as a truism of modern logic, though I should have thought that many philosophers would not in fact subscribe to the conventionalism embodied in the premiss. More importantly, even granted this suspect doctrine of the nature of necessity, it is far from clear that the desired conclusion follows, for all that seems to be implied by this conventionalism is that a necessary statement requires a certain special form of support. That is, the necessity, and thereby the truth of a necessary statement, is determined by the sense of the terms in which it is couched, the sense being in turn determined by certain linguistic conventions. Or, we might say with more plausibility: if an existential statement is necessary, then its necessity is vouched for by facts about the meaning of certain words, taken in conjunction with various logical laws.[1] At any rate, something more is needed if we are to demonstrate that no *existential* statement could have its truth guaranteed in this way. Indeed, it is a notable feature of the argument that nothing peculiar to the notion of existence is invoked in the premiss, but it would seem just as reasonable to conclude that no statement of the form $\Pi x C \phi x \phi x$ can be necessary. Thus, given the conventionalist premiss, why should someone not say: ' Therefore, no conditional statement can be necessary ', or ' Therefore, no subject-predicate statement can be necessary ', or ' Therefore, no identity statement can be necessary '? There may be some peculiarity of existential statements which forces us to deny that they, though not these others, may be necessary, but the argument gives no indication as to what this might be. Furthermore, not only does the idea of existing fail to occur in the argument in any essential way, but the

---

[1] This is still not an adequate account of necessity. The truth of (20), for instance, depends on whether, *as a matter of fact*, the Morning Star and the Evening Star are one and the same.

D

same holds for the term 'necessary': you might just as well argue that no existential statement can be possibly true, for whether or not a statement expresses a possible truth depends on the meaning of the words in it. Again, I have seen it argued that no existential statement can be necessary, on the ground that 'exists' is not a predicate.[1] But this conclusion follows only if there are no sorts of necessary statement other than those of the subject-predicate form. Surely, if existential statements are not of this form, then there must on this view be different reasons for holding them to be contingent than are available for subject-predicate statements.

I am not claiming that there are in fact existential statements which are necessarily true, but only that the arguments to the contrary are not sufficiently conclusive to throw doubt on the inference from $L\phi a$ to $L\Sigma x\phi x$. And yet, although we may grant that there could be such statements, we may well be reluctant to accept all those which (22) would appear to sanction. Thus I am willing to concede the necessity of indefinitely many truths concerning particular natural numbers, but at the same time I wish to claim that there might not have been any numbers at all. Or, to take a less disputable example, although this page could be said to possess at least three dimensions as a matter of necessity and not merely as a matter of fact, it is conceivable that nothing having three dimensions should have existed. Assuming this position to be consistent, we may adopt one of two possibilities with respect to (22), either questioning its validity, or so interpreting $L\Sigma x\phi x$ that it does not conflict with the view that the existence of a ϕ is no more than contingent.

The first possibility could be developed in the following way. I said above that (22) appears to be a simple application of the law $CCpqCLpLq$. Now nobody is likely to deny this law, but it might be contended that a valid application of it is given by (21) rather than (22): if a is necessarily ϕ we may infer that there is something which is necessarily ϕ, as already argued; not, however, that there is necessarily something which is ϕ, since this would involve an illegitimate dissociation of the adverb 'necessarily' from the verb which it originally qualified. In general, if we introduce some qualification of the verb 'is' in the predication 'a is ϕ', this is no guarantee that the first occurrence of this same verb may be

[1] See T. Penelhum, 'Divine Necessity', *Mind*, LXIX (1960), p. 180.

similarly qualified in the consequence of this, viz., ' There is something which is ϕ.' What makes the inference appear plausible is the typographical ordering ' $L-\phi-a$ ', which obscures the fact that ' necessarily ' is properly located as a qualification within the predicate. However, consider once more the case of a universe confined to individuals a, b, c. We may agree that there is a presumption made to the effect that ' necessarily ' may be displaced from within the predicate in the way mentioned, yet hold that such a dissociation is nevertheless legitimate, since to deny (22) in the case of this restricted universe would commit one to accepting, by a few simple transformations, the contradictory formula $MKL\phi aKKNL\phi aNL\phi bNL\phi c$. Consequently, there is a strong presumption in favour of the validity of (22) in the general case.

I am not certain that this vindication of (22) is entirely satisfactory. However, I shall not discuss it further, but instead take up the second possibility, which calls for an acceptable reading to be devised for $L\Sigma x\phi x$. That this formula cannot be taken to mean ' It is necessarily true that there should have been a ϕ ' is clear if it occurs in the context of (22). Various weaker interpretations are nonetheless possible, and in keeping with the interpretation relative to a restricted universe, we might decide to read $L\Sigma x\phi x$ as ' It is necessarily true that at least one of the things which exist is ϕ.' It should be emphasized that this is to be understood as an assertion about what must be the case only with respect to those things which do in fact exist. It is not intended to be an assertion as to what must hold in each and every possible world, whatever might happen to exist therein. This more general formulation is precisely what I wish to avoid, but given the interpretation intended, we may now hold that (22) is valid, and claim that even given the truth of $L\phi a$, there still might not have been anything which was ϕ, depending on whether or not it is possible to deny the assumption written into $L\Sigma x\phi x$.

The position I am advocating may be clarified by considering once more the situation which arises in the case of statements concerning numbers. Ordinarily, we are quite happy to admit that there is necessarily a least prime number, without regard to the question whether the existence of numbers in general is a contingent matter. Given the natural numbers, various necessary truths may be propounded concerning their individual character-istics and relations to one another: at least one is so-and-so, infinitely many are such-and-such—pure arithmetical propositions affirming non-contingent facts about this totality. On the other hand, when it is asserted that no existential statement can be necessary, this is, or at least should be intended in a much stronger sense, according to which the whole framework within which these propositions are necessary is affirmed to have only a con-tingent existence. We could, then, attribute necessity to the existent statements made within the theory of numbers, but at another level claim for this system the status of a contingent human creation. This distinction between two sorts of necessary existential statement is, I believe, an important one. There is nothing perplexing about $L\Sigma x\phi x$ when it is so interpreted that (22), or $C\Sigma xL\phi xL\Sigma x\phi x$ is valid, but there is something puzzling in the notion of a necessarily true existential statement which could be asserted unconditionally, in the sense that it did not require for its truth the assumption of a given totality of objects.

It is worth mentioning here the associated problem of inter-pretation which arises with the modal ' possible '. It may be possible that there should have been a ϕ, and yet not possible that one of the things which in fact exist should have a been a ϕ. For instance, we may reasonably claim that there could have been such things as ghosts, even though none of the past or present occupants of the universe are such that they could have been ghosts. Accordingly, if we read the formula $CM\Sigma x\phi x\Sigma xM\phi x$ as ' It is possible that there should be a ϕ, only if something is such that it could be a ϕ ', we thereby restrict the range of possibilities to what is provided for by the limited potentialities of actual beings. Since this restriction is not obviously warranted, we should, if we wish to maintain $CM\Sigma x\phi x\Sigma xM\phi x$, render the antecedent as ' It is possible that one of the things which (in fact) exist is a ϕ '. This reading of $M\Sigma x\phi x$ is parallel to that suggested for $L\Sigma x\phi x$, and, as before, it is the philosophically interesting interpretation which we have been obliged to reject for the sake of the proposed implication.

I shall now conclude by returning to the analogy with which I began. In the case of tense-operators, the preservation of intuitively reasonable inferences calls for care in reading the quantifier when it occurs embedded in a context in which the precise tense is significant. A similar situation arises when we turn from distinctions of tense to those of mood. Properly understood, quantification into modal contexts is unproblematic— which is not surprising, since in generalizing from $L\phi a$ to $\Sigma x L\phi x$, no displacement of the modal operator is involved which might generate difficulties not already present in $L\phi a$. However, the exact interpretation of the quantifier does become a matter for debate when it is actually prefaced by L, and I have tried to present one possible reading which does, I hope, do no more than preserve those inferences which we should wish to see maintained.

IDENTITY-STATEMENTS

D. Wiggins

I WANT to try to show (i) that there are insuperable difficulties in any term+relation+term or subject+predicate analysis of statements of identity, (ii) that, however important and helpful the sense-reference distinction is,[1] this distinction does not make it possible to retain the relational or predicative analysis of identity-statements, and (iii) that a realistic and radically new account is needed both of '=' and of the manner in which noun-phrases occur in identity-statements.

Till we have such an account many questions about identity and individuation will be partly unclear, and modal logics will continue without the single compelling interpretation one might wish.

The connexion of what I am going to say with modal calculi can be indicated in the following way. It would seem to be a necessary truth that if $a=b$ then whatever is truly ascribable to a is truly ascribable to b and vice versa (*Leibniz's Law*). This amounts to the principle

(1) $(x)\,(y)\,((x{=}y) \supset (\phi)\,(\phi x \equiv \phi y))$

Suppose that identity-statements are ascriptions or predications. Then the predicate variable in (1) will apparently range over properties like that expressed by '($=a$)'[2] and we shall get as a consequence of (1)

(2) $(x)\,(y)\,((x{=}y) \supset (x{=}x. \supset .y{=}x))$

There is nothing puzzling about this. But if (as many modal logicians believe), there exist *de re* modalities of the form

$\square\,(\phi a)$ (*i.e.*, necessarily (ϕa)),

then something less innocent follows. If '($=a$)' expresses a property, then '$\square\,(a{=}a)$', if this too is about the object a, also ascribes something to a, namely the property $\square$ ($=a$). For on a naive and pre-theoretical view of properties, you will reach an expression for a property whenever you subtract a noun-expression

[1] G. Frege, 'On Sense and Reference', *Translations from the Philosophical Writings of Gottlob Frege*, ed. P. T. Geach and M. Black (Oxford, 1952), pp. 56–78.
    [2] Quotation marks are used under the convention that they serve to form a designation of whatever expression would result in a particular case from rewriting the expression within the quotation-marks with genuine constants in the place of free variables and dummy-expressions.

with material occurrence (something like ' a ' in this case) from a
simple declarative sentence. The property $\Box$ ($=a$) then falls
within the range of the predicate variable in Leibniz's Law
(understood in this intuitive way) and we get

(3) $(x)\,(y)\,(x{=}y \supset (\Box\,(x{=}x).\supset.\Box(y{=}x)))$

Hence, reversing the antecedents,

(4) $(x)\,(y)\,(\Box\,(x{=}x).\supset.(x{=}y)\supset\Box(x{=}y))$

But ' $(x)\,(\Box\,(x{=}x))$ ' is a necessary truth, so we can drop this
antecedent and reach

(5) $(x)\,(y)\,((x{=}y).\supset.\Box(x{=}y))$

Now there undoubtedly exist contingent identity-statements.
Let ' $a{=}b$ ' be one of them. From its simple truth and (5) we can
derive ' $\Box\,(a{=}b)$ '. But how then can there be any contingent
identity-statements?

Five reactions to this are possible.

1. We may, like Quine, reject *de re* modalities altogether and
deny that any modal propositions do refer to individuals. According to this suggestion ' $\Box(a{=}a)$ ' ascribes nothing to a at all.
Under this interpretation of modality a is not mentioned in ' $\Box$
$(a{=}a)$ ' but only for instance the *sense* of ' $a{=}a$ '. Leibniz's Law
cannot therefore be deployed to derive (5).

This extreme view, however sympathetic one may be to it,
is rather too specialized a reaction to (5). For, if a is b, (1) still
licenses substitutions of designations of a for designations of b in
all extensional contexts. Notoriously these substitutions can
change the truth-grounds and purport of identity-statements
in a way which is still in need of explanation. (See the first
objection in Section II below.)

2. We might accept the result and plead that provided ' a '
and ' b ' are proper names nothing is amiss. The consequence
of this is that no contingent identity-statements can be made by
means of proper names. I shall give reasons in Sections III and
VII below for being discontent with this solution.

3. The derivation of (5) might be blocked by simply giving
up Leibniz's Law. But the law cannot be given up so lightly. If
a *is* b, how can a have genuine properties b hasn't, or b have
genuine properties a hasn't? I think one's reaction to (5) ought to
be to try to make the definition of ' property ' clearer, not to
fly in the face of common sense.

4. The derivation of (2) itself, via x's predicate ' ($=x$) ',

might be blocked by insisting that when expressions for properties are formed by subtraction of a constant or free variable, then every occurrence of that constant or free variable must be subtracted. ' $(a=a)$ ' would then yield ' $(\ =\ )$ ', and (2) could not be derived by using ' $(\ =x)$ '. One would only get the impotent

$$(2')\ x=y \supset (x=x.\supset .y=y)$$

The paradox could still be derived however. Suppose that a is contingently b. Then $\diamondsuit \sim (a=b)$; *i.e.*, it is possible that not $a=b$. This gives the predicate ' $\diamondsuit \sim (a=\ )$ '. This is true of b. Then by (1), if $a=b$, this predicate is true also of a. This yields ' $\diamondsuit \sim (a=a)$ '. But ' $(x)\ \square\ (x=x)$ ' is a logical truth and implies ' $\sim \diamondsuit \sim (a=a)$ '.

5. The derivation of (5) might be blocked in another way, a way I shall recommend. One might deny that ' $a=a$ ' is of the same form as ' ϕa ' or ' Raa '. If the thesis of this paper is correct it is simply a mistake to regard $(\ =a)$ as a member of the range of the predicate variable in (1). Leibniz's Law is true of properties, But a thing's identity is not among its properties. It seems to me that this suggests a satisfactory solution to these puzzles which is not *ad hoc*. Independent arguments will be adduced to show that it is a mistake to count a thing's identity amongst the predicates true of it.

I

Definition of Identity-Statement

I begin by isolating, I fear very roughly, the one and only class of utterances to which theses (i), (ii) and (iii) are intended to apply. I shall call these statements ' identity-statements ', but my definition will turn out to be a stricter and narrower definition than the one usually assumed.

For a sentence to express an identity ' is ' or '=' must stand between two noun-phrases which, if they are distinct, are *serving independently of one another to make genuine references*. By this criterion ' The evening star is the morning star ' and ' Hesperus is Phosphorus ' do express genuine identities. It is my intention that, *in their normal uses*, such sentences as ' Darius was the King of the Persians ' (where the question ' Which individual do you mean to identify by " King of the Persians "? ' is silly) or

' Plato was the first philosopher to distinguish the copula from the identity sign ' should fail the criterion.

In an abnormal context of utterance the latter sentence might conceivably qualify as an identity-statement. For it might in some very special context be intended to express the genuine identity-statement that a definite logician, the author of the *Sophist* (an individual independently identified), and Plato (independently identified again) were one and the same person. In its non-strained normal use, however, the sentence would express not an identity but a predication, and it would say *of Plato* that he discovered, what no other philosopher had earlier noticed, the difference between ' $=$ ' and the copula. Under the first interpretation, the utterance of the sentence pre-supposes the possibility of establishing both references independently of the truth of what is being asserted. Under the second (normal) interpretation, fixing any ' reference ' for the definite description is bound up with the truth of the assertion.

Another example which would normally fail the criterion is ' Point p is the centre of gravity of body b.' If someone who said this were told that his statement was false then, denied further tests, he would not be able to *identify* a point he intended by ' centre of gravity of body b.' He would only be able to say that the point he meant was *whatever* point the weighing test, correctly performed, would determine. To know *which* point this was would involve knowing a true statement of the form ' Point p is the centre of gravity of body b.' To construe both this statement and all statements like it as satisfying the criterion would be to construe them in such a way that an explanation of their meaning and references had to presuppose their truth.

It is difficult to define ' genuine reference '. Because I shall have to refer so much to Frege, I shall assume, without very much conviction, that Frege and Strawson[1] are at least to this extent right about reference—that definite descriptions are at least sometimes straightforwardly referential. (The difficulties of making clear any criterion for being ' genuinely referential ' are certainly some sort of evidence for the rightness of Russell's opposing theory. For the special case of identity-statements at

---

[1] ' On Referring,' *Mind*, LIX (1950), pp. 320–44. This commits me to no thesis about the truth-value of ' The present King of France is bald ' (*vide* M. A. E. Dummett, ' Truth ', *Proceedings of the Aristotelian Society*, LIX (1958–9), p. 153), nor to any attempt to ' save ' the Square of Opposition.

any rate we shall find that in the end we are in fact driven back to something very like Russell's theory.)

It has been thought that it is enough for a definite description to be genuinely referential if (1) it is a part of its sense that only one thing satisfies it, (2) the speaker knows that only one thing satisfies it. This seems to lead to difficulties.

(a) It would impose different analyses on (a) I have not the faintest idea who was the first man to conceive the idea of the wheel. Please tell me ' (satisfying (1) and (2)), and (β) ' I have not the faintest idea who, if anyone, was the first man to conceive the idea of the wheel. Please tell me ' (satisfying only (1)).

(b) Both (a) and (β) have strong affinities to (γ) ' The first man to conceive the idea of the wheel must have been the greatest genius who ever lived.' Yet this comes down to (γ') ' Whoever first conceived the idea of the wheel must have been the greatest genius who ever lived.' Neither (γ) nor (γ') would have to be withdrawn if it was discovered that some prehistoric community had derived the idea of the wheel from some now extinct natural mechanism and nobody had ever *invented* the wheel at all. ' Whoever uniquely ϕs ' is no more a referring expression than ' whoever ϕs '. Uniqueness is irrelevant.

(c) The idea of reference is inextricably tied to the idea of asserting and to truth-grounds. If I am to assert that ϕa I must know what thought I express by ' ϕa '. This means that I must know the truth-grounds of what I assert. This involves knowing what thing it is which has to be ϕ in order for my statement to be true. I must either be acquainted with a, or be satisfied that (adequately for the purposes in hand) I am able to identify a indirectly, that I am in a position to go about the task of pinning a down in space and time. The mere satisfaction of criteria (1) and (2), however, by themselves, does not guarantee that a man could even *make a start* in identifying the term satisfying the description. Such total inability even to get started in indirectly identifying a thing might nevertheless take the characteristic form of asking questions in which the description was used and used in such a way as to satisfy criteria (1) and (2).

These considerations suggest that there are at least four sorts of situation in which a sentence will contain two apparent definite descriptions with uniqueness built into their sense. Only in one case, the fourth, are both referential.

Simple predication

Pointing to a man I say (δ) ' That man standing there was the first man ever to climb Everest '. Let this be the case where (*a*) my audience and I have no other information about climbers of Everest except that someone or other first climbed Everest and (*b*) our interest is entirely in the impressive looking man pointed to. ' First man to climb Everest ' cannot here be referential. For it may only be by virtue of the *truth* of (δ) that we can identify any putative reference for it. But what if (δ) is false? (δ)'s meaning what it means (and so the reference of its terms) cannot depend on its being true: I conclude that only the *first* term is referential in (δ).

Location

The same example (δ) will suffice. In this case I have led my audience to the room in order to show him directly, in the best possible way, who first climbed Everest. Our interest is in identifying or locating that famous mountaineer. He could also have been indirectly located by an adequate definite description (which would be referential). 'Aristarchus of Samos, the third century Greek, was the first man to conceive that the earth went round the sun ' (said in reply to the question, ' Who first conceived . . .? ') would be an example of this sort. Some such direct or indirect location of a thing (or some in the context undisputed possibility of location) would seem to be a *prerequisite* of genuine reference to the thing. If so, the term cannot be referentially used in the proposition by which the thing is located. Again, only the first term is referential in (δ).

General propositions

(γ) and (γ') above (neither term is referential).

Genuine identity-statements

' The evening star is the morning star ' (both terms are referential).

The best I can offer to make ' genuine reference ' precise is the following: A speaker refers to something by an expression *e* if (i) he is in a position (and thinks he is) to accept and answer informatively the question ' Which particular are you identifying by *e*? ' and (ii) he is in a position to answer this question without making use of the fact that his statement is true, and (iii) he knows (and thinks he knows) how to locate (directly or indirectly) the item which he means to identify by *e*.

Requirement (i) rests on the fact that to express a thought of the form 'ϕa' I must know what the thought is, and so what particular I mean by ' a '.

Requirement (ii) rests on the evident truth that statements must be capable of falsity. Elucidation of the reference of a noun-phrase in a statement r must be independent or r's truth-value. Otherwise r could not be false.[1]

Requirement (iii) is an attempt to make a ruling about when the question ' Which particular are you identifying by e? ' has been adequately answered. The strictness with which it is interpreted depends on the interests and subject matter in hand, and the need for some such requirement is clearer than the form it should take.[2] In one context it may be assumed that some locational knowledge k is adequate and a further question may be posed or statement made about the thing so identified. In another context discontent may be felt with k as locational knowledge and the question posed ' Who or what is it which uniquely ϕs? ', where ' ϕ ' is the description k suggests. In the first case ' the ϕ ' or ' the thing which uniquely ϕs ' (or whatever description k suggests) will be genuinely referential. The speaker is content with his locational knowledge. In the second case he is not, indeed he *wants* a *further* location. From this it follows that ' the ϕ ' cannot be intended here as a genuinely referential expression. For the speaker is *ex hypothesi* wanting to know what particular satisfies the description ' the ϕ '. That requirement (iii) yields varying results according to what a speaker regards as adequate, *i.e.* according to his interests, seems to me not a disadvantage but an advantage of the criterion.

II

Six Objections to Taking Identity as a Relation

So much for the isolation of the class of statements to which I wish to deny predicative or relational analysis, the fourth class above. That this analysis is still widely accepted I take to be indicated by the fact that many people seem quite happy with the

---

[1] *Vide* Plato, *Theaetetus*, 188–9; *Sophist*, 237 ff.

[2] As will be evident, the formulation of the requirement is suggested by Strawson, *Individuals* (London, 1959), ch. I *et passim*. One of the many difficulties of formulating a ' knowing which I mean ' criterion is that the interrogative pronoun ' which ' of indirect questions can play as many roles as any noun-phrase. If I say the King of France does not exist I identify or locate nothing but I ' know which particular I mean.'

doctrine that in the sentence ' a is the same as b ' ' the same '
bears the ' numerical ' sense if it is meant that identity holds
between a and b and the ' qualitative' sense if it is meant that a
resembles b. To distinguish sorts of *sameness* cheerfully in this
manner can only be possible if one believes that the sentences are
otherwise of a comparable logical form, that differences in the
senses of the sentences must be traced to differences in the senses
of the words ' the same ', and, in particular, that a and b are no
less logical subjects in the ' numerical ' than the ' qualitative '
case.[1] It seems to be believed that the sense-reference distinction
will relieve the view of all paradox and difficulty.

Everyone who is discontent with the predicate or relation
plus two subjects theory seems to believe that Frege's earlier
two-signs theory,[2] revived by Wittgenstein[3], is substantially
correct. This view still has distinguished adherents.[4] I shall
touch upon it in Section III below.

My own view is that neither theory is correct.

The first argument to show that identity-statements are not of
the subject-predicate or relational form is this: The content of a
subject-predicate or relational statement certainly seems to be
determined by (a) what its term(s) is (are), and (b) what is said to
be true of those terms. If this principle is correct, and if identity-
statements are predicative or relational, then 'the evening star=
the morning star' and 'the evening star=the evening star ' should
have the same content. (So should 'Hesperus is Phosphorus' and
'Hesperus is Hesperus '.) But how can they have the same content
if the first is contingent and the second non-contingent?

The second difficulty is not a discovery of philosophers. It
is the awkwardness, noticed by every intelligent speaker, of ' They
are one and the same thing '. This can easily enough be avoided
by careful phrasing, but it points at something more serious. A
man who asserts that $a=b$ thereby commits himself to there being
only one thing he is referring to by ' a ' and ' b '. So when it is
asked what is ascribed to the logical subject of the utterance, the
upholder of the predicative analysis cannot refuse to allow that it is

---

[1] It is rather that assertions of different logical form force on the constituent
' the same ' different roles, in the ' numerical ' case that of indicating that a and
b are some one substance, *e.g.* planet, in the ' qualitative' case the role of indicating
that there is a predicate which both *satisfy*, a respect in which they *resemble*.
[2] *Begriffsschrift*, §8 (Geach and Black, *op. cit.*, pp. 10–12).
[3] *Tractatus* 4.23—4.243 and 5.53—5.5352.
[4] P. T. Geach, ' Subject and Predicate ', *Mind*, LIX (1950), pp. 461–82.

identity. Nor can he refuse to allow that this comes down to self-identity. Now there is no absurdity in a relation which holds between a thing and itself. A man may kick, feed, make provision for, &c., himself. The trouble with self-identity is that (unlike these reflexive transactions between part and whole, whole and environment) it is true of any individual whatever. If ' self-identical ' marks nothing off, how can it be a predicate or ascribe a genuine property? And how can contingent statements, in particular, result from its ascription?

It is perhaps just worth mentioning that the notion of *coincidence* (or *being continuous with*) gives us no help here. If ' The evening star coincides with the morning star ' means that their complete life-history is one and the same, or that tracing the evening star and tracing the morning star prove to be tracing the same planet, well and good. But then we have not advanced in saying what relation or predicate self-identity is. If on the other hand the sentence means that two series of segments of a ' four-dimensional worm ' join up into a continuous whole then the problem has simply been deferred. The evening star is a persisting thing, a planet with a *continuous* history in space and time, not a segment or a series of segments of a four-dimensional worm, nor a temporal stretch or series of temporal stretches of the planet Venus. The evening star segments are not the morning star segments at all. ' Coincides ' only gets us somewhere in our problem about a planet when we change the subject from a planet to planet-segments. The same original puzzle can be generated for planet-segments.

The third objection arises as an objection to what someone might regard as a promising attempt to construe identity as a relation. It might be said that the relation of identity marks off the pair consisting of an object and itself from pairs consisting of diverse objects. Thus $\{d, d\}$ and $\{b, b\}$ and $\{c, c\}$, it might be said, are marked off by the relation of identity from $\{d, b\}$ and $\{d, c\}$ and $\{c, b\}$. So the relation of identity might be thought to divide the class consisting of all possible pair classes intelligibly and exhaustively into two, pairs whose members satisfy the relation and pairs whose members do not, resembling in this every other respectable relation. But of course $\{x, x\} = \{x\}$. The division which is in fact effected is identical in upshot and intention to a division between unit classes and pair classes. The principle of bisection, so far from being a vindication of the relational theory, is in fact fatal to it. To say that $\{x, y\}$ belongs with the first set of pairs is tantamount to the numerical statement that there is but one individual here. (Note the idiom ' one and the same '.) Notoriously, statements of number cannot have individuals as logical subjects. They are complex statements about what falls under a concept.

If the degenerate ordered pair $\langle d; d\rangle$ is taken instead and is contrasted with the ordered pairs $\langle d; b\rangle$, $\langle d; c\rangle$, $\langle c; b\rangle$ . . . , then analogous results follow at one level up. For $\langle d; d\rangle = \{\{d\}\}$.[1] The division will be a division between classes whose members are unit classes and classes whose members are a unit class and a pair class $\{\{d\}, \{d, c.\}\}$.

As a fourth objection it is perhaps worth mentioning that relations have to have terms to hold between and hence presuppose the identification of these. So surely they presuppose the identity of these. How then could identity itself (or, its negation, diversity) be a relation?

As a fifth objection one could ask ' How would one teach identity as a relation? ' Does one show someone a thing, a, tell him to go on looking at it, and then when he's done a bit of looking say ' This is the thing I first showed you. Now you understand that this, namely a, has to this, a '—then one points to something else, b—' what that, b, has to that, b, and what this, a has not to that, b '? The man would already have had to understand identification, hence identity, in order to take in the lesson.

Still, it may be said, of the five objections so far urged the fifth and third rest on mere analogies, and the others simply show that identity is a very odd relation or predicate. They don't show it isn't one.

The sixth objection seems to me, with the first, conclusive but it is a long business to prove this. For they are essentially Frege's objections[2] and he seems to have thought that his answer, the sense-reference distinction, enabled him both to master the objections, call identity a relation,[3] and accommodate identity-statements within the subject+predicate schema, if he wished, by the device of reading ' $=$ ' as ' is none other than ' where ' is ' is allowed the normal function of the copula.[4]

---

[1] Provided one defines an ordered pair $\langle x,y\rangle$ with Kuratowski as $\{\{x\},\{x,y\}\}$.
[2] ' On Sense and Reference,' in Geach and Black, op. cit., p. 155.
[3] *Vide Grundgesetze der Arithmetik,* I § 4, in Geach and Black, op. cit., p. 155.
[4] ' On Concept and Object,' in Geach and Black, op. cit., p. 43–4.

The objection may be put like this. Self-identity is guaranteed to every individual. If this is what statements of identity say about their logical subjects then all statements of this kind should be logically true, or anyway logically guaranteed by the mere existence of a reference for the referring expressions in the sentences by which they are made. Yet while some statements have this logical guarantee, for instance ' The evening star = the evening star ' does, others have not. ' The evening star = the morning star ', is a proposition which Greeks and Babylonians had some trouble to establish. Statements of self-identity should not exclude anything if self-identity is analytically guaranteed. Self-identity must by its nature be so guaranteed. Yet some, but not all, statements of identity *do* seem to exclude something. To put the same thing another way, some identity-statements are false in spite of a reference existing for their noun-phrases, others cannot be false if a reference exists for their noun-phrases.

I should wish to say that these six difficulties must be traced to the assumption that identity-statements *assert something* (which then has to be the relation or predicate self-identity) *of the references* of their noun phrases. But this deduction can only be justified by demonstrating the inadequacy of other solutions and answers to the objections.

III

The Begriffsschrift *and* Tractatus *theories of identity.*

In the simplest terms, what is required to do justice to the fact that ' The evening star=the evening star ' (P) has a different logical status and different sort of truth-condition from ' The evening star=the morning star ' (Q) is a theory which will explain the difference in what is *said* in each statement and which will build this difference into *the import of each statement.* Both the *Begriffsschrift* theory and the sense-reference theory (which I shall examine in Section IV) purport to do this.

The *Begriffsschrift* explanation is that in the statement Q *each* noun-phrase occurs autonymously or stands for itself. The judgment says that the two expressions have ' equality of content ' or that the same content is given by two ways of determining it, one being given by ' the evening star ' and the other by ' the morning star '. In statement P there is only one expression, so we learn nothing. This differentiates it from Q, from which we can learn something.

The theory does not leave the different logical status of P and Q bare of explanation but, as Frege said, it gives the wrong explanation. It also gives rise to an infinite regress.

It gives the wrong explanation because the Greeks and Babylonians made an astronomical not a linguistic discovery when they established Q. The analysis does no justice to this. Wittgenstein was able to ignore Frege's problem in the *Tractatus* when he revived the theory because he held a version of the theory of descriptions and could deny that the planet was a genuine constituent in any proposition. For him the dispensable identity sign only figured between logically proper names, or between variables ranging over owners of logically proper names; and he thought the answer ' No ' would have to be given to the question ' Can we understand two names without knowing whether they signify the same thing or two different things? Can we understand a proposition in which two names occur without knowing whether their meaning is the same or different? '[1] But, as we shall see, it is not so clear as Wittgenstein implies that the answer is ' No ', if we take the only sort of proper names one can really believe in, ordinary ones.

The regress which the two-signs theory causes, at least in Frege's formulation, arises in the following way. Asking for the sense of ' $a = b$ ' I am told ' a ' and ' b ' have the same content, or designate only one thing. Unless something is said to justify calling a halt here, the explanation generates a new statement of the same form as the original explicandum—' The content or designatum of " a " = the content or designatum of " b ".' Applying the same explanation to this we get ' The content or designatum of " the content or designatum of ' a ' " = the content or designatum of " the content or designatum of ' b ' ".' But evidently we never can reach in this way what seems to be needed to carry the explanation through, a statement only about signs.

In Wittgenstein's formulation of the theory this regress, admittedly, does not arise because the identity-sign says nothing about the content of expressions. It is simply a permission to substitute one expression for another. The regress is blocked, however, at the price of making it logically impossible to state an informative identity by means of proper names. Thus the analogue of the evening star puzzle cannot arise, it seems, for bearers of proper names. Yet if we reject simples and assign

[1] *Tractatus*, 4.243, tr. D. F. Pears and B. F. McGuinness (London, 1960).

E

proper names to workaday persisting things of whose complete spatio-temporal history we may have only partial knowledge, then it is quite unclear why the puzzle cannot arise for this kind of bearer of a proper name. If we had to know all about a planet in order to name or identify it we could never get started in learning anything about the planet's history.[1] If on the other hand one can use a proper name without knowing *all* about its bearer's history then one can formulate a non-trivial identity-statement by means of proper names, *e.g.*, ' Hesperus is Phosphorus.'

There is undoubtedly something worth salvaging in the Russell-Wittgenstein theory. I shall return to it when I have rendered the sense-reference option unattractive.

IV

The Sense-Reference Theory of Identity-Statements

Frege hoped when he abandoned his earlier for his later view[2] to give both a better answer than the linguistic one to the puzzle of non-trivial identities and an explanation of the apparent falsity of the version of Leibniz's Law which he had assumed without qualification in the *Begriffsschrift*, that if symbol x and symbol y have the same conceptual content then x can always replace y and conversely.

I have no general quarrel at all with the theory, which suggests a beautiful and powerful theory of meaning for decidable propositions[3] of great generality and explanatory power. Indeed it can be employed, I think, in the statement of a correct analysis of identity-statements. What I shall suggest after expounding it is this, *and only this*, that whatever Frege thought,[4] the sense and reference theory cannot save any subject+predicate or term+ relation+term analysis of identity statements. It overcomes none of the six objections of II.

The theory, which I shall not expound exactly as Frege originally expounded it, can be seen as originating in three insights which are not in any way special to the analysis of identity:

(*a*) that to know the meaning of an utterance is to know what it is for it to be true, which latter is no more and no less mysterious

---

[1] An ancient puzzle. *Vide* Plato, *Meno* 80D, *Theaetetus* 188.
[2] *Vide* ' Function and Concept,' ' On Sense and Reference' and *Grundgesetze der Arithmetik*, I, §§ 6–7, in Geach and Black, *op. cit.*, and ' The Thought,' tr. A. M. and M. Quinton, *Mind*, LXV (1956), passim.
[3] In Dummett's sense of ' decidable ': *vide* ' Truth,' *loc. cit.*
[4] And this is not perhaps certain: *vide infra.* p. 60, fn 1

than our ability to accept or reject a given counter, conceived as making an assertion, in an orderly or regular way according to the way the world is;[1]

(b) that the faculty of speech, in particular the capacity to produce and understand novel utterances,[2] can only be explained by showing how utterances are built up step by step from simpler components (whose own meaning is given by explaining the part they play as a feature in the primitive utterances acceptable or rejectable as above at (a)); and

(c) that we must distinguish how an expression signifies from what it signifies.

The third insight is central to our present concerns. If we are to explain, what has to be explained, how a language consisting of a finite number of elements can generate an infinite number of possible strings of elements each of which strings can be used to indicate one of an infinite number of possible states of affairs, then we cannot explain the meaning of any expression *e* by particular allusion to, or particular explanation of, what *e* signifies on a particular occasion of use. We can only get the kind of explanation we need if we have an account of what part *e* plays in determining the content or truth-grounds of *any arbitrary* message in which it occurs.

How does requirement (c) work out for each main syntactic category of expression? A simple or genuine proper name *n* gets its sense simply in virtue of having been assigned to something. What it has been assigned to is its reference. One point of insisting on what may seem, anyway in this simple case, the excessively abstract distinction between *how n* designates what it designates and *what n* designates, and one point of being discontent to mention only reference even here, is the need in theory of meaning to explain how the use of *n* helps to determine the assertibility-conditions or truth-grounds of *all* sentences containing it. In the sentence ' The capital of Denmark is a beautiful city ' the proper name ' Denmark ' does not designate any constituent of which anything is stated by the whole utterance. *That ' Denmark ' designates Denmark*, (so the sense of ' Denmark '), is what must figure in the explanation of how the complex designation ' capital

---

[1] For a more accurate account *vide* Dummett, *loc. cit.*, p. 150.
[2] Cp. M. A. E. Dummett, ' Nominalism ', *The Philosophical Review*, LXV (1956), pp. 491–505, *ad init.*

of Denmark ', which introduces the subject of the sentence, Copenhagen, designates what it designates.[1] In the case of complex designations (definite descriptions, &c.) there is less temptation to confuse sense with reference. An explanation of their signification which omitted explanation of how they picked out what they picked out would be manifestly incomplete.

The distinction between sense and reference is more obscure for predicates but there is no doubt that Frege thought a similar distinction held,[2] and that he can be defended on this score. Certainly nothing can be designated by any predicate in the way something is designated by a proper name or definite description. (Russell's non-self-predicable paradox would exclude the possibility[3] even if it could not in any case be seen to be absurd.) But this does not show that some analogous distinction is not required. In any complete thought of the subject-predicate form (ϕa) or term +relation+term form(Rab) one isolable element is *what a is* or *what a has to b*,[4] namely that which is ascribed to a. This element, the concept, can only be understood, admittedly, in its containing framework of predication, and can only be alluded to by an indirect locution, (*e.g.*, ' what the predicate ' ϕ ' stands for '),[5] but it can be spoken of. Moreover a perfectly good sense can be given to quantification over such elements (*e.g.*, ' There is something you are which I am not, namely an upholder of identity as a relation ').[6] Now suppose that in theory of meaning we were to confine our attention to such elements. We could explain, perhaps, how the word ' round ' ascribes what it ascribes in ' a is green and round '. But what could we make of ' red ' in ' a is other than red ' or ' a is coloured the complementary of red '? Redness is not in fact *ascribed* in this sentence to anything, as it is

---

[1] I have not here given Frege's original explanation of the need for the distinction between sense and reference (nor his account of the sense of proper names. *Vide* p. 66, fn. 1). For this explanation to some extent depends on commitment to his own explanation of the puzzle about identity-statements, an explanation one may need to supplant. It is, however, based on something he later said which seems unquestionably right (*vide* M. A. E. Dummett, *op. cit.*, *The Philosophical Review*, LXV (1956), p. 229.)

[2] *Vide* M. Dummett, ' Frege on Functions: a Reply ', *The Philosophical Review*, LXIV (1955), p. 96, and *op. cit.* (1956), p. 229.

[3] *E.g.*, *vide* P. T. Geach, ' Subject and Predicate ', *loc. cit.*, p. 476.

[4] *Vide* M. Dummett, *loc. cit.* (1955) and P. T. Geach, ' Class and Concept,' *ibid.* (1955), pp. 561–570.

[5] *Vide e.g.* Geach in P. T. Geach and G. E. M. Anscombe, *Three Philosophers* (Oxford, 1961), p. 156. There is a well known difficulty here, that the concept *horse* is not a concept (*vide* Geach and Black, *loc. cit.*, p. 46).

[6] *Vide* M. Dummett, *loc. cit.* (1955) and P. T. Geach, *loc. cit.* (1955).

in ' *a* is red '. We must explain the sense of ' other than red ' by allusion to the *sense* of ' red ' (a sense which suits it to ascribe redness in those sentences where redness *is* ascribed and where ' red ' has a reference). We need both an account of how concept-words go to determine what is ascribed in any sentence (and so help to determine truth-grounds) and an account in any particular case of what they ascribe in that particular case. The first is the sense of a concept-word. The second (which is dependent on the first) may quite harmlessly be called its reference.

Three ways might suggest themselves of extending insight (*c*) above to the complete sentence. We might say

(1) that sense of name : bearer of name :: sense of sentence : fact, or

(2) that sense of name : bearer of name :: sense of sentence : truth-value of utterance of sentence, or

(3) that sense of name : bearer of name :: sense of sentence : proposition expressed by sentence.

Frege, inspired by the paradigm of a function in arithmetic, thought the analogy between name and sentence would be complete and inevitably chose (2)[1]. ((1) would have made false propositions meaningless. (3) would have made it a mystery how sentences ever *said* anything, for one can refer to propositions without saying anything true or false.) This analogy cannot however be complete. For to the theory of the True as the *reference* of true utterances (with its accompaniment, the assertion-sign) there are two decisive objections.[2] In weakening the analogy so that the sense of a sentence merely determines some one thing, possibility (3) must receive as much scrutiny as (2). But (2) is clearly to be preferred, and on grounds quite independent of Frege's identification of the sense with the proposition or the thought (which, as we shall see, is open to question). For an understanding of the constituent words and derivation of a sentence *s* must give us a way to the meaning of *s*. This cannot be

---

[1] (2) was also the inevitable choice because of the doctrine that the reference of a sentence was a function of the references of its parts (*vide* M. Dummett, *loc. cit.* (1958–59)). This doctrine is reported to have been abandoned (*vide* M. Dummett, *loc. cit.* (1956), p. 229), and I have attempted to expound the whole theory in a shape it might have assumed when the doctrine had been given up.

[2] *Vide* M. Dummett, *loc. cit.* (1958–9) and T. J. Smiley, ' Propositional Functions ', *The Aristotelian Society*, Suppl. Vol. XXXIV (1960), pp. 31–46.

other than a way to the *truth-grounds* of *s*. There is only one thing these can determine and this is the truth-value.

We are now in a position to state the theory of sense and reference in its general form for a simple language *L* containing (1) proper names; (2) simple concept-words; (3) complex designations and complex concept-words built out of (1) and (2); (4) sentences built up out of (1), (2) and (3) in accordance with simple derivation schemata; (5) logical constants; (6) sentences compounded from (4) and (5).

The sense of a sentence is determined uniquely (i) by the manner in which the sentence expressing it is built up in an orderly way out of, say, proper names or complex designations, and concept-words, (ii) by the senses of these constituent designations and concept-words.[1] Conversely the sense of a word is determined by the senses of the thoughts in whose expression it is used and the derivational structure of those thoughts, (*i.e.* (i) above).

The sense of a word is the contribution it makes to the determination of the sense of any sentences containing it. Knowing the sense of a sentence *s* (*i.e.* understanding a thought) is knowing the truth-grounds of what is said by any utterance of *s*.[2] One knows these when one knows what counts for and against acceptance of the utterance and has learned to assign the truth-value true or false to the utterance according to how things are.

Thus the sense of a word is a function of the senses of sentences containing it and the sense of a sentence is a function of the senses of its constituent words. There is no circularity here. We could begin with an initial corpus of simple and complete sentences, *c*, and teach a man directly the behavioural skill of accepting or rejecting particular uses of them.[3] When it was seen what syntactic features these sentences shared, the contribution made by the presence of any feature *f* (*i.e.* the powers of any particular word) could be secured by noticing (roughly) how acceptability-conditions or truth-conditions of members of *c* varied concomitantly with the occurrence and manner of occurrence, or the

---

[1] We might add, if we wish to give a general account applicable outside the realm of timeless truths: (iii) the circumstances of utterance and those extra-linguistic factors which help to elucidate the reference of demonstrative and token reflexive referring expressions.

[2] *Vide* G. Frege, *Grundgesetze der Arithmetik* I, § 32.

[3] *Vide* M. Dummett, 'Truth,' *loc. cit.*, *passim*.

absence, of *f*. The powers of words thus fixed, *c* could be extended and more complex sentences could be constructed out of the common features of members of *c* and by iteration of the primitive patterns of sentence construction given in *c*.

The theory as here presented does not depend on there being any close analogy between the relation of name, sense and bearer on the one hand and sentence, thought and truth-value on the other hand. For to deny that sentences have a reference at all (as one should), and to deny therefore that the True and the False are the references of sentences, is to leave absolutely undisturbed the insight that whether the sentence *s* makes a statement which is true is jointly determined by the sense of *s* and what is the case. Frege can say the sense of any expression (name or sentence) in conjunction with what is the case determines its reference. We may say (1) that the sense of a referring expression (with the facts) determines its reference, (2) that the sense of a sentence determines (with what is the case) whether or not its utterance yields a true statement.

A diagram will represent all this information for the sentence scheme ' ϕa '.

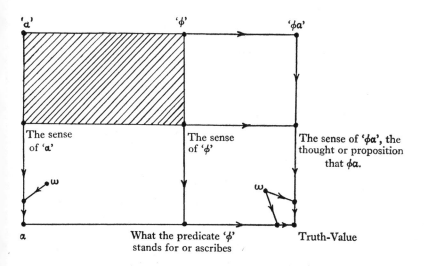

Key: ' ω ' stands (i) for factual information one would need to pin down (with demonstrative and contexual aids) a reference for a referring phrase ' a ', (ii) for further factual information one would need to assign a truth-value to ' ϕa '.

The difference in purport of P ('The evening star is the evening star') and Q ('the evening star is the morning star') can now be explained. The descriptions 'the evening star' and 'the morning star' have different senses. P and Q will therefore have their senses determined by elements of a different sense and therefore their own senses will be different. The suggestion is that this explains the difference in how each's truth-value is determined. The following diagram represents Q:

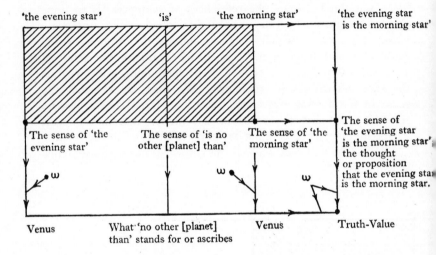

'the evening star'   'is'   'the morning star'   'the evening star is the morning star'

The sense of 'the evening star'   The sense of 'is no other [planet] than'   The sense of 'the morning star'   The sense of 'the evening star is the morning star', the thought or proposition that the evening star is the morning star.

Venus   What 'no other [planet] than' stands for or ascribes   Venus   Truth-Value

In the diagram for P the sense of 'the evening star' would occur twice on the middle horizontal. The thoughts expressed by P and Q are thus differently determined.

V

General Difficulties of the Sense-Reference Approach

The sense-reference distinction explains admirably why I must be in possession of interesting information to say that the evening star is the morning star. I could not bring off two references to the planet in these diverse ways if I were not in possession of such. But how is this information *built into what I say* if the sentence is construed in the normal way as about the planet? As Frege himself remarks, ' If words are used in the normal way what one intends to speak of is their reference ';[1] and nothing might seem more self-evident than this. Why then should *the way* in which the subject(s) in the sentence ' The evening star = the morning star ' are picked out by definite descriptions affect what is *said* about it (them)? How has the question ' What is asserted of it? ' and the answer ' Self-identity ' been improved upon? It surely does not affect what I say of my brother when I say he wants a drink whether I refer to him as ' my brother ' or as ' the man over there with the discontented expression ' or as ' the man in the Wellington boots '. What is said is that he wants a drink. Similarly if a predicative analysis of Q is insisted on and the logical subject is still a planet what is still said is that the planet is self-identical. But everything is self-identical. So how could some self-identities be logically guaranteed and others not logically guaranteed? The same old difficulty is with us as before. This relational analysis is simply not suited to *explain* how the manner of reference affects content. (Asserting that it does is not explaining it.)

It should be remarked that this deduction is very much in accord with Frege's own approach. He rightly regards Leibniz's Law as in *some* form obviously true and believes, in my opinion rightly, that every apparent breakdown of it must be properly explained. Whenever the law in fact breaks down he shows, I think plausibly, that the apparent reference of a sign is not its real reference and that this can be seen *independently of the fact that substitutivity has broken down*. What Frege does not seem to concede is that unless we are to renounce Leibniz's Law, or renounce the self-evident principle which he himself propounds, the principle which Carnap calls the principle of subject-matter —' a sentence is about (deals with, includes in its subject matter) the nominata of the names occurring in it '[2]—or renounce the predicative (' is none other than ') account, then there remains a difficulty about statements of identity. For the substitution of ' evening star ' for ' morning star ' in Q does not change either the (alleged) logical subject nor what is asserted of that logical subject. How then can it change the character and truth-grounds of the

---

[1] ' On Sense and Reference,' in Geach and Black, *op. cit.*, p. 58.
[2] R. Carnap, *Meaning and Necessity* (Chicago, 1947), p. 98.

statement made by the sentence?[1] Yet it does do so. It is easy enough to see why it should if we have a Russellian view of definite descriptions. But then we do not need the Sense-Reference theory specially to account for identity-statements and it is certainly no special help there.

VI

Specific Difficulties in the Sense-Reference Approach

These difficulties can be given a representation in the diagrams of Section V.

In the theory as it stands in the essay ' On Sense and Reference ' a truth-value can be reached by two paths, as a function of references and as a function of senses. This causes a preliminary difficulty in the explanation of the differences between *P*'s and *Q*'s senses. (1) The determination of truth-value for *P* and *Q* via *references* is exactly the same. Both are about Venus, and both have as predicate term what the predicate ' none other than ' ascribes. Under this aspect of the theory *P* and *Q* have their truth determined in the same way and should have identical truth-grounds. But in fact they have not. (2) If the referential determination of truth-value is dropped then we are left only with the determination of truth-value by the sense of the sentence, this sense being determined by senses of parts. There is nothing wrong with this, though the necessity which identity-statements create to limit the theory in this way at least points to the conclusion for which I am arguing, that the terms of identity-statements are not referential in the standard way.

Another difficulty can be put by reference to the diagram. We are told that *P* and *Q* have a different sense and are intended to conclude from this that they say different things, have different sorts of truth-ground, or express different thoughts or propositions. We cannot however allow Frege simply to define sense and thought

[1]Although I do not know of anywhere where Frege explicitly mentions the difficulty or draws the conclusion I am pressing, I think that something like it can be seen at the back of his mind in his address ' Function and Concept ' (which was given in 1891 and contains plentiful allusions to the forthcoming ' On Sense and Reference '). Here he says ' what is expressed in the equation " $2.2^3+2=18$ " is that the right-hand complex of signs has the same reference as the left ' (Geach and Black, *op. cit.*, p. 22). Perhaps this is not so much a backsliding into the *Begriffsschrift* view as a symptom of discomfort at having to say that 2.2^3+2 and 18 are the logical subjects of a relation. One senses that Frege felt that the Sense-Reference theory ought to allow him room to say something else.

into equivalence by mere fiat. There must be some examination of the prior question whether or not the same thought can be expressed in different ways.[1] Can expressions composed of parts of different sense really never say the same thing? Cannot the same thing ever be said in different ways? If it can then it seems a difference in sense is not enough to explain a difference in what is said. To explain at all the difference in truth-grounds of P and Q, and provide a difference in purport, the sense-reference theory must *force* us to admit they say different things.

The weight of Frege's own authority favours not the negative but the affirmative answer to our question. In ' On Concept and Object ' (published in 1892, one year after ' On Sense and Reference ') Frege says ' We must not fail to recognize that the same sense, the same thought, may be variously expressed. . . . If all transformations of the expression were forbidden on the plea that this would alter the content as well, logic would simply be crippled; for the task of logic can hardly be performed without trying to

---

[1] If we decided that it could, and that there was a distinction worth making between sense = lexical force (what does x mean?) and sense = proposition (what does he mean in saying x?), and if we decided that the criterion for ' same proposition ' necessarily depended on identity in context of reference and identity of ascription, then the diagram would have to be redrawn as follows:

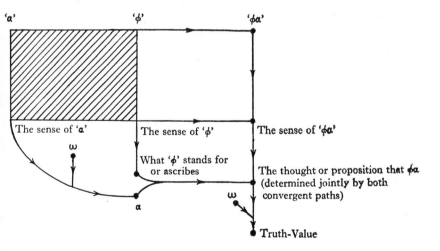

The proposition or thought expressed by ' ϕa ' is now in part determined both by the senses of the constituents of ' ϕa ' and by the references of those constituents.

recognize the thought in its manifold guises. Moreover all definitions would have to be rejected as false '.[1] If this is given one strong interpretation a difference in the senses of P and Q yields no automatic explanation of the difference in their truth-grounds. For P and Q may still say the same thing (assert the self-identity of a planet) even though they have a different sense.

Someone might object at this point that Frege could and would have chosen to reply to my question that no expressions of different sense can say the same thing, and that he could have limited the transformations alluded to in the quoted passage to logical transformations. ' Evening star ' and ' morning star ' are not logically guaranteed the same reference. Apart from transformations which are licensed by logic alone or by dictionary equivalences, Frege would have said there cannot be two ways of saying the same thing.

This uninviting possibility must be explored. (I say ' uninviting ' because the supposition has no plausibility independent of the puzzle discovered about identity-statements. That puzzle may be soluble in other ways.) My objection to the suggestion is that it makes the individuation of facts and propositions a complete mystery.

Let us suppose that it is in virtue of the same fact that it is true that my brother wants a drink (R), that the man in gum boots wants a drink (S), and that the man with fair hair and a discontented expression wants a drink (T). For, let us suppose, these are one and the same person. Now either the individuation of facts marches in step with the individuation of what utterances say or it does not. We will explore both possibilities.

Suppose that it does, and that there is a one-one correlation between facts and true propositions. Then if R, S and T say something different (which is what we must suppose if expressions with a different sense never say the same thing), the facts in virtue of which R, S and T are true will be different facts. But then it is a complete mystery why to settle the truth of R is ipso facto to settle the truth of S and T. If these are true in virtue of different facts ought we not to have to check separately? But, it may be said, the man in gum-boots with sad expression *is* your brother, that is why no separate check is needed. The counter-objection is, does not this show that R, S and T are true in virtue of the same fact,

---

[1] Geach and Black, *op. cit.*, p. 46. Cp. *ibid.*, p. 80.

which is contrary to this hypothesis? Why, *given* the identity, does one investigation suffice?

Let us explore the other possibility. This is, as always, that it is not possible to say the same thing with expressions of a different sense and (the other option for facts) that the individuation of facts need not, though it may sometimes, march in step with the individuation of what utterances say. It is now easy enough to explain why one investigation settles R, S and T in spite of the circumstance that R, S and T say something different. The trouble is rather that we need some neutral access to the fact in virtue of which R, S and T are true, access which is not mediated by propositions R, S and T. How are we to refer to this fact neutrally?[1] By the use of proper names, it may be suggested. ' F. P. T. Wiggins wants a drink ' (U) will then give us access to that in virtue of which R, S and T are true, and will be the common fact incapsulated in the facts that R, that S, that T. It would be important for Frege (though it would not be for anyone who thought you could say the same thing with expressions of different sense and therefore that you could allude to the same fact by ' that '-clauses of different sense) that this proper name be devoid of descriptive content (except perhaps the information that its bearer was a man). If it had descriptive content we should have another proposition of the same genre as R, S and T and we should be no further forward.

The difficulty is now of course that proper names have to be assigned and their bearers individuated. This brings us back to descriptions and demonstratives. Although there is no particular description, except ' man ', of which the proper name ' F. P. T. Wiggins ' is not independent, it does not follow that the use of proper names is independent of the possession of descriptions over and above 'man '.

[1] There is nothing wrong with the supposition that one can refer to facts. Of course if the proposition that P were about the fact, or referred to the fact, in virtue of which it was true that P, then false statement would become impossible. This is what most people have had in mind when they said that propositions indicated, but were not about and did not refer to, facts. But alluding to facts is not the same as stating them, and nobody has ever proved that alluding to them was as such impossible. And it would seem to destroy the possibility of any theory of evidence or truth to suppose that one could not allude to them. It is absurd to let justifiable discontent with the correspondence theory (to which nothing in the text commits me) precipitate one into denying that there must be something in virtue of which true propositions are true (*vide* M. Dummett, ' Truth ', *loc. cit.*, p. 157). If one did deny this how would one explain why one set of consistent asertions was better than another?

How then about using demonstratives instead of proper names? The interdependences of that in virtue of which it was true that R, true that S, and true that T, would rest on the circumstance that the truth of each depended on one and the same fact, sc. (W), that this man wants a drink. There are certainly oddities about this suggestion—for one thing it would seem one could only give a satisfactory neutral reference to a present and directly identified state of affairs. Waive the oddity and suppose the answer satisfactory. It raises again in a new form a familiar problem.

If the truth of W is necessary and sufficient for the truth of R, S and T then how can R, S and T have an extra purport over and above the sense of W? It is no longer clear then that difference in *purport* is guaranteed by difference of sense.

Applying this conclusion about R, S and T—namely that they are not yet demonstrated to have different purport—back to P and Q we find that difference in sense does not give any explanation, clear or unclear, of the difference in their purport or truth-grounds. But their purports and truth-grounds are different.

VII

Solutions which reject a referential analysis of the noun-phrases

If we reject the predicative or relational analysis of identity-statements how shall we analyse these statements, and how shall we contrast them with, and relate them to, predicative and relational statements?

We might try to build those individuating facts which make reference possible into the analysis of propositions in some other way. It might be suggested that you could certainly say the same thing by means of R, S and T, namely that W, but that the propositions that R, that S, that T, each had an extra content derived from the manner of reference to the particular, my brother. This suggestion might certainly have been made in defence of Frege. Oddly, it leads almost inevitably, though by quite a different route from Russell's, to a Russellian analysis of the identity-statement Q:[1]

$(Q1)$ $(\exists x)$ $(\exists y)$ [(Evening star x) & (w) (Evening star $w. \supset .w{=}x$) & (Morning star y) & (z) (Morning star $z \supset z{=}y$) & $(y{=}x$)]

Whether or not Russell's treatment of definite descriptions is in general correct, identity-statements, at any rate, turn out to be second-order statements about concepts.

[1] *Vide* ' On Denoting ', *Mind*, XII (1905), pp. 479–93.

This analysis leads to difficulties and amendments and these lead in their turn to further difficulties. Some of these must be reviewed.

(1) If the identity of indiscernibles is not to be presupposed and if we are to be spared complete description of the evening star and the morning star in the attempt to secure the intended reference, then some demonstrative element must be introduced into the predicates in the first four conjuncts following the quantifiers. One of Strawson's objections to the theory of descriptions can indeed be met in this way.[1]

(2) The identity sign still figures between variables. These must be supposed (if we reject objects of acquaintance, simples &c.) to range over the bearers of common or garden proper names. Is the occurrence of the identity-sign between proper names (or their surrogates), any easier to understand than its occurrence between definite descriptions? Or do the evening star puzzle and all our objections to taking identity as a relation now fail to apply? Surely if planets can have proper names the puzzle arises all over again; and however often we redeploy the Russellian analysis by forming definite descriptions to correspond to these apparent proper names we shall always be left with an analysis containing ' $=$ ' between variables, variables which range over bearers of proper names.

The charm of the *Tractatus* theory is that it stops this regress of explanation, and suggests a reading of ' $=$ ' which is not relational. It would allow informative identities to be reduced to statements about concepts while on a lower tier identity-signs between variables could be explained by allusion to the possibility of intersubstitution of proper names without change in truth-grounds.

(3) Reflection on the sense of proper names may prompt us to try to save the *Tractatus* explanation. The descriptions ' pupil of Plato and teacher of Alexander ' and ' teacher of Alexander born at Stagira' exploit different facts to pick out their reference. Genuine proper names however get their sense not by picking out something which satisfies them but by being assigned to something. (This is, I take it, what Mill,[2] Russell and Ryle[3] have meant

---

[1] ' On Referring,' *loc. cit.*   [2] *A System of Logic*, I.i.5.
[3] ' The Theory of Meaning,' *British Philosophy in the Mid-Century*, ed. C. A. Mace (London, 1957), pp. 239–64.

by denying them any connotation.) In Frege's theory of sense and reference any sign whose presence contributes to the determination of a truth-value (and no less, therefore, any signs conventionally assigned to pick out one object) must have a sense. Though the theory did not solve the puzzle of identity-statements it is in general acceptable enough. We may certainly accept that proper names must have a sense as well as a reference. Frege's own explanation of the sense of normal proper names (of the ordinary kind) seems to be no help to the *Tractatus* explanation.[1] If Frege's explanation were right informative identity-statements could certainly be made by use of proper names. But other explanations of their sense are available.

The concept under which the bearer is picked out[2] will not alone suffice to yield a sense, or anyway the sort of sense demanded. (For ' *Rab* ' and ' *Rba* ', if *a* and *b* were picked out under the same concept, would have the same sense if this concept gave the sense.)

What does remain to bestow the requisite sense, it could be said, is the fact that the sign has been assigned to the particular it has been assigned to, that particular being individuable and traceable through time in whatever way it is individuable and traceable.[3]

It seems to follow that any two genuine proper names of the same object will have the same sense. To appeal against this to differences in circumstances of assignment or learning, it might be said, is to leave without explanation the fact that we constantly overcome contingent details like this in finding access to the sense of words. We must do so if the senses of words are not to collapse into the mere subjectivities which Frege himself ought to have been the first to reject in this case (as he did in other cases) as having nothing to do with meaning or logic.

If this were right then the *Tractatus* explanation of ' $=$ ' between variables of quantification might be correct and the problem would be solved. All statements made by the use of ' $=$ '

---

[1] *Vide* ' The Thought,' *Mind*, LXV (1956), pp. 297–8.

[2] P. T. Geach, *Mental Acts* (London, 1956), p. 60.

[3] That there is no favoured description or characterization ' ϕ ' of a proper-named individual *a* which would yield the requisite sense can be proved in the following way. Make any choice for ' ϕ ' other than the substance-concept under which *a* is identified (which, being multiply satisfied, does not yield the complete sense of ' *a* '). Then it will have to be a contradiction to say ' not ϕa '. For *being* ϕ would be a part of the sense of ' *a* '. But facts which serve to identify and form definite descriptions can be and characteristically are contingent.

between genuine proper names would automatically have trivial truth-grounds like *P*. The trouble is this. If proper names have sense in this way then do we in fact *have* any genuine proper names? Are ' Hesperus ' and ' Phosphorus ' proper names at all? Do we know *all* about the history of the planet Venus? The account gives an ideal of a proper name to which, it seems, the ones we actually use (and think we understand the sense of) can only approximate. Surely I need the full apparatus of referential devices (including presumably proper names) to get the complete knowledge of the spatio-temporal history of the planet Venus which would be a prerequisite of my correctly understanding all the identity-statements which were made about Venus by the use of pairs of *genuine* proper names. For this knowledge would be a prerequisite of my understanding the identity-statements in the right way, that is as statements with truth-grounds as trivial as those of *P*.

(4) There are a number of ways in which we could attempt to expel ' = ' from its position between variables. We could modify and simplify the Russellian translation to read:

(*Q2*) (*x*) (*M.S.x* ≡ *E.S.x*) & (the number of the concept *both M.S. and E.S.* is 1)

or

(*Q3*) (x) (*M.S.x* ≡ *E.S.x*) & (only one thing falls under the concept *E.S. and M.S.*)

How illuminating is any of these translations? Analysis *Q2* may seem itself to involve an identity-statement, a numerical one. Arithmetical identity-statements are certainly not exempt from the sort of difficulties we have been trying to overcome. I think that a case could be made for saying that statements of the form ' the number of the concept *F and G* is 1 ' were analogous to what I called in Section I ' locations ', and for denying therefore that they were strictly identity-statements at all. But even if this were admitted it could be retorted that locations depended upon the ascription of predicates a part of whose sense involved uniqueness; and it could be maintained that it needed to be shown that this uniqueness-element could be understood without recourse to ' = '.

Similarly it could be objected to Analysis *Q3* that, though it avoided the hypostatization of numbers and therefore avoided any overt appearance of identity-statement, the *analysis* of numerical

F

statements taken in this way uses identity essentially. For the analysis will have to resemble Frege's suggestion: ' The number 1 belongs to a concept F, if the proposition that a does not fall under F is not true universally, whatever a may be, and if from the propositions " a falls under F " and " b falls under F " it follows universally that a and b are the same '.[1] Frege finds this analysis deficient in any case, but, even if it could be saved, ' $=$ ' would not have been expelled in the way we desired.

(5) At this point I suppose I could say that, in spite of the fact that further analysis of $Q2$ and $Q3$ reintroduces ' $=$ ' essentially, still $Q2$ and $Q3$ do illuminate the real nature of identity-statements. You cannot expect to have *number* and *identity* and *uniqueness* analysed simultaneously. $Q1$—$Q3$ do, after all, suggest some sort of answer to our problem. For given any particular contingent identity-statement, p, one can always find by means of $Q1$—$Q3$ a translation of p which is about how concepts are satisfied, and which demonstrates how p itself can be contingent.

(6) Some people, however, will certainly not be content with this situation as it is, and it may be worth seeing what could be done to allay that discontent by further attempts to expel ' $=$ ' completely. In a further attempt on $Q1$—$Q3$ the usual reductions of arithmetic to logic could be employed taking ' ϵ ' as primitive and using the definition.

$$(x=y) : \equiv . (w) \ (x \ \epsilon \ w) \ \equiv \ (y \ \epsilon \ w)$$

to expel ' $=$ ' at all points. It is a fatal objection to this that this definition of ' $=$ ' presupposes that we can individuate all sets. How can we decide about whether the unit sets $\{a\}$ and $\{b\}$ are identical without knowing whether or not $a=b$?

A more heroic course would be to analyse ' The number of the concept F is 1 ' as ' There are as many Fs as there are unit sets of the null set '. The null set would be defined as $\hat{x} \ (\phi x . \sim \phi x)$. (This description-operator for sets would present difficulties however.) The unit set of $\hat{x} \ (\phi x \sim \phi x)$ would be defined as the set whose members had every property that $\hat{x} \ (\phi x \sim \phi x)$ had. ' Equinumerous ' would have to be defined by simply writing the identity of indiscernibles definition of identity ' $(\phi)(\phi x \equiv \phi y)$', wherever ' $=$ ' occurred in the normal definition. This, or any similar construction, could hardly command less confidence with

[1] *Grundlagen der Arithmetik*, § 55 (J. L. Austin, *op. cit.*, p. 67).

the reader than it does with me. I shall suggest a reason for the resistance we meet in all these attempts in the next section.

(7) If the analyses *Q1—Q3* have any power to illuminate at all, as (5) suggested they did, and if it is correct that noun-phrases in identity-statements really indicate *concepts*, then one obvious objection must be met. In Section I it was said that identity-statements were statements with two genuinely referential terms. Some trouble was taken to insist on this. Now it is said that identity is some sort of predicate of concepts. The answer to this charge would have to be that referential terms in identity-statements must be given a double-analysis.[1] In *Q2*, for instance, ' evening star ' and ' morning star ' will have to be said to occur first referentially thereby indicating the requisite concepts *evening star* and *morning star*, and then to stand, in a second rôle, for the composite concept itself, *what it is to be the evening star and the morning star*.

VIII

Conclusion

We have had recourse to some pretty Heath Robinsonsian devices. Nothing much less artificial will, I suspect, suffice to exhibit the connexions, such as they are, abstract and implausible, between predications and identity-statements. In fact, I think, it can be demonstrated that both forms of statement are primitive.

Predication presupposes identification. Identification presupposes the possibility of re-identification. This last presupposes the possibility of identity-statements. On the other hand, identification and reference presuppose identification under some description, which presupposes predication. If identity presupposes predication and predication presupposes identity then both must be primitive. What we have been trying to do in

---

[1] I think such devices would also have to be employed in the analysis of such sentences as ' John, James, Peter and Judas are four in number ', ' Mr. Truman exists ' and perhaps in the case of most or all apparent *de re* modalities. It is always a difficulty to know how exactly to form the corresponding concept from a corresponding name. What exactly does Quine's ' Trumanizes ' mean? Two explanations are possible, I think. We may make the assumption that no proper name has more than one bearer. Then the concept ' Trumanizes ' will be ' man with the name " Truman " '. This assumption, though convenient, is false. The other way would be to take from the context of utterance whatever location the speaker would in fact use in a direct or indirect identification and form the concept from this. This formation of the concept then rests ultimately on the possibility of demonstratives.

Section VII is ' reduce ' the primitive functions of individuation and ascription one to the other. It is not surprising that we met resistance. Nor is it surprising that we needed the identity of indiscernibles to bring the thing off at all.

To despair of the kind of analysis attempted in Section VII is not to despair of all clarification of the rôle of identity-statements in speech and thought. An explanation of their purport which seems to me not wholly useless and which brings out their primitive role, is this: *To utter an identity-statement is to give to understand that one will name or refer to one object in two acts of reference.* In the interesting case the two referential acts will be distinct references (not 'evening star' and 'evening star'). If there is to be any singling out of persisting things at all,[1] there must be the possibility of amplifying and supplementing any act of singling out. This is the role of identity-statement. Persisting things are not simple things with only one face. The life-history of a persistent thing is a contingent matter and an indefinite number of singlings out may be needed in tracing it through space and time. If there are persisting things to single out and ascribe properties to there must be contingent identity-statements, or their possibility.

The word ' one ' occurs essentially in this explanation. Its presence must be accounted no more disturbing, and no less disturbing, than the inevitable presence, for instance, of tensed verbs (or something like them) in the explanations we give of the sense and use of statements about the past. It seems that we have to be content simply to succeed in indicating an activity which can be recognized. This is disappointing. Yet it was surely too much to hope for, that *identity*, *cardinality* and *reference* should be completely and wholly disentangled from one another in some *final* analysis of these notions.

It is not now difficult to see why inter-substitutivity of identicals breaks down in identity-statements. The point of an identity-statement, its content and its purport, lies in the particular referring expression actually produced, and in these referring expressions *exhibited in use.* Hence the content of an identity-statement includes, *e.g.*, *what it is to be the evening star* and *what it is to be the morning star.* (For some one thing is picked out as

---

[1]And there is a good case for saying that this is a prerequisite of there being anything we could recognize as thought. *Vide* S. Hampshire, *Thought and Action* (London, 1959), ch. I.

satisfying these concepts.) Not even proper names are inter-substitutable. For in its use every proper name has to carry with it an identificatory backing, or the possibility of one. (How otherwise could the difficulty of multiple assignment be overcome? How in fact could the sense of proper names begin to be clear?) 'Hesperus' and 'Phosphorus' cannot normally be expected, in a determinate context of utterance and use, to have the same identificatory backing. So to change 'Hesperus is Phosphorus' into 'Hesperus is Hesperus' *would* be to change what the former identity-statement, in a determinate context, exhibits and asserts.[1]

---

[1] The foregoing essay was written and conceived before the publication in England of Geach's *Reference and Generality*. In the light of his arguments about relative pronouns, I should certainly wish to amend or redeploy some of the arguments of Section II. But others remain untouched; and so, I think, does Frege's original problem, and with it the desirability of some non-relational analysis, like the one attempted in Section VIII.

Given the contingency of 'Hesperus is Phosphorus' it is, of course, not very surprising that a substitution which makes use of this contingent premiss can transform the logical truth of 'Hesperus is Hesperus' into the contingent truth 'Hesperus is Phosphorus'. (An analogous remark could be made about another paradox, the paradox of analysis.) Nor are arguable exceptions to the alleged sufficient condition of propositional identity *same subject and same predicate* very difficult to find if we allow definite descriptions a quasi proper-nominal status. The hard residual problem, in view of the availability of the Russellian analysis of definite descriptions, is the occurrence of '=' between genuine proper names, or between variables, the termini of Russellian analysis. So what ultimately has to be explained is the contingency of the proposition 'Hesperus is Phosphorus'. If we persist in thinking of identity-statements as reducible to a predicative or relational form, then we face the problem: It could not apparently be a necessary truth that Hesperus is the same planet as Phosphorus. For this truth depends on, and indeed is, a contingent fact about the empirically discoverable life-history of the planet Venus. On the other hand, it cannot apparently be a contingent fact. 'Hesperus' and 'Phosphorus' are names of one and the same persisting planet. But how then might Hesperus have been Phosphorus? Hesperus might not have had the other *name* 'Phosphorus', but (*pace* the *Begriffsschrift*) 'Hesperus is Phosphorus' is not about names. Hesperus might not have satisfied the *description* which backs the name 'Phosphorus' (e.g. 'morning star'), but according to the relational or predicative view the proposition is not about descriptions or concepts. It is about a planet. But then there is no way on the predicative or relational view for the proposition to be either necessary or contingent.

The analysis of VIII in no way prohibits a formal system from *representing* identity as a transitive symmetrical reflexive relation, provided one is clear about the difference between it and everything else which goes under the name of a relation. Indeed the logical properties of identity demand this treatment in such a context.

Unlike the performative analysis of 'good', which uses the notion of *approval*, a notion only intelligible in terms of 'thinking good', the perhaps semi-performative analysis of identity in VIII makes use of an arguably separable and independently intelligible notion, that of reference.

AN APPROACH TO EXPLANATION[1]

S. BROMBERGER

The word explanation occurs so continuously and holds so important a place in philosophy, that a little time spent in fixing the meaning of it will be profitably employed.

J. S. MILL.

I

PHILOSOPHERS of science should be able to state the truth-conditions that govern the occurrences of ' to explain ' when that verb functions as in *e.g.*:

(1) The kinetic theory of gases explains why the state equation of vapours near condensation differs markedly from that of an ideal gas.

These truth-conditions determine what must be true of any doctrine or proposition rightly said to explain something. Thus they constitute standards that play a crucial part in the critical analysis of any alleged piece of information or theory, and their explicit formulation is needed by anyone who wishes to know in general when and how specific scientific contributions meet these standards.

What are these truth-conditions? Most answers proposed up to now strike me as missing the heart of the matter or as being at best about quasi-technical homonyms of ' to explain '. In this essay I shall propose an answer of my own. It too has weaknesses: it is unfinished and it raises a number of problems whose solution is not available at present. I think, however, that it sets matters in the right perspective and that it provides foundations for relevant further inquiries.

' To explain ' does not always function as in (1) above. Consider the following two statements:

(2) Someone explained to somebody how World War II might have been avoided.

[1]Dr. Paul Benacerraf, my former colleague at Princeton University, read and criticised earlier versions of this essay. His interest and penetrating comments were of invaluable help to me and led to the removal of some serious errors. It is with pleasure that I acknowledge here my great indebtedness to him, but I do not wish to suggest thereby that he necessarily agrees with the theses or arguments or even with the approach of this paper.

(3) Newton explained a long time ago the variations of the tides.
(2) unlike (1) can generate the questions ' where? ', ' when? ',
' using what words? ', *i.e.* (2) unlike (1) implies the occurrence of
some datable and placeable exchange of utterances. (3), on the
other hand, can give rise to ' when? ' but not to ' using what
words? '

The truth-conditions of statements in which ' to explain '
functions as in (2) or as in (3) must obviously be different from
those in which it functions as in (1). They are also of less direct
concern to philosophers of science. In what follows I shall
nevertheless give them a good deal of attention. I shall, in fact,
begin with a long discussion of statements like (2). Nothing very
deep lies behind this. It happens to be a convenient way of
introducing certain notions that are at the heart of my approach.

Towards the end of this essay I shall turn to ' explanation ' and
explain what an explanation is.

A word of caution. The verb ' to explain ' and the phrase
' explanation of ' are often followed by the *oratio obliqua* of certain
questions and these questions fall naturally into groups: one can
explain why, or how, and have explanations of what really happens
whenever such and such, or of what causes what, &c. Many
writings ostensibly about explanation are best understood as not
about explanation at all but as about what is called for by the
questions belonging to one or the other of these groups. That
should not be true of this paper. It is *not* about causality, or
reality, or why, or how; it is about explaining and explanation and
only about that.

II

Let us begin by asking what it is for someone to explain something to someone, where the ' something ' can be specified by
means of an indirect question.[1] In other words, what are the truth-
conditions common to such statements as ' John is explaining to
Rosalie how ozone differs from ordinary oxygen ', ' Rudolph
explained to Susan what " functor " means ', ' He will explain to

---

[1] ' INDIRECT QUESTION is the grammarian's name for a modification of what
was originally a question, such that it does not stand by itself as a sentence, but
is treated as a noun serving for instance as subject or object to a verb outside of
it. Thus the direct question *who are you?* indirect question, *I asked who he was
...*' H. G. Fowler, *Modern English Usage* (London 1954), page 268.
   I shall use ' indirect question ' and ' question in *oratio obliqua* form '
interchangeably.

you what you should do '? More formally, what are the truth-conditions governing statements of the form 'A E to B W ', where 'A' and ' B ' indicate positions occupied by expressions through which a person or persons are mentioned (*i.e.* proper names, singular descriptions of specific people or groups of people, personal pronouns, ' somebody ', ' someone ', &c.) where ' W ' indicates a position occupied by an indirect question, and where ' E ' indicates a position taken up by a tensed version of ' to explain '.

Two things may be noted immediately: (*a*) Many kinds of indirect question can occupy the position indicated by ' W ', and they may open on a variety of interrogatives—' Why ', ' How ', ' Whence ', ' Whither ', ' What '—but not *every* indirect question is at home there; some would be out of place, awkward, reminiscent of Eisenhower prose, *e.g.* ' what the distance in miles between London and Paris is ' or ' whether it will rain tomorrow ' or ' what time it is ' or ' which sister Sam married '. A good analysis should show why some indirect questions do not sit well in these contexts.

(*b*) In these statements ' to explain ' functions as an accomplishment term. 'Accomplishment term ' is used here in the sense given to it by Zeno Vendler.[1] It indicates a place within a fourfold classification: activity terms, accomplishment terms, state terms, achievement terms. What follows is a brief account of this classification.

The first two classes, *i.e.* activity terms and accomplishment terms, include all those verbs that have a continuous present or, more exactly, whose continuous present makes sense as the main verb in answer to ' what is x doing? ', *e.g.* ' to run ', ' to eat ', ' to

---

[1] Z. Vendler, ' Verbs and Times ', *The Philosophical Review*, 66 (1957).

I believe that I have reproduced the distinctions that Vendler must have had in mind when he wrote his paper, but I do not rely on his criteria. He writes ' . . . if I say of a person that he is running a mile or of someone else that he is drawing a circle, then I do claim that the first one will keep running till he has covered the mile and that the second will keep drawing till he has drawn the circle. If they do not complete their activities, my statement will turn out to be false.' This is a mistake: if either the runner or the drawer should be interrupted before finishing, the statement will not ' turn out ' to be false. I have tried to avoid such objections by attending to the use of the simple past. But Vendler saw what had to be seen.

Note that the rest of the discussion does not require that the classification be exhaustive. Nor does it require that a given verb or verbal phrase occur as a member of the same class in every context. ' To explain ', as we shall see, does not *always* function as an accomplishment term. The principle at work here is analogous to that in virtue of which some verbs can be transitive in some types of contexts but intransitive in others.

talk ', ' to lunch ', ' to speak '. They are used to describe episodes that require and occupy stretches of time, stretches at any moment of which the continuous present applies. The last two classes exclude these.

The difference between activity terms and accomplishment terms is readily seen when we compare their simple past tense. Both types have a simple past tense which implies that the continuous present was applicable at some moments in the past. The simple past tense of an activity term is applicable as soon as such moments have passed, and implies only the existence of such moments in the past. Aristotle walked. This implies that during some moments in the past Aristotle was walking. It does not tell whether or not Aristotle is through walking. The simple past tense of accomplishment terms implies more. It implies that relevant activities took place in the past, but furthermore that they have come to an end. And not to a mere stop, but to a conclusion. In other words, the simple past tense of accomplishment verbs entails that something has been finished, completed, that might, in principle, have been left unfinished, incomplete, that might have been stopped before coming to its logical end. Typical accomplishment verbs are ' to fill ', ' to draw a circle ', ' to write a letter ', ' to die '. During the appropriate sorts of goings on, it is true that Jane is filling a pillow, Zachary is drawing a circle, Rachel is writing a letter, Socrates is dying. But to say that Jane filled the pillow, that Zachary drew a circle, that Rachel wrote a letter, that Socrates died, is to imply that all the stuffing is in, that all the points of the perimeter have been joined, that the final salutation is on paper, that he is dead. Otherwise, all that may be said is that she was filling a pillow, that he was drawing a circle, that she was writing a letter, that he was dying.

Thus accomplishment terms differ from activity terms in being associated with distinctions between what constitutes completion and what constitutes mere stopping, mere interruption. As Vendler points out, activity terms lend themselves to such questions as ' How long did so and so do such and such? ' *e.g.* ' How long did Aristotle walk? ', but accomplishment terms call rather for ' How long did it take so and so to do such and such? ' *e.g.* ' How long did it take Jane to fill the pillow? '[1]

---

[1] Verbs that normally function as activity terms may, of course, be constituents of verbal phrases that function as accomplishment terms, *e.g.* ' to write ' in ' to write a letter ', ' to walk ' in ' to walk to the store ', &c.

The difference between state terms and achievement terms is of less immediate relevance. Briefly, state terms (*e.g.* ' to know ', ' to love ', ' to want ', in their non-episodic senses) have present indicatives that apply throughout intervals of time, and that are true of something at more than one moment even if true of it only once; achievement terms (*e.g.* ' to win ', ' to hit ', ' to join ', in their non-episodic sense) have present indicatives that are true of something at one particular moment only, unless they are true of that thing more than once.

It should be clear that in 'A E to B W ' contexts, ' to explain ' functions as an accomplishment term: it can appear there in the continuous present; episodes filling intervals during which a continuous present applies need not but may be followed by moments at which truth demands the substitution of the simple past; finally, the use of the simple past does imply that the person mentioned as subject of the sentence completed something.

A good analysis should therefore make explicit the nature of the completion implied by statements in 'A E to B W ' form in which ' to explain ' occurs in the *simple past tense*; it should bring out what must be the case for a statement in 'A explain*ed* to B W ' form to be true.

Let us now turn to the task of providing such an analysis. To expedite the discussion, I shall refer to episodes whose completion can be conveyed by a statement of the form 'A explain*ed* to B W ' as *explaining episodes*. I shall also refer in a general way to whatever person or persons would be mentioned at 'A' as the *tutor*, and to whatever person or persons would be mentioned at ' B ' as the *tutee* in the episode; when I speak of ' the question ', I shall mean the question whose *oratio obliqua* form would appear at ' W '.

In what follows I shall examine and reject a series of hypotheses each of which is a tentative analysis. My purpose in following this procedure is twofold: to bring out negative truths that are of intrinsic interest, and to discover the conditions that an acceptable doctrine must satisfy. Each demonstrable defect of these tentative analyses will correspond to such a negative truth and to such a condition. Confidence in the last hypothesis will have to rest to a great extent on the fact that it has none of the defects of its predecessors and that it apparently has none of its own. Some fatal flaw may of course have escaped my attention. But I can think of no procedure that will yield conclusive results here.

This one has a certain advantage: if defects of the last hypothesis do eventually come to light, they will show that I stopped too soon, but they will not vitiate the negative conclusions nor invalidate the negative conditions already established.

First hypothesis.

A statement of the form 'A explained to B W' is true if and only if an episode has occurred

(*a*) at the beginning of which the tutee did not know the right answer to the question;

(*b*) in the course of which the tutor presents to the tutee all the facts that he, the tutee, must know to know the right answer to the question;

(*c*) at the end of which the tutor has presented all the facts mentioned in (*b*);

(*d*) at the end of which the tutee knows the right answer to the question.

The hypothesis avoids the implication that in every explaining episode someone actually asks the question. This is as it should be. The truth of 'Salviati explained to Sagredo what the grounds are for saying that similar solids are to each other in the sesquialteral ratio of their surfaces' does not imply that Sagredo asked the question, though we can discover by reading the dialogue that he did.

The hypothesis nevertheless still contains unnecessary conditions. Initial ignorance on the part of the tutee is not necessary, is not implied: we all know of the father who explained to his son how babies come into the world only to be told ' I knew all that; I thought that you were going to tell me something about birds and bees!' Nor is ultimate knowledge on the part of the tutee necessary: 'Max explained to Alonzo what the difference is between using and mentioning a term' does not entail that Alonzo now knew, that he was convinced, or that he even paid any attention.

Eliminating (*a*) and (*d*) and rephrasing (*b*) and (*c*) into

(*b'*) in the course of the episode the tutor presents the facts that one must know to know the right answer to the question;

(*c'*) at the end of the episode the tutor has presented all the facts mentioned in (*b'*),

would avoid these unwanted implications, but it would not take care of another objection, to wit that the hypothesis (or its revised

version) does not provide a set of *sufficient* conditions. At twelve
o'clock yesterday, I did not know the height of the Empire State
Building; I met Henrietta, who knew and who told me ' 1,250
feet '. Now I also knew. This episode meets all the requirements
of the first hypothesis, but it does not rate the description
' Henrietta explained to me what the height of the Empire State
Building is.'

Of course, no episode can rate the description ' Henrietta
explained to me what the height of the Empire State Building is '.
This may suggest that the sentence is perhaps not well formed,
that it is grammatically rather than semantically deviant. The
point is not without interest since we want to know why some
questions do not function properly as direct objects of ' to explain '.
However the following two illustrations bring out that more than
mere syntax is at play here; they show that some strings of words
are a proper direct object of ' to explain ' in some circumstances
but not in others.

First illustration: maximum security prison, walls that can't be
scaled, guards in every hall, dogs, &c. A prisoner manages to
escape by digging a tunnel. The tunnel has been found, but no one
can figure out how the dirt from the excavations was disposed of; all
the possibilities that occur to anyone have to be rejected for one
reason or another. The prisoner is now recaptured. He is made to
describe his escape. He is clearly aware of the fact that his jailers
are baffled, and in the course of his description, he reveals how he
disposed of the dirt from his tunnelling.

I take it that there can be no objection to saying that the
prisoner explained to his jailers (in the course of his account) how
he disposed of the dirt from his tunnelling.

Second illustration: similar jail, similar escape, but in this case
it is easy to see how the prisoner may have disposed of the dirt;
he may have dropped it into the moat under his window, or he
may also have carried it out in his pockets to a garden where he
was not closely watched. But still, the jailers do not *know* how the
prisoner disposed of the dirt, whether he used the moat or his
pockets. The prisoner is recaptured, made to describe his escape,
and he tells how he disposed of the dirt (the moat) from his
tunnelling.

Here as in the previous example, the conditions of the first
hypothesis are satisfied, but I take it that ' The prisoner explained

to his jailers how he disposed of the dirt from his tunnelling ' is out of place, distorts things, smacks of exaggeration, is at best a near truth.

It would not do of course to say simply that the prisoner did not explain to his jailers how he disposed of the dirt from his tunnel, and to let it go at that. This would suggest that he refused to explain, or failed to explain, or prevaricated, or perhaps did not address himself to the question at all. Normally some such thing is conveyed by the explicit denial that someone explained something on some specific occasion. Thus in the present instance that sort of denial would be misleading. The description does not apply, but neither does its denial. Not an unusual situation; one does not want to say simply that the Empire State Building is not happy, for this would suggest that it is melancholy. But one can't say that it is happy either.

Admittedly, however, the statement that in the second illustration the prisoner explained how he disposed of the dirt from his tunnelling, ceases to be glaringly odd when one limits one's mental picturing to the scene in which the prisoner describes his escape; more of the epistemic background must be kept in mind, *i.e.* that what was said, though informative, merely settled for the audience *which* of the means of which it was already aware had actually been used, and that the prisoner realized this.

It should not come as a surprise that this first hypothesis must be rejected. A correct perspective on the nature of explaining episodes would reveal the difference between what is conveyed by statements of the form 'A explained to B W ' and statements of the form 'A told B W '. The one just examined would obliterate that difference.

The first hypothesis requires that what the tutor tells the tutee be true. However there is such a thing as explaining incorrectly, and a report that little Suzy explained to her brother what little girls are made of, does not imply that what she said is true. Seen in this light, the requirement may seem uncalled for. But this would be an illusion. Statements of the form 'A explained to B W ' *do* imply that the tutee was given correct information. The addition of ' incorrectly ' does not add a detail that could have been left unspecified without affecting the truth of the statement; it *qualifies* the whole statement, and has the force of a partial denial: to have explained incorrectly is *not* to have explained, but to have been engaged in something akin to it. The same effect can be achieved through ironic, or sarcastic, or condescending intonation.

Admittedly, however, statements of the form 'A explained to B W' are open to strict and to loose usage. Strictly they imply that the tutor uttered verities. But one does not have to know that he did, to use such a statement; it is enough to assume that he did. And a loose usage allows the tutor's views about the truth of what he said to prevail altogether over those of the user, and it does not rule out such statements even where the latter believes that what the tutor told the tutee was false. Such usage, however, is apt to mislead when one's listener does not know better.

The hypothesis also entails that the question itself must be sound, *i.e.* must have a correct answer. Here too, there is a strict and a loose usage. The former rules out questions that are based on false presuppositions, the latter countenances them. ' Max explained to Alonzo why the Gödel incompleteness theorem is of no epistemological significance ' would normally commit the user of the sentence to the view that the Gödel theorem is of no epistemological significance: the statement, unless qualified, implies this. Implications of this kind are still-born whenever speaker and listener agree and know that they agree that the question is unsound.[1]

P-predicament.

The statement of the second hypothesis must be postponed until the term ' p-predicament ',[2] needed for its formulation, has been introduced.

Consider the following two questions:

(A) What is the height of Mt. Kilimanjaro?

(B) Why do tea kettles emit a humming noise just before the water begins to boil?

I know the answer to neither. However I am not equally ignorant with regard to both. This is brought out to some extent by the fact that I am prepared to say that *I do not understand* why tea kettles emit a humming noise just before the water begins to boil,

---

[1] The discussion from here on will be limited to the strict usage. The looser usage is best handled after the analysis of the strict usage, but I will ignore it altogether as of little interest.

[2] The ' p ' of ' p-predicament' may be thought of as standing for 'puzzled' or ' perplexed ', but mnemonically only. As will become obvious, one need not be either puzzled or perplexed to be in a p-predicament.

whereas I am not prepared to say anything of the sort about what the height of Mt. Kilimanjaro is. We will say that I am in a p-predicament with regard to (B) but not with regard to (A). What is the difference?

I take (A) to be a sound question, *i.e.* to admit of a right answer,[1] to rest on no mistaken assumptions or false presuppositions; there is such a thing as Mt. Kilimanjaro, and it is the sort of thing that has a height. I also believe the following about the answer: (*a*) it can be put as a number followed by a unit of length; (*b*) if given in feet, the number must lie between 100 and 30,000; (*c*) if not in feet, then the number must be such that conversion into an equivalent number of feet would yield a number between 100 and 30,000; and (*d*) the number could be obtained through certain measuring operations that need not be described here. These conditions on the answer, even when combined with my other beliefs, do not uniquely determine an answer to (A); acceptance of them does not settle the question for me. But acceptance of them does require that I consider a number of expressions as not possibly being, on my view, formulations of the right answer. These make up a varied lot: ' 12 feet ', ' I don't know ', ' Look it up in the encyclopedia ', ' Morton White ', ' 19, 321 lbs ', &c.[2] Still, I can think of many expressions which do not belong in that lot, *e.g.* ' 15,000 feet ', ' 8,000 feet ', ' 3 kilometers ', and others.

I also take (B) to be a sound question: tea kettles do emit a humming noise just before the water in them begins to boil. I have views about its answer too: (*a*) it must be statable in the form of a sentence or conjunction of sentences preceded by the word ' because '; (*b*) this sentence or conjunction of sentences must include—perhaps among other things— description of something

---

[1] Throughout this discussion, ' right answer ' must be understood somewhat narrowly. I am using ' right answer to Q ' (where Q is a question) to cover a possible reply to Q if and only if a statement of the form 'A told B W ' (where ' W ' must be thought of as replaced by the *oratio obliqua* of Q, and 'A' and ' B ' by expressions through which two persons are mentioned) would be true of any episode in which the reply had been given by the person mentioned at 'A' in response to the asking of Q by the person mentioned at ' B '. This excludes such possibly ' correct ' answers as ' I don't know.' Certain questions do not admit of a right answer, *e.g.* ' Who is the present king of France? '

[2] Significant distinctions exist among the expressions that I must reject. The first three would, under most circumstances, count as replies when uttered in response to an utterance of (A), but very special circumstances are called for in the case of the last two. Furthermore, as a reply to (A) the first must convey a falsehood, the second may convey a truth, the third can convey neither a truth nor a falsehood. These distinctions are not relevant to our present purpose.

that actually happens whenever water is about to begin boiling; and (c) this description must entail that on each such occasion something sets air to vibrate with an amplitude, frequency, and overtones corresponding to the loudness, pitch, and quality of the noise in question. As before, the conditions do not add up to an answer, even when supplemented with my other beliefs. Acceptance of them again requires that I reject a number of expressions as incapable of being, on my view, formulations of the right answer. These too make up a varied lot: ' Because Cleopatra had a short nose ', ' I don't know ', ' Look it up in the encyclopedia ', ' Ruth Otto ', ' 19,321 feet ', ' &c. ' But this time I am unable to conceive of any others, *i.e.* I can think of nothing, I can imagine nothing, I can conjure up nothing, I can invent nothing, I can remember nothing, that can survive confrontation with what I take to be conditions on the right answer. And this is clearly a consequence not only of the character of those conditions but also of the limits of my intellectual repertoire.

To recapitulate then:

(i) I take both (A) and (B) to be sound questions, to admit of a right answer.

(ii) I know, or believe I know, enough about each answer to be able to eliminate a number of possible utterances, *i.e.* of expressions, as not being formulations of it.

(iii) In the case of (A) I can think of some possible utterances that I cannot eliminate in this way.

(iv) In the case of (B) I can think[1] of no expression that I cannot eliminate in this way.

Let us say of anyone who stands with regard to any question Q in the relation in which I stand to (B) that he (she, they) is (are) in a p-predicament with regard to the question Q. In other words, *A is in a p-predicament with regard to Q if and only if, on A's views, Q admits of a right answer, but A can think of no answer to which, on A's views, there are no decisive objections.*

'A is in a p-predicament with regard to Q ' is a neologism, but the meaning of each statement of that form is intimately related to the meaning of some statement of the form 'A does not understand q ', with ' q ' replaced by the *oratio obliqua* form of the

---

[1] ' Can think of no expression ' and ' can think of no answer ' as short for ' can imagine nothing, conjure up nothing, invent nothing, remember nothing, conceive nothing . . .' does not cover the familiar states of momentary amnesia during which one has the answer ' on the tip of one's tongue ' but cannot utter it.

question mentioned at ' Q '. Any statement of the form ' I am in a p-predicament with regard to Q ' implies and is implied by the corresponding ' I do not understand q.' In other words, the two kinds of statements are interchangeable when the person speaking is the person spoken about. The relation is a little more complicated when the speaker is not the person spoken about. In those cases 'A is in a p-predicament with regard to Q ' should convey what would be conveyed by an ' I do not understand q ' uttered by the person mentioned at 'A'—with one difference to be specified in a moment—but need not convey what would be conveyed by the corresponding 'A does not understand q'. This is a consequence of the following:

(a) Any 'A does not understand q ' implies that the question alluded to at ' q ' is sound. Thus its use by anyone conveys (pragmatically implies) that the user believes the question to be sound. Its cognate 'A is in a p-predicament with regard to Q ' does not imply that the question is sound, but only that it is sound on the views of the person mentioned at 'A'; its use by anyone should therefore not convey that the user takes the question to be sound, (except for a first-person A). In other words, the meaning of 'A does not understand q ' requires that the opinion of the user concerning the soundness of the question be dominant, but the meaning of 'A is in a p-predicament with regard to Q ' requires that the views of the person mentioned, about matters relevant to the soundness of the question, be dominant.

(b) An 'A does not understand q ' statement may be used to report or describe situations in which *either* (1) none of the answers that the person mentioned at 'A' can conceive is an answer that that person can accept—and this includes situations in which the person spoken about can conceive of the right answer, but cannot accept it in the light of his or her other beliefs—*or* (2) none of the answers that the person mentioned at 'A' can conceive is the right answer—and this includes situations in which that person can conceive of one or more answers that he or she can consistently accept. These statements are thus marked by an ambiguity, and demand contextual clues that indicate whose conditions on the answer are at play, the speaker's or those of the person spoken about. 'A is in a p-predicament with regard to Q ' suffers from no such ambiguity; it refers only to the sort of situations described under (1) above, *i.e.* the meaning is such as to require that the

G

relevant beliefs of the person mentioned at 'A' be dominant. Here too the difference vanishes when the person spoken about is the person speaking.

An illustration will fix these two points. Neither Sam nor Rebecca know or think they know the answer to ' How did God make Eve, a whole human being, from just one bone? ' Rebecca, a pure but simple soul, knows of no reason for dismissing the view that He first broke Adam's rib in as many pieces as He needed parts for her body, that He then stretched and shaped each of these into one of these parts, that He next assembled them into the well known configuration, and that He finally blew life into the whole. Sam cannot accept this answer. He knows about the principle of conservation of matter, about the differences in chemical composition of muscles, hair, bones, skin, nerves, stomach, appendix. But he cannot think of anything that he would find acceptable. Max the atheist would reject the whole question. Sam would be right in saying that he himself is in a p-predicament with regard to the above question, and it would make sense for Max (or anyone else) to say that Sam is in a p-predicament with regard to the question, even though Max could not rightly say that Sam does not understand how God created Eve. But Sam, or Max, or Rebecca (or anyone else for that matter) would be mistaken in saying that Rebecca is in a p-predicament with regard to the question, since she can think of at least one possibility that she need not reject. Nevertheless, Sam would be correct in saying that she does not understand how God created Eve. No one should say that Max is in a p-predicament with regard to the question.

There is one respect in which an 'A is in a p-predicament with regard to Q ' statement not made by the person mentioned at 'A' conveys less than its cognate ' I do not understand q ' when uttered by that person. The latter statement conveys that that person knows or believes that he or she does not understand q, but the former does not entail that the subject knows or believes that he or she is in a p-predicament with regard to Q, and could not convey it.

Being in a p-predicament with regard to a question may sound like greater ignorance than merely not knowing the answer. It isn't. Being in a p-predicament usually calls for more learning than does mere ignorance. Sam would not be in a p-predicament with regard to ' How did God make Eve? ' had he not studied chemistry. It was once suggested to me that the noise emitted by tea kettles just before the water begins to boil might come from surface vibrations set off by air bubbles released before vapour bubbles begin to form. For a while thereafter I was not in a p-predicament with regard to ' Why do tea kettles emit a humming noise just before the water begins to boil? ' Since then I have had occasion to observe the phenomenon a little more closely, and I have satisfied myself that these air bubbles are too small and too few to account for the noise in question. I would not be in a p-predicament today had I not learned these facts. Or again, I am not in a p-predicament with regard to ' What is the relation between the Debye temperature θ and the temperature at which the atomic heat of a solid element is equal to 3R/2? ' I hardly know enough to understand the question; the only condition that I associate with it is that the answer must be statable as a mathematical function of θ, but I can construct indefinitely many of those![1]

Second hypothesis.

A statement of the form 'A explained to B W ' is true if and only if an episode has occurred

(*a*) at the time of which the tutor knows the right answer to the question;

(*b*) at the beginning of which the tutee was in a p-predicament with regard to the question;[2]

(*c*) at the beginning of which the tutee thought of himself as in a p-predicament with regard to the question;

(*d*) during which the tutor knows, or believes, or at least

[1] All my examples have been homespun cases. To lend dignity and significance to this discussion it would no doubt be better to use illustrations taken from the history of science. I have not done this because the analysis required to show that some scientist was in a p-predicament with regard to some question at some time would be very long and very complex: it would demand an examination of theoretical background, available evidence, implicit assumptions, &c. But it is obvious that there have been times in the history of science when scientists were in a p-predicament with regard to some question, *e.g.* when a maximum height to which water can be pumped was known but the concept of atmospheric pressure had not yet been discovered; when the mathematical representation of energy distribution for black body radiators was known but the quantum hypothesis had not been thought of or admitted; when the Michelson and Morley results were known but the Special Theory of Relativity had not been advanced, &c.

[2] This implies of course that the question must have a right answer.

assumes that, at the beginning of the episode, the tutee was in a p-predicament with regard to the question;[1]

(e) in the course of which the tutor presents the facts that in his opinion the tutee must learn to know the right answer to the question;

(f) at the end of which all the facts mentioned in (e) have been presented to the tutee by the tutor;

(g) at the end of which the tutee knows the right answer, and knows it as a result of, and in virtue of what he has been told by the tutor in the course of the episode.

Some of these clauses obviously do not stand for necessary conditions. (b) and (g) would require initial ignorance and ultimate knowledge of the right answer by the tutee. This is uncalled for, as we saw in the comments to the first hypothesis. But (c) and (d) are not necessary either. (c) too implies initial ignorance of the right answer. (d) (and incidentally (c) again) would imply that the following correct account is incorrect. Until the age of five I was convinced that babies grew in cabbages. My older brother knew this about me, and on my fifth birthday, as a present, he told me the facts of life; on that day he *explained* to me how babies come into the world. At the age of four, I was not, nor did I think myself to be in a p-predicament with regard to ' How do babies come into the world? ', since I had an answer, though admittedly a false one. My brother knew this about me, and the statement that he explained to me how babies come into the world does not imply the contrary, *i.e.* does not imply that he thought or assumed that I would not have been able to come up with an answer compatible with my total set of beliefs. This is in general true of statements of the form 'A explained to B W '. They do not imply that the tutor (or tutee) believed or assumed that the tutee would have been or should have been puzzled (in a p-predicament way) by the question before the explaining episode.

---

[1] 'Assumes ' throughout this discussion must carry a heavy load. To assume may simply be to take for granted. It may be something else. When I give an examination to my students, I always tell them to assume that they are writing for someone who knows nothing on the subject; but I do not wish that they take for granted that I know nothing on the subject. I always assume that they know very little philosophy when I prepare a lecture for them, though I often have no strong convictions on this. To assume is thus sometimes to go on the assumption that. It can also be to take for granted *and* to go on the assumption that. In stating these hypotheses, I have assumed that ' to assume ' may do the job of a disjunction of all these possibilities.

If we eliminate all these conditions, however, we are left with (a), (e)—' learn ' being perhaps replaced by ' learn or know '— and (f), a set enough like the revised first hypothesis to be recognized immediately as not sufficient.

On the other hand, this hypothesis in its original form, unlike the first one, does seem to provide a set of sufficient conditions. I don't know how one can prove this. My own conviction on the matter rests on the fact that I am unable to construct any illustration that meets these seven clauses yet is not an explaining episode. It helps, in this connection, to look at the counter-examples showing the insufficiency of the previous hypothesis.

The first counter-example, it will be recalled, consisted of an episode in which I was told the height of the Empire State Building, something I had not known before, but knew thereafter. But ' What is the height of the Empire State Building? ' is not a question with regard to which I was or could have been believed to be in a p-predicament (the same, by the way, is true of ' What is the height of Mt. Kilimanjaro? ').

The second example was an episode in which a prisoner told how he had disposed of tunnelling dirt, and, in effect, settled in the mind of his audience which of a number of obvious methods he had actually used. Here again the tutee, i.e., his audience, was neither known nor thought to be in a p-predicament with regard to the question. This illustration was contrasted at the time with another one, in many respects similar, but which was clearly recognizable as an explaining episode, i.e. as properly describable by an 'A explained to BW ' statement. That latter episode, notice, does satisfy the present hypothesis.

The present hypothesis has a minor virtue that may strengthen its *prima facie* plausibility as a set of sufficient conditions. The etymology of a word, we have often been told, often provides the key to the analysis of its meaning. The origins of ' to explain ' and of its French cousin *expliquer* go back to expressions used to speak of making smooth by removing folds and wrinkles. But what were these ancestral folds and wrinkles? The literature contains a number of suggestions. In *La Thèorie Physique*, Pierre Duhem offers the following one: ' To explain [expliquer], *explicare*, is to strip reality of the appearances in which it is wrapped as in veils, in order to see this reality naked and face to face.' There

is a more Lockean[1] and more plausible possibility compatible
with a more modest reality. The second hypothesis would support
it. People who contemplate a question with regard to which they
are in a p-predicament are prone to frounce their foreheads, to
screw up their faces, to knit their brows, and they usually shed
most of these folds and wrinkles and present a smoother countenance upon being told the answer. We know that one who remedies
a p-predicament often explains in this sense which, if original is
now obsolete. Is this account correct? Perhaps not. (And yet . . .
the first quotation under ' to explain ' in the O.E.D. is ' He must
caulm and explain his forehead ', 1569; and the second one reads
' Their faces are explained and flattered by art ', 1650.) For our
purpose, that does not really matter. It is enough if the account
reminds us that sentences of the form 'A explained W to B ' are
aptly chosen to report episodes in which a tutor turns someone
who could truly have said ' I don't understand W ' into someone
in a position to assert ' I know W ', and if it provides the occasion
for seeing that the hypothesis does justice to this fact.

All this suggests that the clauses making up the second hypothesis should perhaps be divided into three classes: first, some that
are necessary conditions, i.e. (a), (e), and (f); secondly, some that
are totally dispensable, i.e. (b), (c), and (g); and thirdly, one that
is not necessary by itself but is a member of a set of conditions
whose *disjunction* is a necessary condition, i.e. (d).

At the beginning of this discussion I pointed out that a good
analysis of explaining episodes should show why some indirect
questions are out of place as direct objects of ' to explain '. An
account could be built on the second hypothesis. That account
would not rest on any of the ' totally dispensable ' clauses listed
above, and may therefore be part of the truth. To the extent to
which it strikes one as such, it will confirm my suggestion that the
present hypothesis is a disjunct of the truth that we are after. I
will therefore give a rough sketch of that account.

Indirect questions beginning with ' whether '. These represent
questions whose right answers must be either ' yes ' or ' no '.

---

[1] ' It may also lead us a little towards the original of all our notions and
knowledge, if we remark how great a dependence our words have on common
sensible ideas: and how those which are made use of to stand for actions and
notions quite removed from sense, have their rise from thence, and from obvious
sensible ideas are transferred to more abstruse significations, and made to stand
for ideas that come not under the cognizance of our senses;' John Locke, *Essay
Concerning Human Understanding*, Book III, ch. 1, sec. 5.

But no tutee can be thought to be in a p-predicament with regard to such a question. If the views held by him require that he reject both ' yes ' and ' no ' as each violating some belief or assumption of his, then he cannot take the question to be sound, to admit of a right answer. But then he cannot be in a p-predicament with regard to the question either, since one can only be in a p-predicament with regard to questions that one can consistently think of as having a right answer. On the other hand, if he is not compelled to reject both ' yes ' and ' no ', he cannot be in a p-predicament either. Could a tutee be in a situation in which he can think of ' yes ' (and have to reject it) but not of ' no ', or vice versa? Perhaps, but then the question is one that he does not understand, and indefinitely many answers will be open to him. In the case of these indirect questions, then, nothing corresponds to the sort of knowledge or belief or assumption called for in (d) and the conditions of the hypothesis cannot be satisfied.

Indirect questions beginning with, e.g. ' What is the height of . . . ? ', ' What is the weight of . . .? ', ' What is the distance between . . .? ', i.e. questions calling for an answer expressible in the form of a number and a unit of measurement. A tutee who knows or thinks he knows the form of the answer and who knows or thinks he knows appropriate units of measurement, must either reject every number, in which case he cannot take the question to be sound, or there is some number that he does not have to reject. But how could he be in a p-predicament in the latter case? To be able to conjure up further answers he need only be able to generate numbers. One *can* imagine situations in which a tutor believes that he is dealing with a partly educated tutee unable to count, yet able to reject the possibilities that would occur to him. But in those cases, if the conditions of the hypothesis are satisfied, an 'A explained to B what . . . ' would be true. And in the others (d) could not be satisfied. In the remaining cases, i.e. where the tutee does not think that he knows the form of the answer, he is in a situation analogous to the one that I described as mine with regard to the question about the Debye temperature, and thus not in a p-predicament because in no position to reject possibilities apt to occur to him. If the tutor believes that this is the situation, (d) is not satisfied. One can also imagine cases where the tutee is thought of as in a position to reject every kind of unit of which he is aware but as not aware of the right kind of unit. In those cases, however,

'A explained to B W ' statements will be true, if the conditions of
the hypothesis are all satisfied.

Indirect questions beginning with ' which '. These represent
questions that also open on the word ' which '. An interrogative
sentence beginning with the word ' which ' is not the formulation
of a question unless and until it becomes associated with a specific
set of alternatives that include the right answer, if any. Anyone
thought to be in a position to have views on the soundness of the
question must also be thought to know the members of that set.
But then (*d*) cannot be satisfied. The tutor must either believe
that the tutee should reject every member of the relevant set and
ipso facto should reject the question itself as without correct
answer, or the tutor must believe that one alternative at least is an
open possibility on the views of the tutee. Either belief rules out
thinking that the tutee is in a p-predicament with regard to that
question.

B-predicament.

The third hypothesis too requires the introduction of a new
phrase, ' being in a b-predicament with regard to a question '. A
statement of the form 'A is in a b-predicament with regard to Q '
(in which 'A' must be replaced by an expression referring to some
person or persons, and ' Q ' by one referring to some question) is
true if and only if the question mentioned in it admits of a right
answer, but that answer is beyond what the person mentioned can
conceive, can think of, can imagine, *i.e.* is something that that
person cannot remember, cannot excogitate, cannot compose.

My position with regard to ' Why do tea kettles emit a humming noise just before the water begins to boil? ' can be used to
bring out the difference between a p-predicament and a b-predicament. I am in a p-predicament with regard to that question.
I am also in a b-predicament with regard to it, since I am unable
to think of the right answer. However there was a time when I was
in a b-predicament with regard to the question *without* being at
the same time in a p-predicament with regard to it, *i.e.* when I was
able to entertain ' because the surface of the water is made to
vibrate by escaping air bubbles that form before vapour bubbles do'
as possibly the correct answer. Note that it is possible to be in a
p-predicament with regard to a question *without* at the same time
being in a b-predicament with regard to it. This is the case when

someone is in a p-predicament with regard to a question that in fact admits of no right answer. It is also the case when someone rejects the correct answer to a question with regard to which he is in a p-predicament. Such would be my situation if the air-bubble theory were correct. Such was Kepler's situation with regard to 'What is the shape of planetary orbits?' while he refused to admit the possibility of elliptical paths.[1]

Third hypothesis.

A statement of the form 'A explained to B W' is true if and only if an episode has occurred

(*a*) at the time of which the tutor knows the right answer to the question;

(*b*) during which the tutor knows, or believes, or at least assumes that at the beginning of the episode, the tutee was in a b-predicament;

(*c*) in the course of which the tutor presents the facts that, in his opinion, the tutee must learn to know the right answer to the question;

(*d*) at the end of which all the facts mentioned in (*c*) have been presented to the tutee by the tutor.

This hypothesis includes or implies none of the clauses shown so far to stand for conditions that are not necessary conditions. It does not require initial ignorance or ultimate knowledge of the answer by the tutee, and it does not require that the tutor think the tutee to have been in a p-predicament at the beginning of the episode.[2]

Like the second hypothesis, the third seems to be a set of sufficient conditions. Again, I can't prove this, but again I am unable to construct a case that meets the requirements of the hypothesis but

---

[1] 'A is in a b-predicament with regard to Q' is in some respects closer to 'A does not understand W' than is 'A is in a p-predicament with regard to Q.' It requires a sound question. Its truth is independent of the opinions held by the person mentioned concerning the soundness of the question or concerning the conditions that the right answer must satisfy. Notice however that 'A is not in a b-predicament with regard to Q' unlike 'A understands W' does not require that the question be sound.

[2] Someone in a b-predicament with regard to a question cannot know the answer to that question, but (b) is phrased to allow for explaining episodes at the beginning of which tutees do know the answer. (c) and (d) furthermore are phrased to allow for explaining episodes in which tutors exert themselves in vain, are not understood, are not listened to attentively, &c., *i.e.* explaining episodes at the end of which the tutee still does not know the answer.

is not an explaining episode. Those that brought out insufficiency before won't do so here. I was not nor could I have been believed to be in a b-predicament with regard to ' What is the height of the Empire State Building?' Our prisoner while the protagonist in a non-explaining episode was addressing an audience that was not and that was not thought to be in a b-predicament with regard to the question. But his audience was believed to be in a b-predicament (as well as a p-predicament) in the explaining episode. Furthermore, the illustration showing that (*d*) of the second hypothesis is not a necessary condition, satisfies the conditions of the present hypothesis: my brother knew that I was in a b-predicament with regard to ' How do babies come into the world? '

Speculative etymology may stir the relevant intuitions here too. The prototypic folds should now be brought to mind by the story of the excitable Frenchman who, when shown an old fashioned telephone requiring the earpiece to be held in one hand and the mouthpiece to be held in the other, protested: ' Mais alors, comment s'explique-t-on? '. Words often seem too weak to cure a b-predicament, gestures seem called for, unfoldings of arms, openings of hands. These may have been the original topic of 'A E to B W ' descriptions! The O.E.D. fails us at this point, but not completely; under ' to explicate ' we find ' When he intendeth his business to purpose, then he standeth upon his feet, explicateth and displayeth his limbs ' 1620.

This hypothesis too will support an account of why some indirect questions are out of place as direct object of ' to explain '. Its outlines are readily drawn; the details would get us into the arid territory of erotetic logic.

Indirect questions beginning with ' whether '. To believe that someone is in a b-predicament with regard to a question whose right answer must be either ' yes ' or ' no ' is to believe that someone is incapable of thinking of either ' yes ' or ' no '. This isn't merely to believe or to assume that the person is unable to accept, or to conceive of himself as accepting either ' yes ' or ' no ' as the correct answer; it is in effect to impute to that person the inability to come up with the thought of ' yes ' or ' no ' as even the wrong answer. On the present hypothesis, an 'A E to B whether . . . ' statement cannot be true unless some tutor (i) believed or assumed some tutee to be that colossally dull and yet (ii) undertook to convey information to that tutee. But (i) and (ii) are pragmatically incompatible with one another: the occurrence of (ii) would establish the falsehood of (i). Thus the conditions of the hypothesis cannot be met in these cases.

Indirect questions like ' What is the height of . . .?' 'What is the weight of . . .?', &c., i.e. indirect questions calling for a number followed by a unit of measurement. The cases involving units of measurement familiar to practically everyone can be dealt with in the same way as indirect questions beginning with 'whether'. The fact that a tutor undertakes to inform a tutee is prima facie evidence that he does not believe or assume that one specific combination of a number and an obvious unit of measurement surpasses what the tutee can conceive. Normally the conditions of the hypothesis are not fulfilled.

The cases involving less familiar dimensions and less familiar units are a little more complicated. Indirect questions standing for questions of that sort *can* serve as direct object of 'to explain'. Their aptness in that role depends, however, on how much the tutor tells the tutee. Thus (1) ' Picard explained to Mme. Rouge what the difference of potential between the poles of his car battery is ' is not warranted if Picard merely said to Mme. Rouge ' The difference of potential between the two poles of my battery is six volts.' But then that would be prima facie evidence that (*b*), (*c*), and (*d*) are not satisfied. But (1) is *not* unwarranted if Picard presented Mme. Rouge with a lengthier exposition, one designed to convey not only the sound of the answer, but its meaning as well, *i.e.* designed to put her in possession of notions not previously in her intellectual repertoire. This too is compatible with the hypothesis.

Indirect questions beginning with ' which '. To hold that a tutee is in a b-predicament with regard to a question beginning with ' which ' a tutor would have to assume that the tutee associates with it the same set of alternatives that he does: these alternatives are part of the very identity of the question. The tutor would also have to assume that one of these alternatives is the right answer. It is therefore impossible for a tutor to believe or to assume that some tutee is in a b-predicament with regard to such a question.

The third hypothesis cannot be a set of necessary conditions. Consider the following example:

I am the Dr. Watson to some Sherlock Holmes. Yesterday

morning we were called to investigate a crime. The body was found in a room with a fireplace, two windows, one door. According to irrefutable evidence, the doors and the windows were locked from the inside, by the victim, before he was killed, and were not touched again until investigators entered the room. The chimney is too narrow to allow the passage of a grown man. Walls, floor, and ceiling have been checked; there are no secret doors, no hidden outlets. The victim did not commit suicide: he was killed by a bullet in the head, wasn't wearing gloves, and the fingerprints on the gun do not match his.

How did the assassin leave the room?

All day yesterday I was in a p-predicament with regard to that question. The only answers that occurred to me were ones that I was forced to reject: through the door, the North window, the South window, the chimney, the floor, the ceiling, the walls.

At dinner time, my Sherlock Holmes, who knew my condition, explained to me how the assassin had left the room: through the chimney. He was a midget, small enough and slender enough to get through it.

This counter-example does not come as a surprise. The third hypothesis can't be a set of necessary conditions if the second hypothesis is a set of sufficient ones, since these two hypotheses can be independently satisfied. The midget case is merely an explaining episode that accords with the second but not with the third. But it confirms the hunch that the final doctrine must contain a disjunctive clause.

Fourth and Last Hypothesis.

The essential characteristics of explaining episodes are the following:

(*a*) the question is sound, *i.e.* admits of a right answer;

(*b*) the tutor is rational and knows the right answer to the question at the time of the episode;

(*c*) during the episode the tutor knows, or believes, or at least assumes that at the beginning of the episode the tutee was in a p-predicament with regard to the question,

or that, at the beginning of the episode the tutee was in a b-predicament with regard to the question,

or that, at the beginning of the episode, the tutee was in either a p-predicament or b-predicament with regard to the question.

(*d*) in the course of the episode the tutor presents the facts that, in his opinion the tutee must learn to know the right answer to the question;

(*e*) in the course of the episode the tutor also provides the tutee with such instruction as he (the tutor) thinks necessary to remove the basis of whichever of the states mentioned in (*c*) he deems the tutee to be in;

(*f*) at the end of the episode all the facts mentioned in (*d*) and (*e*) have been presented to the tutee by the tutor.

I have expressed this hypothesis in the material mode, and have included three clauses, *i.e.* (*a*) and (*c*) and (*f*), that are superfluous since (*a*) is implied by (*b*), and (*c*) and (*f*) by (*d*) and (*e*). I have chosen the material mode because the hypothesis concerns more than our understanding of an English verb.[1] The superfluous clauses are apt to be overlooked and deserve an explicit statement.

A word about (*e*). (*e*) excludes from the class of explaining episodes those episodes in which the tutor provides no more information than might have been put in the form ' The answer to Q is . . . ', *e.g.* 'The answer to " How did the assassin leave the room? " is " through the chimney ".' In one sense, such statements, if true, contain all that one has to learn to know the answer to the question. But they cannot make up the total substance of explaining episodes.

It is easier to indicate what (*e*) excludes than to indicate what it is designed to include. A fully adequate treatment of what is involved would take us far afield. Here I shall merely evoke the relevant facts through illustrations.

Picard of a previous example, it will be recalled, knew or believed, or at least assumed, that Mme. Rouge was in a b-predicament with regard to the question ' What is the potential difference between the two poles of Picard's car battery? ' How could he

---

[1] There is another reason for using the material mode. Put in the formal mode, this hypothesis provides only truth-conditions for statements in the form 'A explained to B W ', *i.e.* with ' to explain ' in the simple past tense. But we are interested in all 'A E to B W ' statements, regardless of the tense of the verb. Extending the above conditions to include cases with other tenses would require the discussion and resolution of difficult problems about the relationship among truth-conditions of statements in every respect alike but for the tense of the verb. The use of the material mode should enable us to visualise the relevant points in a way that is adequate for present purposes; *e.g.* the continuous present is applicable while an explaining episode is going on, the past tenses if it took place in the past, the future tenses if it is to take place, &c.

know, or believe, or assume this? He knew that the answer has to
be expressed in volts. He also knew that ' volt ' is what some have
called a ' theory laden term ', *i.e.* he knew that before one can
understand the term ' volt ' one must become aware of certain
phenomena and of principles, concepts, ideas, and facts used to
represent, to reason about, and to record these phenomena. He
furthermore knew or believed, or at least assumed that Mme.
Rouge did not possess the background just alluded to, that she
had never acquired the modicum of factual and theoretical knowledge required to understand ' volt '. He assumed that she could
not have conjured up the answer because he assumed that she
literally did not have the ideas that she would have had to have.
The basis of her alleged b-predicament with regard to the question
presumably went deeper than mere ignorance of the words needed
to formulate the answer; to remove it Picard had to enlarge her
conceptual repertoire, *i.e.* he had to teach her some elements of
electricity.

Removal of the basis of a b-predicament or p-predicament
with regard to a question will in general require instructions
about matters not covered by a mere statement of the answer, but
the above example ought not to mislead us into thinking that it
always requires *theoretical* instruction. Remember how my
brother, on my fifth birthday, removed the basis of my b-predicament. Even less theory will often do. Picard does not know who
the author of *De Fabrica* was. He is in no position to think of the
answer because he has never heard of Vesalius. To remove the
basis of his b-predicament with regard to ' Who was the author of
De Fabrica? ' one must do more than give him the name of the
author; to explain to him who the author of *De Fabrica* was one
must tell him who Vesalius was. But this demands no abstract
principles or theoretical notions. Or consider the case of someone
assumed to be in a p-predicament but *not* in a b-predicament with
regard to some question. I was in a p-predicament with regard to
' How did the assassin leave the room? ' because I took it for
granted that the culprit was a full-sized, normal human being.
The correct answer was ruled out for me by a false assumption.
In all such cases removal of the basis of the p-predicament
requires instructions that lead one to *revise* one's views. (Einstein
had to do something of the sort when he explained why no interference pattern had been observed by Michelson and Morley.

In his episode theory had to be expounded, but not so in that of Holmes.) Holmes would not have explained how the assassin had left the room had he merely said ' through the chimney ', but the additional information was short and pedestrian.

What is to be said in behalf of this fourth hypothesis?

If the second hypothesis (with its ' totally dispensable ' clauses removed) and the third hypothesis are each a set of sufficient conditions, then this one must also be a set of sufficient conditions. This hypothesis does not contain, either explicitly or implicitly any of the conditions that we have had occasion to reject as not being necessary ones. It includes all the conditions that we have had occasion to recognize as necessary ones. It lends itself to an account of why some indirect questions are out of place as direct objects of ' to explain '. (The account is readily constructed by combining those suggested by the second and third hypothesis.) It even lends itself to the speculative etymology to which the second and third ones lend themselves. I, for one, cannot think of an episode that fits all the clauses in this hypothesis and that is not correctly described by an 'A explained to B W ' sentence, nor can I imagine an episode that is so describable but that does not fit all the clauses of this hypothesis.

There is one possible objection that ought perhaps to be considered. We speak on occasion of someone's having tried to explain something to someone without having succeeded, and we often imply thereby that at the end of the episode the tutee did not know the answer. This may suggest that ultimate knowledge is necessary after all, since to have tried to explain something to someone without succeeding is no more to have explained something than to have tried to scale Mt. Everest without succeeding is to have scaled it.

But the fourth hypothesis accommodates these utterances in a natural way. Statements of the form 'A tried to explain to B W but failed ' cover unfinished explaining episodes, *i.e.* episodes in which (f) is not satisfied, and which therefore do not meet the truth-conditions proposed here. They cover episodes in which a tutor comes to realize that he is not being listened to and gives up; they cover episodes in which he is prevented from finishing; they also cover episodes in which he withholds nothing yet realizes that there are some things, things that have not occurred to him, that the tutee must be told to become properly informed under (e). Notice that

they do *not* cover episodes in which all the conditions of our hypothesis have been satisfied, but at the end of which the tutee is
still ignorant because of *his* failure to attend properly.

All this does not amount to a proof of the fourth hypothesis,
but it goes a long way to establish a presumption in its favour.

III

I now turn to statements of the form 'A E X to B ' and 'A E to
B X ' where 'A' and ' B ' indicate positions occupied by expressions
through which some person or persons are mentioned, where ' E '
indicates a position occupied by a tensed version of ' to explain ',
but where ' X ' is *not* replaced by an indirect question.

Statements of that form, also describe, or report, or record the
occurrence of explaining episodes. ' To explain ' in each functions
as an accomplishment term, and their truth entails that the truth-
conditions of some 'A E to B W ' statement (with identical
replacements for 'A', ' B ' and ' E ') are satisfied. Their own truth-
conditions should therefore be readily obtainable from those of
'A E to B W ' through some appropriate modifications.

Where ' X ' is simply replaced by ' something ' (*e.g.* ' Sam
explained something to Rebecca ') the question is simply left
unspecified, and we can adapt the fourth hypothesis by substituting
for (*a*),

(*a₁*) There is a sound question, *i.e.* one that admits of a right
answer.

The remaining cases fall under two headings, those in which
' X ' is replaced by a noun-phrase (*e.g.* ' Hector's behaviour ', ' the
laws of electro-statics ') and those in which it is replaced by a statement in *oratio obliqua* form (*e.g.* ' that bones contain no dextrose ').

First those in which a noun-phrase occurs. In 'A E to B W '
statements the question is specified by an indirect question. However, questions can be specified in other ways and some noun-
phrases in some contexts can fulfill that function and can serve as
surrogates of indirect questions. Thus ' Hector's behaviour ' will
stand for ' why Hector behaves (or behaved) in the way he does
(or did) ' and ' the origins of the word " explain " ' will stand for
' what the origins of the word " explain " are '. The precise
description of the relevant transformations is something that we
must leave to grammarians. The fourth hypothesis will cover
statements with such noun-phrases if we amend the definition of

' the question ' on page 6 to read ' the question whose *oratio obliqua* form or a surrogate for whose *oratio obliqua* form would appear at the position indicated by " W " or " X ".'

Some occurrences of noun-phrases do not convey enough information to be considered as surrogates of indirect questions. Mere knowledge of English is not sufficient to produce the question in an episode described by ' Mme. Rouge explained the third chapter of *Moby Dick* to Picard '; one must be acquainted with the third chapter of *Moby Dick* and know something of the questions to which it gives rise. The vagueness characteristic of such statements must be preserved in an adequate formulation of their truth-conditions. But this is easy to achieve. Simply replace (*a*) of the fourth hypothesis by

(a_2) There is a question about the topic mentioned at the X position that is sound, *i.e.* that admits of a right answer.

Notice that though such noun-phrases are vague, they are nevertheless almost indispensable. For instance, the third chapter of *Moby Dick* gives rise to a cluster of questions. It can happen that a tutee is not in a p-predicament with regard to any one of these questions taken in isolation, and that he is able to admit each as sound, but that he is nevertheless not in a position to think of a *set* of answers (to that set of questions) that he can consistently admit as possibly correct. This will happen when every non-objectionable answer that he can think of to one isolated question would require him to reject every non-objectionable answer that he can think of to another isolated question. Even more complicated situations arise. A question with regard to which a given tutee is in a p-predicament, may itself rest on a presupposition that the tutee trusts simply because it is the only non-objectionable answer that he can think of to some other question. Giving him the correct answer to the latter may teach him that the former has *no* right answer, and may thus ' cure ' him of his p-predicament. In all such situations ' the question ' is complex and is made up of disjunctions and conjunctions of more elementary ones. In each case it can no doubt be put in *oratio obliqua* form but the result must be unwieldy and awkward within an 'A E to B W ' statement.[1]

---

[1] To simplify the discussion I have written as if the actual cognitive state of the tutee were essential rather than what the tutor believes or assumes about that state, and I have ignored b-predicaments altogether. The necessary adjustments are obvious enough, and do not merit the further circumlocutions that their exposition would require.

H

This point is worth remembering. Often the question in an explaining episode cannot be told from an 'A E X to B ' description of that episode. This may lead us to overlook the essential connection that links explaining to questions.

Now briefly the cases in which the direct object of ' to explain ' is a statement in *oratio obliqua*. The nature of these statements is obvious enough: they reproduce, if not the words, at least the gist of what the tutee was told. To pass from a description containing such a statement to a description containing a question in *oratio obliqua* one merely has to phrase the question calling for the statement. This is sometimes easy. But not always. A given statement may convey the answer to more than one question. Moreover the alluded to words may have conveyed not the content of the answer but part of the background. Some explaining episodes, as we know, require that the tutee be corrected about some assumption, and others that he be informed of matters that will put the answer within his intellectual grasp. To know the role played by something that the tutor told the tutee one must know more than what he said. This will be reflected in a statement of truth-conditions obtained by substituting (a_1) again for (a). ' There is a sound question, *i.e.* one that admits of a right answer '; and by supplementing (f) to read 'At the end of the episode all the facts mentioned in (d) and (e) have been presented to the tutee by the tutor, and these include the facts described by the statement at the direct object position.'

IV

I pass now to statements in which ' to explain ' does not function as an accomplishment term. First, those of the form 'A explained W ' in which 'A' still indicates a position occupied by an expression through which a person is mentioned. When one says that Newton explained why there are tides, one need not mean that some explaining episode took place in which Newton was the tutor. One may mean that Newton solved the problem, found the answer to the question. Similarly ' Sherlock Holmes explained how the assassin left the room ' may convey that Holmes solved the riddle. Here ' to explain ' functions as an achievement term, not as an accomplishment term.

The fourth hypothesis does not require but is compatible with the occurrence of explaining episodes at the beginning of which the tutee is really in either a p-predicament or b-predicament with regard to the question, and by the end of which he actually has learned the answer and has had the grounds of his predicament corrected. I shall call explaining episodes of that sort *proper explaining episodes.*

A proper explaining episode involves a change in the tutee: at the beginning he does not know the answer to the question; in the course of the episode he learns certain facts, or (vel) he gains certain ideas and concepts, or (vel) he becomes aware of certain principles; at the end of the episode, he knows the answer, and he is competent to act as tutor in explaining episodes whose tutees are in a p-predicament or b-predicament with regard to the same question as a result of not knowing some or all the facts, ideas, concepts, or principles that our initial tutee has acquired in our initial episode. In other words, he is changed into someone who can explain the matter.

The kind of transformation just described can be brought about without benefit of tutor and without the occurrence of an explaining episode: research, re-examination of beliefs and assumptions, conceptual inventions, explorations, prodding for inspiration, exploitation of good luck, or grace may enable one to transform himself by himself into somebody able to explain something. To have succeeded in this sort of endeavour is to have explained something in the sense of ' to explain ' to which we are now attending.

The connection, then, between the truth-conditions of 'A E W ' and 'A E to B W '—put in the material mode—is that to have explained something in the sense now under consideration is to have become able to explain something in the sense discussed in the fourth hypothesis, as a result of one's own endeavours and ingenuity.[1]

V

Now finally the statements of the form ' T explains W ' in which ' T ' is *not* a position occupied by an expression through

---

[1] As an achievement term ' to explain ' is also often used to credit people with certain scientific discoveries. ' Newton explained why the tides vary with the phases of the moon ' may serve to mark the fact that Newton was the one who solved the riddle, who found the answer to a question with regard to which everybody had been in either a p-predicament or a b-predicament. To have explained something in this sense is to be one of the first to have explained it in the sense just analysed in Section IV, *i.e.* to be one of the first to have been in a position to explain (in the sense of Section II) it to a tutee.

which persons are mentioned. *E.g.*, ' The Special Theory of Relativity explains why no interference pattern was observed by Michelson and Morely ', ' Lumumba's prison record explains why he hated everything Belgian ', ' The fact that the assassin was a midget explains how he was able to leave the room without touching door or window.' In such statements ' to explain ' functions as a state term.

One might expect a characterization of the truth-conditions of these statements to require a list of the kinds of references that may be made at ' T '. But this would draw us into a veritable philosophic Sargasso Sea: theories, facts, events, propositions, items of information, discoveries, principles. . . . The list seems to have no end, and each of its entries may ensnare and choke us. Fortunately no such list is needed.

The transformation of someone into someone who can explain something does not always include an explaining episode. We noted in the previous section that one can achieve this by oneself. The change can often be initiated by informing the tutee of things that will put him in a position to work out the answer and to correct by himself the deficiencies responsible for his predicament. About any question W with regard to which someone might be in either a p-predicament or a b-predicament, one may ask: *What must someone who is in a p-predicament or a b-predicament with regard to that question learn, or of what must he be made aware to become able to explain W?* Any noun-phrase that is the right answer to *that* question may appear as the subject of a statement of the form ' T explains W '. Furthermore *such a statement is true if and only if the subject at ' T ' is related to the question represented at ' W ' in the way that a right answer to a ' What must someone in a p-predicament or b-predicament with regard to W learn, and of what must he be made aware to become able to explain W? ' question is related to the question at ' W '.*[1]

This question-using way of putting things is clearly a question-begging one. What is the relation referred to in the above bi-conditional? Under what conditions does it hold? One wants here a set of standards, a set of criteria, and an explicit general procedure that determine whether something that purports to

---

[1] The use of the past tense of ' to explain ' here is worth noticing. It implies that the conditions for the above relation do *not* hold though they were once thought to hold.

explain something does indeed do so. This I cannot give for the present. Getting what is wanted here must wait for developments in at least two areas: (*a*) erotetic logic, (*b*) the theory of p- and b-predicaments. Notice, by the way, that the latter is not to be thought of as the concern of psychology. Situations in which people are, or are not, in a p- or a b-predicament with regard to some questions depend on logical factors first, and on psychological ones only incidentally. For instance, some theories generate questions that, according to other theories, rest on unsound presuppositions. That this is so, is in each case, a matter of logic. It follows, however, that one who subscribes to one of the former theories can be in a p-predicament with regard to questions with regard to which someone who subscribes to one of the latter theories will not be in a p-predicament. Or again, two systems of assumptions and of concepts may differ in that only one is capable of generating answers to questions to which both provide presuppositions. This again must be a matter of logic. But it follows that one who relies on a specific system of assumptions may necessarily be in a p-predicament or b-predicament with regard to a question to which someone else, aware of different systems, will be able to envisage answers, perhaps even correct answers. The object of a theory of p- and b-predicaments must be to provide a general and systematic treatment of all such possibilities and of their grounds.

One last point before we leave ' to explain '. Everyone in a p-predicament or b-predicament with regard to a specific question does not always need the same instruction. A may be in a p-predicament with regard to the question as a consequence of one set of objections to the right answer; B may not share those particular objections but may have some of his own; C may not be in a p-predicament at all but only in a b-predicament; D may be in both. Though the question is the same, in each case a proper explaining episode may have to correct different shortcomings and inform on different points. Therefore the truth of statements of the form ' T E W ' is relative to something left unmentioned by them, *i.e.* the basis of the p-predicament or b-predicament with regard to the question. Such statements taken out of context may thus suffer from a peculiar ambiguity: they are true when viewed against such and such nescience, but not when viewed against such and such.

VI

What is an explanation?

An explanation may be something about which it makes sense to ask: How long did it take? Was it interrupted at any point? Who gave it? When? Where? What were the exact words used? For whose benefit was it given?

It may also be something about which none of these questions make sense, but about which it makes sense to ask: Does anyone know it? Who thought of it first? Is it very complicated?

We are not dealing here with two kinds of explanation, but with two senses of the word ' explanation ', one that refers to a certain type of didactic performance, and instances of it, the other that refers to something more abstract, to something that con- stitutes the cognitive substance of such performances. I will therefore speak of a *performance sense* of ' explanation ' and of a *text sense* of ' explanation '.

Each instance of *the* explanation (in the performance sense) of something coincides with an explaining episode; the two form necessarily co-extensive classes. Thus the explanation of some- thing by someone is merely the performance by someone of the rôle of tutor in an explaining episode.

Instances of *an* explanation (in the performance sense) of something form a wider class. They cover not only genuine explaining episodes, but also episodes corresponding to what I have called a looser use of ' to explain ', *i.e.* episodes in which the tutor *thought* that he was explaining something, but was mis- taken and did not know the answer to the question, or did not give it.

The text sense of ' explanation ' is more elusive. Ontological snares cover the genus within which its reference subsists, and should discourage a straightforward extensional explication. Some- thing is *the* explanation (in the text sense) of something if and only if it is the right answer to a question formed from:

(1) What must one tell someone in a p-predicament or a b-pre- dicament or either a p-predicament or b-predicament with regard to Q in order to explain (in the accomplishment sense) W to him?

by putting a question at the position indicated by ' Q ' and the *oratio obliqua* form of that question at the position indicated by

' W ', the resulting question being understood as calling for an actual utterance of what must be said to the tutee, not a description of what must be said.

Anything that is *the* explanation (in the text sense) of something is obviously an explanation of something. But everything that is *an* explanation (in the text sense) is not necessarily the explanation of anything. *An* explanation (in the text sense) of something is simply *an* answer to a question formed from (1) in the above way. Thus an explanation, like an answer to a question formed from (1), may be right or wrong, clear or unclear, confirmed or disconfirmed, complete or incomplete. Like an answer to such a question, its rightness or wrongness is relative not only to the question that would be cited at the place indicated by ' Q ', but also to the known or assumed basis of a known or assumed predicament.

The remarks made in Section V should no doubt be repeated here. The account of the nature of explanation just given falls short of what is eventually wanted: it fails to provide the sort of insight that can be translated into explicit standards and into a pattern of analysis applicable to all explanations and capable of deciding their correctness; it fails to make explicit the criteria that make correct explanations *correct* explanations. But as I remarked before, an adequate account that tells us all we want to know about explanations in general must wait until prior problems have been solved. This discussion merely brings us to the problems, and merely suggests an approach.

STRAWSON AND ONTOLOGICAL PRIORITY

J. M. E. Moravcsik

This paper consists of three parts. In the first part a few general remarks are made concerning ontological theories. The second part consists of a critical examination of what Strawson says about ontological priority. The third part consists of a statement and refutation of Strawson's claim that material bodies, in his sense, are ontologically prior to all other types of particular which are specified in ordinary language.

I

Some of the most important questions of ontology are: (i) Do ' is ' and ' exist ' have only one sense, or are they multivocal? (ii) What exists, and what existential assumptions should we be committed to? (iii) What important dependencies are there among the various types of existing entity? In the first half of this century, ontological investigations within analytic philosophy were concerned almost solely with the second of these questions. One of the main reasons for this preoccupation was the prevalent feeling that an allegedly clear and rigorous way had been found to state this question and to formulate answers to it. As a result, under the heading of ontology we find mostly proposals, or attacks, of so-called ' reductionist theses '. During the last fifteen years reductionist programmes have lost their importance in view of such difficulties as the paradox of analysis and the well-known problems of synonymy. Strawson's recent book[1] marks a renewed interest in ontology by concentrating on the third rather than the second of the questions mentioned above. Of course, any treatment of the third question involves taking some stand with regard to the second. Strawson's position—only briefly argued—is anti-reductionistic, *i.e.*, it assumes the existence of both particulars and universals. The usual objections which arise in connection with reductionist programmes cannot be raised against Strawson's ontological investigations. But we must see if other, equally

[1] P. F. Strawson, *Individuals* (London, 1959). All further references are to this book unless otherwise indicated.

damaging, objections might not arise in connection with the type of investigation which Strawson conducts.

Later I shall criticize Strawson's account of ontological priority, but first I would like to show that the notion of ontological priority has sufficient clarity to merit investigations which rely upon it. In general, to say that x is ontologically prior to y means that the existence of x is a necessary condition of the existence of y, but the existence of y is not a necessary condition of the existence of x. There are two difficulties with this formulation. One is to decide which conditions to count as ontological dependencies. If we apply the formula without restriction, fathers will turn out to be ontologically prior to their offspring, though this is clearly not the sort of dependency with which we are concerned in ontology. Thus mere causal conditions are to be excluded. In some vague sense, the relevant condition must be a ' logical ' one. Though much more needs to be said here, the difficulty of further specification is not an overwhelming one. For we can see intuitively at least what kinds of condition will be relevant, and if we find a number of borderline cases, this will not in any way vitiate the concept. The other difficulty is that there are many different kinds of conditions of existence, and it is not clear that all of the dependencies will always run the same way. Thus, for example, Plato claimed that Forms were ontologically prior to particulars, and one of his reasons for this assertion was that particulars need be the instantiation of Forms, but that Forms need not be instantiated by particulars in order to exist. Assuming this to be true, we must note that this does not prove Forms to be ontologically prior to particulars in any *unqualified* sense; there might be other dependencies which would run in the opposite direction. Thus any claim of ontological priority must have attached to it a specification of the relation(s) with respect to which the dependency is claimed to hold. Inasmuch as there may be an infinite number of such necessary relationships between any given types of entities, one can never make a claim of ontological priority *simpliciter* (unless one can show that a certain dependency, running one way, excludes the possibility of any dependency running the other way). In this way the specification of the respect in which ontological priority is claimed overcomes the second difficulty. The realization of this helps us toward a better understanding of the history of philosophy. For in this light we can see not only the conflicting claims of priority made, but also that many of these claims are based on different dependence-relationships. With respect to contemporary work in ontology, we shall remain on safe ground as long as the proper specifications are made.

II

Strawson's account of ontological priority is restricted to types of particulars.[1] His formula ties ontological priority to dependence with respect to identifiability, and thus it has to be viewed as a new study of dependencies. The key to this account of ontological priority is, of course, the notion of identification. The explanation of this notion is also restricted to the realm of particulars. Despite these restrictions one might be able to extract from Strawson's account a general explanation of what it is to identify as well as the corresponding relation of priority.[2] Strawson's formula is as follows: A type of particular b is dependent from the point of view of identifiability on another type of particular a, if and only if particulars of type b cannot be identified without reference to particulars of type a, but particulars of type a can be identified without reference to particulars of type b.[3] Such a dependence of identifiability is obviously relative to whatever conceptual scheme is under consideration. With respect to this dependency, we must see how it is related to ontological priority. The connection seems to be the following: If the identifiability of bs depends on reference to as, then it also depends on the existence of as, provided that we accept the claim that the existence of as is a necessary, though not a sufficient, condition of reference to as. Thus the connection between the kind of dependency that Strawson examines and ontological priority holds only if we assume that one cannot refer to that which does not exist. We shall ask later whether Strawson's sense of ' identify ' and ' refer ' allows us such an assumption.

[1] *Ibid.*, p. 17.

[2] Such a general account must be given if the conceptual apparatus of the first half of the book is to carry the burden which is placed on it by the second half. For here Strawson wants to illuminate the subject-predicate and universal-particular distinctions with the aid of the notion ' introducing a term into a proposition '. But this technical notion of term-introduction, which covers universals as well as particulars, is explained with reference to the notion of identification. Thus any adequate explanation of the distinctions drawn in the second half of the book depends on a general account of identification. No such account is given in the book. For ' term-introduction ' see pp. 146, 158–9, 181, 183.

[3] *Ibid.*, p. 17.

Strawson explains his notion of identification as something relative to a hearer-speaker situation.[1] A speaker S identifies a particular p to a hearer H if and only if S uses an appropriate referring expression (*e.g.*, a proper name or a definite description) to refer to p, and H identifies p as what S referred to. A sufficient, but not a necessary, condition of H's success in identifying p is H's sensibly discriminating p, knowing that it is the particular referred to by S.[2] Strawson admits that there are cases in which p is not sensibly present to S and H, but he believes that particular-identification in these cases can be ultimately linked to the cases where p is sensibly present.

From this summary of Strawson's account we can see that the success of identification depends on certain relations between the beliefs of S and H. In order to see these relations more clearly, let us draw a few distinctions. Let us call an ' individuating statement ' any statement which by its form singles out one and only one entity. We must distinguish the class of individuating statements which are true of any given entity from the criteria which determine the identity of that entity. The predicate expressions in individuating statements are definite descriptions. We can divide definite descriptions into two kinds, those that do and those that do not contain any reference to spatio-temporal location. Let us note that individuating statements containing either kind of predicate can be made both of universals and of particulars. (An example of a predicate of the relevant sort, containing reference to spatio-temporal location, is '— is the virtue best illustrated by Achilles in his fight with Hector '. An example of the relevant sort which takes a particular as its subject and does not contain reference to spatio-temporal location is ' — is the fastest runner '.) Thus whatever the criteria for the identity of universals and particulars may be, they do not restrict the kinds of individuating statement which may be true of either kind of entity.

Strawson thinks, however, that there are certain other conditions which restrict what he would call the availability of individuating statements for purposes of identification. One might imagine that apart from questions about criteria of identity, all further problems of availability would be matters of contingent

[1] *Ibid.*, pp. 16 ff.
[2] *Ibid.*, p. 18.

fact—of interest to the linguist and psychologist only. But
Strawson argues that there are necessary conditions which impose
a special kind of limitation on availability. For example, he
claims—successfully, it seems to me—that individuating statements about particulars which contain predicate expressions
without reference to spatio-temporal location are not available
for purposes of identification, for we could never be certain that
there is no duplicate somewhere in the universe of the entity
characterized in purely qualitative terms by the individuating
statement in question.

The persuasiveness of this argument should not prevent us
from asking questions about the kind of necessity which is invoked
in this claim. It is evident that what is argued for is not a truth of
logic, and that it is not a ' matter of definition ' (whatever this may
mean). Thus the claim is not analytic—in any sense in which this
notion is at least partially clear to me. Strawson never deals
directly with this issue, and our only clues are his occasional
allusions to Kant's transcendental method. Yet it seems that unless
we can give a satisfactory explanation of the kind of necessity
invoked here, we cannot regard the dependency which Strawson
is investigating, nor the claims of priority which are based on this
notion, as adequately clarified. For we have no adequate interpretations for the locutions '—can be identified ' and '—cannot be
identified '. It should be added that whatever limitations there
may be in identifying universals and particulars, they are not in
any way correlated with the kinds of criteria of identity which
hold for these types. Thus criteria of identity for universals will
not contain any reference to spatio-temporal location, but this
does not exclude the possibility of there being universals which
cannot be identified in Strawson's sense without reference to
spatio-temporal location.[1]

----

[1] Yet Strawson is arguing for this exclusion in the second half of the book,
and he bases on this alleged feature the universal-particular distinction. I find
two kinds of counter-example to this claim. The first is the class of universals
involving relations to places; e.g. ' being a landowner in Woonsocket, R.I.'
Surely these universals cannot be identified in Strawson's sense without reference to locations. If it is said that these examples are not bona fide universals,
we can go on and consider as counter-examples primitive qualities from the
range of sensory universals, e.g., colours, tastes, &c. The criteria of identity for
these would not include reference to spatio-temporal location, but I do not see
how we could talk of identifying them, in Strawson's sense, in hearer-speaker
situations, with tests of success, &c., without including ostensible reference to
samples with definite spatio-temporal location.

Let us now consider the criteria for successful identification. According to Strawson, if the particular to be identified is sensibly present both to S and H, then it is sufficient for H's success that he should sensibly discriminate the particular p as the entity to which S referred. This condition seems to me to be inadequate. First, the notion of sensibly discriminating a particular is unclear. In the usual contexts we talk of sensibly discriminating colours, sounds, shapes, &c., in short, of discriminating universals, not particulars. We can extend the notion to cover the discrimination of particulars if we mean by this simply the directing of one's attention to the appropriate segment of one's visual field in connection with someone's gesturing or talking about something sensibly present. But in this sense, though sensible discrimination of sensibly present particulars is a necessary condition for success in identifying, it is not a sufficient condition for this task. In order to see this, we may rely on some of the material discussed in Quine's latest book.[1] Suppose that in the presence of an entity S says, ' That brown thing over there looks furry ', and H, having correctly discriminated through the senses the phenomenon referred to, takes S to have asserted something about a collection of rabbit-parts, whereas S meant to refe· to a rabbit. Strawson's condition is met in this case, but the identification is surely not successful. Another kind of example showing the same inadequacy is the kind of situation in which two people are discussing the same phenomena, in the same language, but within different scientific frameworks. Thus, for example, S might refer to a fire, within our scientific framework, but H, though he discriminates correctly through the senses the phenomenon called to his attention, takes S to be referring to the presence of phlogiston. Again, Strawson's condition is met but the identification is not successful. These examples show that in order to account for success in identification we need to consider as relevant the speaker's and the hearer's conceptual framework as well as their intentions. (We cannot, however, construe reference and identification purely in terms of what is intended by the speaker. For example S might say something, referring to a chubby man puffing a cigar in a corner of the room. H in reply might point out to S that the man in question is Sir Winston Churchill. It will not do to say that S, on account of his intentions and ignorance, did not refer to

[1] W. V. Quine, *Word and Object* (New York, 1960).

Churchill.) Someone might say that my counter-examples are cases of referring to the same thing as different kinds of entity, and that once we distinguish ' referring as . . . ' from ' referring ' *simpliciter*, my examples lose their force. But I fail to make any sense out of ' referring *simpliciter* '. It seems to me that there can be no reference without subsuming the referent under some concept, even though this may be accomplished by some institutionalized gesture rather than verbally.

Another question arising in connection with the criteria of identification is whether what is identified in Strawson's sense must exist. Given the account surveyed above, with its condition for the hearer's success in identifying, it does not seem that such an assumption is justified. It seems rather that for the success of identification in Strawson's sense all we need is that the entity referred to should be assumed to exist by both speaker and hearer. This may seem paradoxical. Someone might say, ' How can we sensibly discriminate that which does not exist? ' But as far as I can make sense out of the notion of sensibly discriminating particulars, the question of existence or non-existence simply does not arise here. When this question does arise, then we are raising it with regard to something which is not only sensibly discriminated, but also subsumed under a concept. I fail to see why one could not, in Strawson's sense, identify phlogiston, or any other entity no longer countenanced by modern science. Thus the connection between this sort of dependency and ontological priority does not seem to hold. It might be better to construe this dependency as indicating priority of ontological commitment, rather than that of ontological priority. In this respect the dependency which Strawson investigates is to be contrasted with the sort of dependencies which Plato and Aristotle were examining.

Let us now consider Strawson's account of the relevant types of particular among which the alleged dependencies are supposed to hold. The delineation of relevant types can be done in two ways: either by enumeration, as Aristotle does, or by some general characterization. Strawson does the latter. He claims that the types of particulars under consideration are those and only those which we encounter in ordinary language. The adequacy of this description seems to depend on how clear Strawson can make what is to be excluded. It does not seem, however, that such clarification is adequately given. For Strawson considers the possibility that entities which fall under the concept ' process-thing ' (as Quine and others have called it) are not ontologically posterior to material bodies—in his sense—and he rejects this possibility on the ground that it is irrelevant since the concept of process-thing is not embodied in ordinary language. It is a concept which ' we neither have nor need '.[1]

This dismissal seems strange when placed side by side with Strawson's own account of what is ontologically basic. He calls this type ' material bodies ', and defines this type as what is three-dimensional, and possesses some qualities of the tactual range.[2] This account of what is the basic type, the one ontologically prior to all others, seems unsatisfactory. First, I doubt if there is such a term as ' material body ' in ordinary language. Both the words ' body ' and ' material ' do have uses in ordinary language, but the combination of the two sounds suspiciously like what is technical, philosophical discourse. But even if we do regard this combination as part of ordinary language, the definition given is much too wide. Let us consider the following collection: saw-dust, rain-drops, a strand of hair, and a dash of fresh paint. According to Strawson's definition, each of these items qualifies as a material body, yet none could be properly described in ordinary English as a body, or as a material body. Further reflection should convince us that there is no word in ordinary English which would answer to Strawson's definition: thus this is not merely a matter of an unfortunate choice of words. What we do find is a variety of more or less similar nouns, such as ' thing ', ' object ', ' material', ' body ', ' matter ', ' stuff ', &c., to cover the range of particulars which answers to Strawson's definition. Though these words exhibit important similarities in their uses, they also show important differences (e.g., some of them are mass-terms and others not). This family of words should be studied carefully if we are to give an adequate analysis of the ways in which we refer to entities in space and time. Strawson's carelessness in this respect results in his dismissal of rival categories as philosophic concepts, while his own candidate for top priority likewise turns out to be a technical concept. I realize, of course, that Strawson's notion of a material body is closer to ordinary language than Quine's notion of a process-thing, but I fail to see that such differences in degree are relevant to an issue such as ours. In short, if Strawson wants

[1] *Ibid.*, p. 57.   [2] *Ibid.*, p. 39.

to adhere strictly to ordinary language, then he cannot use
' material body ' as he defines this word; if on the other hand he is
going to use this term, then he can no longer dismiss Quine's
notion of a process-thing on the ground that it is not part of
ordinary language.

To conclude, although the notion of identification carries
initial plausibility, there are serious shortcomings in Strawson's
account of this concept, and it is not clear that dependencies resting
on this notion can be called justifiably ontological priorities.

III

Let us assume that the notion of particular-identification is at
least intuitively clear, and that we have an adequate grasp of the
relevant types to be considered. Can we accept Strawson's claim
that among these types, with respect to the relation specified,
material bodies are prior to all other types? Strawson presents a
number of arguments in support of this claim. Some of these are
general arguments, while others deal with specific types. These
arguments, if successful, have to show not only that there is no
other type prior to material bodies, but also that there is no other
type enjoying a status equal to that of material bodies. In other
words, Strawson has to show not only that there is no asymmetrical
dependency which shows material bodies to be posterior, but also
that there is no other type which has a mutual, symmetrical
dependency relation with material bodies. In this section I shall
argue that such a symmetrical relationship does hold between
material bodies and types of event, action, and process. (In what
follows I am giving the terms ' event ', ' action ', &c., a wider
denotation than is usual in ordinary language. In doing this I am
departing no more and no less from ordinary language than
Strawson does in his use of ' material body '.)

One of Strawson's general arguments takes as its basic premiss
the nature of the spatio-temporal framework within which we
identify particulars.[1] This framework is said to necessitate that the
basic particulars—the ones prior to all else—should be three-
dimensional, have stability and sufficient richness, and endure in
time. The argument concludes that only material bodies meet this
set of criteria. The key premiss in this argument is the condition
of three-dimensionality. I do not see any considerations support-

[1] *Ibid.*

ing this premiss. Given the nature of the framework within which we identify particulars, it is obvious that basic particulars must be located in space and time, and that they must have stability and richness. The number of dimensions, however, which they or any other type of particular have, seems to me to be entirely a matter of contingent fact, and it has no direct bearing on identifiability. Once this is seen, and the condition of three-dimensionality is dropped, events, actions and processes become as good candidates for basicness as are material bodies. For some events, actions and processes have as much stability in space and time as any material body has, even though the question of dimensionality does not arise in connection with them.

This criticism of Strawson's first argument establishes only the negative point, that the argument does not give sufficient grounds for not construing events and actions as basic as material bodies. In examining critically the second of Strawson's arguments I would like to show what positive reasons we have for regarding events and actions as basic as material bodies from the point of view of identifiability. Strawson's second argument deals with the question of re-identifiability, *i.e.*, the identifying of x at time t_2 as the same entity as x at time t_1, where t_2 is later than t_1. Strawson claims that the re-identification of material bodies, and of this type only, is independent of reference to any other type of particular.[1] He cites in support of this claim the fact that the fundamental requirement for the continuing identity of material bodies in time is continuity of existence in space, and that this requirement does not involve any reference to other types of particular.[2] With regard to this claim, I do not wish to dispute, in this paper at least, that the re-identification of events requires reference to material bodies. But I do wish to show that the re-identification of bodies does require reference to events and processes, and that in view of this we are justified in regarding these types as equally basic, and to construe the identificational dependency as symmetrical.

First, we have to distinguish between the criteria of continuing identity in time, and the ways in which we can ascertain whether those criteria have been fulfilled. For while it is true that the

[1] *Ibid.*, pp. 55–56.
[2] Strawson admits that re-identification requires reference to places, but he thinks that the identification of these in turn rests on the identification of bodies (p. 56).

I

criteria make no reference to particulars of other types, it is not true either that statements of the continuing identity of material bodies in time or that statements containing evidence for such claims can ultimately avoid reference to events, or actions, or processes.[1] For in order to raise questions about the re-identification of any material body, we have to locate two segments of time which the body allegedly occupied and occupies. I do not see how such locating would be possible without reference to events, or times (*e.g.*, ' The knife in front of me now is the same knife with which I cut an orange an hour ago ', or ' The only table in the West Room on January 6, 1963, is the same as the only table in the Georgian Room on December 28, 1962 '). If we attempt to locate these time-segments by reference to other bodies only, we shall not be able to relate them to the observer, and this is surely crucial for re-identification. Furthermore, reference to times presupposes some reference to events.

Turning to the verification of claims of re-identification, it seems that such a process must involve events of observation, and that statements summing up the evidence would have to make reference to them. Thus though part of the evidence for a claim of re-identification may be qualitative sameness (*e.g.*, ' The knife looks the same '), the statements of the evidence would have to connect this with events of observation (*e.g.*, ' The knife looks the same as the one I (or someone else) saw an hour ago '). In short, re-identification involves correlating in certain ways objects, times and places; and this is not possible without some reference— ultimately—to events. Thus the re-identification of material bodies depends on reference to events, and even though the identification of these may depend in some ways on the identification of material bodies, this latter dependency makes the relation simply a symmetrical one, rather than something asymmetrical. If my argument is sound, then Strawson's conception of a ' pyramid ' of priorities is inadequate. In disagreeing with him I want to claim more than merely that there is no homogeneous base

[1] The notion of ' without reference to ', both in Strawson's arguments and in my discussion, must be construed in a wide sense. Strictly speaking, the identification of events does not require reference to material bodies, nor does the identification of material bodies require reference to events. For example, in the statement ' Mickey Mantle's home run was the longest ever hit ' we are not referring to Mickey Mantle. But unless one understood what it is to refer to Mickey Mantle, one would not understand the statement in question. Thus reference to Mantle is still presupposed by the statement in question.

to the pyramid. It seems to me that in identification and re-identification various types of particulars are interwoven in many complex ways. There is no base to the pyramid, because there is no pyramid to begin with.

The same relationship of mutual dependence can be exhibited if one turns to the examination of Strawson's arguments concerning specific types. At one place Strawson argues that events such as strikes can not be basic particulars, for we could not have the concept of a strike without having such concepts as those of tools and factories.[1] To this, however, it should be replied that neither could we have the concepts of tools and factories without having such concepts as those of production, manufacturing, &c. Perhaps Strawson would counter this move by saying that even without the concepts of production and manufacturing we could identify tools and factories as material bodies, whereas without the concepts of tools and factories we could not identify a strike at all. But this brings us back to the previous point, that without reference to events of some sort, *e.g.*, strikes, we could not re-identify factories and tools, and without re-identification, we could not recognize them as material objects. It is also unclear to me why one could not identify processes—strikes or other kinds—without being able to identify any bodies involved.

Strawson's other argument involving specific types seems to rest on drawing illegitimate conclusions from what are contingent features of the English language.[2] In this argument Strawson claims that there is a one-way identificational dependence between animals and births. According to Strawson ' This is a birth ' entails ' There is an animal of which this is a birth ', but ' This is an animal ' entails ' There is a birth which is the birth of this animal ' only in a weaker sense, without any commitment to the existence of births. Strawson's defense of this interpretation of the entailments is that the consequent of the second entailment can be translated into ' This was born ' whereas no such translation into an adjectival expression can be given for the consequent of the first entailment. From this Strawson concludes that we can eliminate quantification over births, but not quantification over animals, and thus the asymmetry is maintained. This seems to me an entirely unwarranted conclusion. First, it is surely a contingent matter that we have in English the word ' born ' and

[1] *Ibid.*, p. 44.   [2] *Ibid.*, pp. 51–52.

that we do not have the word ' animalish ' or some equivalent. Secondly, though I would not want to say that no significant conclusions can be drawn from grammatical disparities, surely we cannot draw from the disparity presented any inference concerning existential import. If we could not count and refer to births, the meaning of '—— is born ' would be different from what it is; the mere existence of this phrase is thus not significant. There are, after all, nouns other than ' animal ' which do have a corresponding adjectival expression, e.g., ' man ' and ' human '. Would Strawson want to say that we can eliminate quantification over men, but not over animals? There is a sense, of course, in which ' This is an animal ' does not entail ' There is a birth which is the birth of this animal '; after all, animals without births are referred to in the Bible, and though we may doubt the veracity of biblical stories, we would not want to say that they are self-contradictory. But of course the same holds for the possibility of births which are not births of animals. Consider, for example, talk about the birth of nations, of gods, &c. Thus this consideration also fails to establish some sort of asymmetry. In general, the view that agents are somehow more basic than actions seems to me unsound. Surely there is a relation of mutual dependence here, both from the point of view of having these concepts, and from the point of view of identifiability. The absurdity of Strawson's view can be seen perhaps more clearly if we consider another pair of terms, ' animal ' and ' eat '. Strawson would have to argue that ' This is an occasion of eating ' entails ' There is an animal which eats on this occasion ' but that ' This is an animal ' entails ' There are occasions on which this animal eats ' only in a weaker sense, such that we could translate the consequent into ' This animal is an eater ' without committing ourselves thereby to the existence of occasions of eating. Frankly, I can make no sense out of the concept of an eater which does not involve occasions of eating, and thus I fail to see how the alleged asymmetry would hold.

In view of these considerations I reject Strawson's claim that material bodies are prior to all else with respect to identification within the realm of particulars. I suggest instead, that there is a mutual dependency between material bodies, events, actions and processes. I have also suggested that much work needs to be done if the kind of dependency which Strawson attempts to formulate and to examine is to be given an adequate explication. My comments, however, leave many questions unanswered. What are other dependencies from the point of view of identification among types of particulars? Why should there be this mutual dependence which I described above? What, if any, are the relations of dependence from the point of view of identification between particulars and universals? To attempt to answer these questions is beyond the scope of this paper. But let me conclude on a constructive note by emphasizing that these further questions arise as a result of Strawson's investigations. It does seem to me to be the case that the work which Strawson began with this book leads to a number of new and interesting philosophical questions the answering of which is an important, and most likely rewarding, task of contemporary philosophy.

IDENTITY AND INDIVIDUATION

M. J. Woods

THIS paper is an attempt first to clarify, and then to explore, the relation between the concepts of identity and individuation. A preliminary clarification is very necessary, as these terms have not been used by recent philosophers in an entirely uniform way. Apart from this conflict of philosophical usage, there is the difficulty that although we are dealing with an intuitive distinction, and trying to give a philosophical account of it, the pre-philosophical intuitions of different persons may not coincide here as much as elsewhere. So I may appear to some people to be imposing a distinction rather than discovering one.

The conflict of usage can be seen if we notice that Miss Anscombe, for example, in her article entitled ' The Principle of Individuation ',[1] discusses under this heading what sort of identity is attributed to a man, given that the cells in his body are constantly being replaced. Professor Hampshire in *Thought and Action*,[2] when discussing what kinds of rule a language needs for it to be capable of being used for singling out constant objects of reference, mentions two kinds of rule; rules of the one kind he calls principles of individuation, rules of the other principles of classification. Principles of classification, for Hampshire, are principles for sorting objects into kinds; principles of individuation are principles for distinguishing objects of a given kind. However, elsewhere Hampshire speaks of a *criterion of identity*,[3] and it is not clear whether he regards a criterion of identity for a class of objects as coextensive with, or included in, a principle of individuation.

On the other hand, principles of individuation have often been distinguished from criteria of identity, as though it were a real question whether the one involved the other. A distinction of this sort is drawn by Strawson in *Individuals* when he separates criteria of distinctness from criteria of re-identification.[4]

[1] G. E. M. Anscombe, ' The Principle of Individuation ', *The Aristotelian Society*, Suppl. Vol. XXVII (1953), pp. 83–96.
[2] S. Hampshire, *Thought and Action* (London, 1959), p. 12.
[3] *Ibid.*, p. 37.
[4] P. F. Strawson, *Individuals* (London, 1959), p. 203 ff.

It will no doubt be readily agreed that, however the two are to be distinguished, the learning of both a principle of individuation and a criterion of identity is a necessary condition of full understanding of a word for a kind of material object; or, more generally, that where there exists an established principle of individuation ('P.I.') and criterion of identity ('C.I.') for the objects falling under a concept, a knowledge of these is a necessary condition of full understanding of the concept in question. Intuitively, the distinction applies most clearly in the case of material objects; secondly, in the case of other directly observed particulars which last over a period of time; thirdly, in the case of particulars which, though not directly observed, are such that a life-history can intelligibly be attributed to them. Thus, to illustrate the third type of case, a comparative philologist might use the concept of a word in a way which invited us to distinguish a P.I. from a C.I. in so far as words were regarded as objects which could have a history and develop with language. This use might be thought to contrast with the everyday use of the notion of a word, which does not seem to invite any such distinction. If it is true that material object concepts are to be regarded as having a C.I. and P.I. built into them, one could say that the question we are discussing is whether two elements in the understanding of a material object concept can be separated; if it should be found that the full understanding of one involves the understanding of the other, we shall have to conclude that the break-down in question is not feasible.

Some qualifications must be made to my statement that all material object words have a C.I. and a P.I. built into their meaning. For example, both are in many cases very indeterminate. Sometimes this is because our interest in distinguishing and enumerating objects of the kind in question is slight, or because their behaviour would make these procedures pointless. In other cases, the indeterminacy exists, but in certain directions only, because rules for individuating and identifying have been made only to deal with cases that actually arise. Examples where indeterminacy of the first sort arises would be objects such as clouds or tidal waves, for which only a very indeterminate C.I. and P.I. exist, both on account of their behaviour and on account of our lack of interest in possessing a determinate P.I. and C.I. The second sort of case can best be illustrated by many technical and quasi-technical concepts which have needed to be refined for their technical use, where the methods of identification and individuation have been altered in response to new cases of doubt as they arose. *Living organism* might be an example of this. These cases are all such that although the C.I. and P.I. are altered to make them yield a determinate answer when they would not have yielded one before, this new determinacy is not ordinarily thought of as changing crucially the character of the concept concerned, provided that the alteration to the rules is not in danger of leading to a different decision in cases decidable already. Thus most of us probably understand a concept like *living organism* yet realize that there could arise difficult cases of identity and individuation for answering which there exist established techniques, even if we do not know what these techniques are. But these cases show merely that the notion of understanding a word or possessing a concept must not be made to bear too much weight.

A more important class of exceptional cases are those where concepts have no determinate P.I. or C.I., and this indeterminacy could not be removed, or could only be removed at the cost of depriving the concept in question of the point which it has in our conceptual system. Some concepts in this class are perhaps best regarded as incomplete. When completed in an appropriate way they could be said to possess both a C.I. and a P.I. Examples would be *heap, lump, fragment*. There are moderately determinate criteria of identity and principles of individuation for lumps of coal, heaps of leaves and fragments of pottery. But there is a large number of other material object concepts, for which there is no built-in C.I. or P.I., which have a place in language which excludes their being given one. The reasons are no doubt various. A familiar set of examples is provided by concepts like the concept *material object* itself. There is no procedure for answering the question ' How many material objects are there in this room? ', and this is not a simple case of indeterminacy which could be removed by linguistic innovation. Similar considerations apply to concepts like *space-occupier*, and also, for different reasons, concepts like *part, segment* and *unit*. These are all notions which would be likely to occur in a general explanation of the notion of a material object. Other fairly general material object concepts seem to approximate to the examples already mentioned; *e.g.*, the concept of an instrument. These examples do not, of course, tell against the view that where a C.I. and P.I. exist for a class of objects, knowing them is a necessary condition of understanding the concept defining the class; but they are counter-examples, though readily intelligible ones, to the thesis that all material object concepts have a C.I. and a P.I. built into them.

It is time now to attempt to clarify the intuitive distinction between a P.I. and a C.I. I shall attempt to clarify it and make it operate for the case of material objects; if this can be done, it will be possible to see how far a parallel distinction can be drawn for other kinds of object, and see how far the class of non-material objects for which the distinction has some point extends.

I have up to now treated the notion of a material object as unproblematic, as though there were complete agreement on what is to be counted as a material object; and probably no such agreement exists. I propose to avoid difficulties, as far as possible, by confining my examples to indisputable cases.

It might be suggested that an approach could be made via a distinction between two kinds of question:

> *Type 1*: Questions of the form ' How many Xs are there?' with or without some further specification (*e.g.*, by a phrase delimiting an area of space) of the objects to be counted.

> *Type 2*: Questions of the form ' Is this X the same X as the X which . . .?'

These are not be taken as formulae from which any question of the two sorts can be derived by substitution, but rather as indicating in a rough way the kind of questions I have in mind. What is essential to a question's being a Type 2 question is (1) that there should be two phrases purporting to identify something under a description, and (2) that there should be a word or phrase ' X ' in each identifying expression such that the question raised is whether the X picked out by one identifying expression is the same X as the X picked out by the other. In the case of Type 1 questions we do not need to consider cases where the objects to be enumerated are identified only by a complex description; for we are concerned only with a possible account of the concepts of a P.I. and a C.I. in terms of these two types of question.

For a person to be able to set about answering a Type 1 question it is clearly necessary that he should know the natural numbers and understand the procedure of counting; he must, in fact, understand in a general way how to answer questions of this sort.

But in addition to this he must have an understanding of the specific concept under which the objects to be counted fall; and it might be suggested that to have sufficient understanding of a concept as will, in conjunction with a general understanding of how Type 1 questions are to be answered, enable a person to set about answering Type 1 questions about objects falling under the concept, is to have a P.I. for the objects concerned.

In a similar way, to be able to set about answering a Type 2 question it is necessary to understand the sense of questions of this general form—to understand the way in which the *kinds* of identifying expression occurring in the question are used. But, besides this, to know a procedure for answering it the person would need to have specific understanding of the concept under which the identifications were made. And it might be thought that to have sufficient understanding of a concept as will, when added to the general understanding mentioned earlier, enable someone to set about answering a Type 2 question asked about objects falling under the concept is to possess a C.I. for the objects in question.

This suggested characterization of criteria of identity and principles of individuation would relate them to the two kinds of question in a very direct way. If this account is satisfactory, it must be possible, at any rate for some objects, that someone should have the specific knowledge to answer Type 1 questions without having the specific knowledge necessary to answer Type 2 questions. (I use the phrase ' specific knowledge ' in order to exclude the general understanding of the forms of question which I mentioned above. It is necessary to exclude it, since a person might be familiar with Type 2 questions as a type without, in a similar way, being familiar with Type 1 questions, and vice versa; but the substantial question is whether someone familiar with both types could know the procedure for answering a question of one type, asked about a kind of object, without also knowing the procedure for answering one of the other type, asked about objects of the same kind. From now on I shall ignore the general knowledge required.)

Criteria of identity and principles of individuation are not, however, related in any such direct way to Type 1 and Type 2 questions, if one wishes to distinguish them. For any rule sufficiently powerful and comprehensive to yield a determinate answer to Type 1 questions asked about objects of a given kind would also determine an answer to the corresponding Type 2 questions. I shall first illustrate this point and then try to explain it.

If an explorer on a sea voyage puts ashore on an island on two occasions then he could ask a Type 2 question about the identity of the island he landed on on the first occasion with the island he landed on on the second. The rule he would make use of in answering this question would be the one which he would also use in answering the Type 1 question 'How many islands have been visited by me to-day?' A rule which determined the answer to the Type 2 question mentioned also determined the answer to the Type 1 question. If a case of doubt arose where the rule gave no determinate answer in one case, the answer in the other would be equally indeterminate. (For example, if a canal intersected what was otherwise a single island.)

Conversely, if someone were able to set about answering the Type 1 question 'How many rooms does this building contain?' he would also know how to set about answering the question 'Is the room with the window overlooking the garden the same room as the room with the bay window?' Any doubt whether a partition divided off two rooms or merely sections of one would entail that some Type 2 question was also in doubt.

To generalize this, I am saying that for any Type 1 question asked about objects of a given kind the rule used in settling it would also be used in settling some Type 2 questions, and conversely. So any rule powerful and comprehensive enough to determine an answer to all Type 1 questions about a given class would also determine an answer to all Type 2 questions, and vice versa. If, therefore, it is suggested that an account can be given of the distinction between a C.I. and P.I. in terms of the distinction between identity questions and individuation questions, distinguished in the way suggested, some restriction must be placed on the *kind* of Type 1 and Type 2 questions relevant to the distinction.

I must emphasize that I am *not* saying that anyone who had actually found an answer to one type of question would also be able to find an answer to one of the other type; only that he would know what the procedure was. Clearly, the observations which might be sufficient to settle one would not necessarily be sufficient to settle the other; but the rule used would be the same.

That this is so can be seen if we consider first what is involved in successful counting. A minimum necessity is that double-counting should be avoided, and that none of the objects to be enumerated should be left out. But the first of these conditions can only be satisfied if the counter is able to answer at least some Type 2 questions about the objects, since to raise the question whether or not double-counting has occurred is to raise a question of identity.

Conversely, any Type 2 question will be answered by the use of a rule which would also be used in answering some Type 1 questions; for every Type 2 question is a question whether two referring expressions pick out one object or two; so that any Type 2 question could be unnaturally rephrased as a Type 1 question. A less unnatural reformulation of a Type 2 question as a Type 1 question would involve the finding of a suitable *frame of enumeration*.

This term must now be explained. In the example mentioned earlier we said that someone who was equipped to answer the question ' Is the island I have now landed on the same island I landed on before?' would also be equipped to answer the question ' How many islands are there which I have visited to-day?', and in this case the qualifying phrase ' which I have visited to-day ' provides a frame of enumeration for the question. A simpler case would be a Type 1 question ' How many animals are there in this cage? ', where the frame of enumeration is provided by the phrase ' in this cage '. This is a simpler case, because the restriction imposed only delimits an area of space, and does so quite explicitly. The island example was less straightforward because both a temporal and a spatial restriction were imposed implicitly by the qualifying phrase. To answer the question would involve enumerating islands along the path traced out by the explorer's journeys, within a time-stretch delimited by the word ' to-day '. But simpler cases can be found where both the temporal and the spatial frame of enumeration are clearly marked and separated. To take a Humean example, ' How many churches have stood on this site since 1090? ' is a question which embodies a temporal frame of enumeration provided by the words ' since 1090 ' and a spatial frame provided by the words ' on this site '. There exist numerous ways in which the frames of enumeration of Type 1 questions are indicated in language. Often a qualifying adjective is used; for example, ' recent ' in ' How many recent eruptions have there been of this volcano?'

But it is not necessary for our purposes to consider in detail how the frame of enumeration of a question is indicated in language; provided sense can be made of a distinction between a temporal and a spatial frame of enumeration, and there do exist cases where each of them is separately marked out, we can give an account of the distinction between a C.I. and a P.I. in terms of them. We can then say that to possess a C.I. for a kind of object is to have a rule for answering Type 1 questions within a temporal frame of enumeration; to possess a P.I. is to have a rule for answering Type 1 questions within a spatial frame of enumeration. This seems to distinguish two kinds of rule satisfactorily, even if the formulation appears to fit our intuitive notions of a P.I. better than it does our intuitive notions of a C.I. That is because where the use of a C.I. is most prominent a Type 2 question is more likely to be involved; the notion of a C.I. has been more commonly connected with Type 2 questions.

How far is it essential that every Type 1 question should be given both a spatial and temporal frame of enumeration? This is a crucial point, very relevant to the problem we are now going to consider, namely how far a C.I. and a P.I. for a kind of object involve one another. For if there were Type 1 questions which had only a spatial or only a temporal frame of enumeration it would look as if it were possible for someone to learn one without learning the other.

Now, one type of frame of enumeration which figures very largely in the situations in which people learn to count objects is the frame of enumeration given by some phrase such as 'currently visible'. The area of space which can be observed from a particular point of observation provides, as it were, a natural spatial frame of enumeration which would often not be explicitly delimited; if it were we should expect demonstratives like 'here' to figure in the phrases by which the area was determined. There does not seem to be any natural frame of enumeration analogous to this in the case of temporal frames of enumeration. If there is one it would have to be something like the specious present; but even if sense can be made of this notion, it would be too short to provide a frame of enumeration that we should have much occasion to use.

This natural frame of enumeration in space has blurred outlines, but that does not prevent us from operating with it. For even where another spatial frame of enumeration is introduced this frequently is a narrower frame of enumeration within the larger one which consists of the portion of space observable from a particular point of observation. I propose to consider now cases where a Type 1 question is asked about a class of objects within a frame of enumeration which is the natural spatial frame of enumeration just mentioned or some spatial frame of enumeration falling within it. Must a temporal frame of enumeration always be provided in these cases? If the Type 1 question is asked ' How many animals are there in this cage now? ', the only temporal frame of enumeration seems to be that provided by the word ' now '. The word ' now ' is presumably to be taken to mark out a fairly short time-stretch which would include the moment when the question was asked; and the length roughly marked out would vary with the context. What is important, however, is that the objects to be enumerated are supposed to exist throughout the time-stretch picked out by ' now ', for these Type 1 questions are essentially questions about the number of simultaneously existing objects of the kind in question. This requirement could be covered by saying that when a Type 1 question is asked about the objects existing simultaneously in the period delimited by ' now ' then the time-stretch picked out by ' now ' is always sufficiently short that the same answer to the Type 1 question would be obtained, using a given principle, if it were asked with reference to any shorter time-stretch within it; that is, the temporal frame of enumeration may approximate as nearly as we wish to a point-instant. This provides us with a reason for saying that we use no temporal frame of enumeration in these cases, since it is in no way relevant to the answer obtainable by the use of the P.I. that it should be regarded as being greater than any specified length of time. It is therefore these cases that ought to be specially considered if we wish to see how far a P.I. presupposes a C.I., since in answering these Type 1 questions no C.I. seems to be actually used, in the sense first suggested.

Is it possible, in an analogous way, to find examples of Type 1 questions with a temporal frame of enumeration but not a spatial? Examples can perhaps be constructed; but, as we have seen, criteria of identity are more commonly associated with Type 2 than Type 1 questions. So in trying to see whether a C.I. implies a P.I. we may perhaps consider Type 2 questions. If it proves to be impossible to settle any Type 2 questions without recourse to both sorts of rule, we may reasonably take it as established that a C.I. involves a P.I., since it is difficult to see how a person could be said to have learned a criterion of identity for a kind of object if he had not been thereby equipped to set about answering *some* questions of either type.

To return now to the question whether a P.I. involves a C.I. The cases most promising for the contrary thesis appear to be those where a Type 1 question was asked with a frame of enumeration which coincided with or was included in an observer's field of observation, and there appeared to be no temporal frame of enumeration. Might someone be able to answer a Type 1 question of this sort without knowing a criterion of identity for the objects in question? It must be borne in mind that we are discussing the question at the moment solely with reference to three-dimensional material objects. So it is not relevant to point out that someone might be able to distinguish X-type *appearances* or *apparent* Xs, in the required way. And this is where the difficulty arises in the supposition that someone might be able to individuate three-dimensional objects without knowing a C.I. For to be in a position to enumerate objects with certainty an observer must be in a position to draw boundaries round them in every dimension; and to do this he would seem to need a C.I. Even if the question at issue were of the form ' How many Xs can I see now?', he would still not be able to satisfy himself of the number of objects within the frame of enumeration unless he could observe the objects from other points of observation than that which defined the frame of enumeration. This argument is connected with the more general point that the identification of something as an X, where X is a material object, involves the claim that the object could also be observed from other points of observation. The fact that we commonly know what the objects we observe are without making a series of observations does not alter the fact that we must know what further observations could be made if we are to understand the sense of the identifications.

It is perhaps worth emphasizing that a person might easily enumerate with success material objects knowing only a P.I. and not a C.I.; I am not saying that this is impossible, only that if someone set about distinguishing objects of a class in order to count them, he would be logically committed to being able to make further observations which he could only make if he had a C.I. Thus, although a P.I. for a kind of material object could be learned independently of a C.I., anyone using it would possibly be faced with situations for which a C.I. was needed. The point is not that criteria of re-identification would be needed for an object not continuously observed but that over any time-stretch a C.I. might be needed even if the object were observed continuously; for the notion of continuous observation of an object itself brings in the identity-criterion of spatio-temporal continuity.

To turn finally to the question whether a C.I. involves a P.I., which we saw could be answered by considering Type 2 questions. It was characteristic of Type 2 questions that two referring expressions occurred in them each of which purported to pick out a material object. But this already imports a P.I., since, as we saw earlier, using a principle of individuation involves drawing a three-dimensional boundary round objects. If the argument which purported to show that a P.I. presupposes a C.I. is correct, there could, similarly, be no use of a C.I. which did not involve the use of a P.I.; for Type 2 questions can only be raised by someone who knows how to pick out objects of a kind from others of the same kind by drawing appropriate boundaries.

Thus a distinction between a criterion of identity and a principle of individuation can be upheld in so far as a distinction can be made between temporal and spatial frames of enumeration for Type 1 and Type 2 questions. When the objects concerned are of such a kind that a distinction of this sort between frames of enumeration cannot be made, the criterion of identity and principle of individuation appear to collapse into one. Thus no viable distinction seems to be capable of being drawn between one and the other in the case of numbers, for instance. But, even in other cases, the use of a P.I. involves the possibility of situations where a C.I. would be needed also; and the use of a C.I. presupposes an ability to individuate objects of the kind in question in a spatial frame of enumeration.

THE LOCATION OF SOUND

R. M. P. MALPAS

IT is convenient to talk of the location of sound, and I shall do so in this paper, but the phrase is open to misinterpretation. I do not mean by ' location ' ' locality ', but ' the act of locating ', and by ' the act of locating ' I do not mean ' the act of establishing in a place ', but ' the act of discovering the place of '. Even so ' location ' is misleading, because it implies that there is such a thing as discovering the place of sounds. Since sounds do not have places there is no such act. ' Telling where sounds come from ' is not ' discovering the place of sounds '. Sounds *come from* places, they do not *have* them. This is not due simply to the fact that sounds, not being physical bodies, do not occupy space to the exclusion of other physical bodies: smells can be said to have places although, lacking as they do some of Locke's primary qualities, they are not physical bodies. Smells as well as their sources are said to be in places: while the source of the smell is the tree in blossom outside the window, the smell of the blossom is actually in the room. On the other hand the chirping of birds which comes from the tree is not in the room although it can be heard in the room. Sounds are like the wind; we assign to them direction, but not position. So a more accurate, if clumsier, phrase than ' location of sound ' is ' telling where sound comes from '. I shall also make use of the phrase ' source of the sound ', meaning by it ' where the sound comes from '.

How do we tell where a sound is coming from? The experimental psychologist might answer as follows:[1] the intensity of sound, that is the amplitude of the sound wave, decreases with distance. Therefore if my right ear is further from the source of sound than my left ear, the intensity of sound at my right ear is less than it is at my left ear. Intervening objects also decrease the intensity of the sound, and this is a factor of greater importance than the diminution of intensity due to the sound passing through the air. The latter is not significant, but the decrease in intensity

---

[1] Here I rely on E. G. Boring, *Sensation and Perception in the History of Experimental Psychology* (New York, 1942).

K

caused by the obstruction of the head is important, and sometimes enables us to locate sounds. This can be demonstrated experimentally. However, when the sound is low, and the wave-length consequently long, the head is quite ineffective in securing a difference of intensity at each ear, because the wave-length is long enough to 'wrap itself' round the head. Experiments show that location by the intensity difference is efficient for high sounds, inefficient for low sounds. But we can locate sounds of low pitch pretty well as efficiently as we locate sounds of high pitch, so intensity difference is not the whole answer.

Another factor besides intensity difference (usefully termed 'dichotic intensity') is the difference in the phase of sound at each ear ('dichotic phase'). Suppose that the wave-length of the sound is greater than the distance between the ears, then the height of the wave at one ear will be greater than its height at the other ear. Since sound waves are in fact pressure waves, this means that the pressure at one ear will be different from the pressure at the other. A sound that is any pitch lower than moderately high (3,000 c.p.s.) has a wave-length longer than the distance between the two ears when the speed of sound is normal. Suppose a sound coming from the right: if the ears are out of phase, then at any moment the height of the wave at one ear will be different from the height of the wave at the other ear. This is also true of a sound coming from the left. What differentiates the two is this: if the sound is coming from the right, at a moment when the pressure in the right ear is higher than the pressure in the left ear, the average of the pressure at each ear will be rising; if the pressure at the right ear is lower than the pressure at the left, the average of the pressure at both ears is decreasing. When the sound is coming from the left the converse is the case. I find this analogy helpful: if I am in a perfectly anchored boat and into the sea bed beside me is fastened a measuring rod which tells me my height above the sea bed, and if I can also tell whether the prow of my boat is higher or lower than the stern, then I can tell whether the waves are coming from ahead or astern. If the waves are coming from ahead, then when my bow is up my height above sea bed will be increasing, and when my bow is down my height above sea bed will be decreasing. If the waves are coming from astern, the converse will be the case. It is clear that the wave-length has to be greater than the length of my boat for this method to work.

Dichotic phase compensates in a fairly satisfactory way for the defects of dichotic intensity; the phase effect is at its best when the intensity effect is at its worst, and vice versa. However, in the area between 1000 c.p.s. and 3,000 c.p.s. the phase effect is beginning to lose its effectiveness and the intensity effect has not yet acquired its full effectiveness. It has been shown that in this area we are bad at locating sounds.

There is another factor in the location of sound which I merely mention (it is not unrelated to dichotic phase): a sound from the right reaches the right ear before it reaches the left ear. The ears are extremely sensitive to this time difference, and use it to locate sounds. Nor do I embark on the question of how sounds coming from in front are differentiated from sounds coming from behind, except to remark that here movement of the head is important. These three explanations were once regarded as competing theories of how we locate sounds. Boring illuminatingly remarks, ' Only after 1920 was it realized that the investigations indicate not three theories of localization, but different means by which the same localization is effected.'[1]

The answer which the experimental psychologist would give to the question ' How do we locate sounds? ' has been indicated. Has the philosopher got a question of his own to ask about sound location, or are all the questions here physiological or psychological ones?

Suppose that a philosopher argued as follows: ' There is still a problem here. The psychologist has perhaps discovered under what conditions we can tell where sounds come from, but this is not to explain *how* we locate sounds. I can bring out the difference between the question " How do we tell? " and the question "What are the conditions for our being able to tell? " by the following example: a prospector has an unusual flair for discovering uranium without the use of instruments. It transpires that he only detects uranium when he is subjected to abnormal radiation. So we might say that the conditions under which he is able to tell that there is uranium about include a dose of radiation. But we have not discovered how he can detect uranium, because we have not yet answered the question " How can he tell that he is being irradiated? " Similarly we have not been told how we tell that a sound is coming from the right, when we have been told under what

[1] *Op. cit.*, p. 387.

conditions we can tell that a sound is coming from the right. The problem is unsolved because we have not been told how we come to be aware of these conditions.'

One way of answering this philosopher would be to say that dichotic intensity, at least, is not at all parallel to a dose of radiation. Whereas we are not conscious of radiation, we are conscious that a sound is louder in one ear than the other. Of course this answer leaves out of account dichotic phase, and questionably identifies loudness with intensity of sound, but it is wrong anyway. ' The sound is louder in one ear than the other ' is not a report of what is heard at all. Contrast this with the remark of a satisfied automobile owner: ' The ticking of the clock is louder than the sound of the engine.' The fact that we can hear that one sound is louder than another sound does not mean that we can hear that one and the same sound is louder in one ear than the other. Well, isn't being deaf in one ear a limiting case of hearing a sound louder in one ear than the other? So surely if I am slightly deaf in my right ear, then I hear sounds slightly louder in my left ear? This is not a good argument. What leads a man to think that he is growing deaf in one ear is that sounds on one side seem to be fainter than they ought to be, not that any sound is at one time heard to be louder in one ear than the other. If a person still insists that he can hear that a sound is louder in one ear than the other, we should suspect that his reason for saying this is that the sound seems to be coming from one side rather than the other. If this is the case he can hardly go on to explain how he locates sounds by saying that the sound sounds louder in one ear than the other. Of course it is a fact that a man is sometimes, though not always, enabled to locate sounds by the fact that the sound is more intense in the region of one ear rather than the other, but this is discovered by the use of instruments, not by ear alone.

The answer ' I can tell that a sound is coming from the right because I hear it louder in one ear than the other ' has a certain appeal because we feel that variation in loudness is an intrinsic feature of auditory experience, whereas spatial characteristics are not intrinsic to our auditory experience, in the sense that we only describe our auditory experience in spatial terms because there are certain intrinsic but non-spatial features of our auditory experience which are correlated with the genuinely spatial features of our non-auditory experience. Here I am paraphrasing some remarks made

by Strawson in support of his thesis that the Auditory World is a
No-Space World.[1] I should add that he does not suggest that we
can say what these non-spatial but intrinsic features of our
auditory experience are. However, the fact that variation in
loudness is something of which auditory experience is intrinsically
capable does not show that variation in loudness as heard by one
ear compared with loudness as heard by the other ear is an intrinsic
feature of experience. It is no more intrinsic to auditory experience than the direction of sound is: indeed it is less so.

Let us return to the uranium prospector. So far it seems that
' He can tell that there is uranium about because he is being
irradiated ' is just as good, or bad, an answer as ' We can tell that
a sound is coming from the right because it is more intense in the
right ear.' Just as the prospector might learn to tell when he was
being irradiated by discovering that when there seemed to him to
be uranium about he was being irradiated, so we have to learn to
tell when the sound is more intense in one ear rather than the
other by discovering that when the sound seems to be coming
from one side it is more intense in the region of the ear on that
side. Now the prospector was introduced to show how a philosopher might express dissatisfaction with the experimental psychologist's account of how we locate sounds. Such a philosopher is
dissatisfied both with the explanation of how we locate sounds
and with the explanation of how the prospector locates uranium.
However he seems to be wrong in feeling dissatisfaction with the
explanation of the prospector's knowledge. Very often we come to
expect A, given B, when A and B have been regularly connected
in our experience, but this is only a special type of conditioning to
expect something in that what leads us to expect is something
experienced. There seems no *a priori* reason why things experienced should be the only things which lead us to form expectations
(I am not talking about justifications for expecting.) I find it not
implausible to suppose that a dose of radiation, even though it is
not something of which we are aware, might lead us to expect that
something unpleasant, perhaps quite specific, was going to happen
to us.

If this is right the prospector's knowledge is not unsatis-
factorily explained just because he is not aware that he is being
irradiated. Does this mean also that there is nothing incomplete

[1] P. F. Strawson, *Individuals* (London, 1959), p. 63 ff.

about the explanation of the location of sounds? There is an important difference between sound location and ' uranium location ' which makes it impossible to account for them in the same way. We have been comparing a very odd way of detecting uranium with the *standard* way of telling where the sound comes from. This means no less than that we learn what the source of sound is by locating sound in this standard way. Thus what occurs when we locate sounds by ear is also what must lead us to understand the notion of where the sound comes from. Consequently a satisfactory account of sound location must explain how we learn the meaning of certain words. It seems clear that the dose of radiation, though it could lead the prospector to think that something was the case, could not lead him to understand the meaning of ' uranium ' or any other word. Are we not forced to explain this impossibility by the fact that he is not *aware* of radiation?

We cannot then ignore the question of what we are aware of when we locate sounds, for it is what we are then aware of that enables us to understand the meaning of sentences such as ' The sound is coming from over there.'

This view has to be defended against an objection. I have mentioned Strawson's claim that spatial characteristics are not intrinsic to auditory experience on the grounds that it is only in virtue of some correlation between auditory and non-auditory experience that we ascribe any spatial characteristics to sounds. This view can easily develop into the view that what we locate when we tell where the sound is coming from is the position of the cause of the sound, and this view *is*, though Strawson's is not, inconsistent with the view that what we discover when we tell where a sound is coming from is unintelligible without reference to this mode of discovering it. For there seems no reason why we should not be able to understand what the *cause of sound* is without appealing to the fact that we tell where the cause of sound is by ear. We understand very well the notion of the cause of a smell without appealing to the fact that when we smell a smell the smell seems to be coming from a particular direction. There is no such fact.

What I have to oppose then is the view that what we really locate when we locate sounds is, quite simply, the cause of sound. ' Where is the sound coming from? ' ' The loudspeaker.' ' The grasshopper's legs.' ' Smith.' It seems not improper to call all these causes of sounds, so what is wrong with equating where the sound comes from, the source of sound, with the cause of sound? But what about echoes? What about the faulty valve which adds an unpleasant hum to the sound of the gramophone? Not all causes of sound are located in the place where the sound comes from. By tinkering with the valves we may discover where the cause of the sound is: we have to use our ears to find out where the sound is coming from. It might be argued that the source of sound must *at least* be the cause, or *a* cause, of the sound. I only wish to assert that it must be something else as well. Nor is it true that the source of sound is where the sound is loudest— another theory which makes the claim that we can account for the notion of a source of sound without bringing in the fact that we tell where this is by ear. Usually the sound is loudest at its source, but this is not necessarily so. Perhaps I hear a loud sound coming from the right, but as I move in that direction it gets fainter until I pass a certain point after which it gets louder again, but now I hear it from the left. If we suppose a medium which has the effect of magnifying sound we can give a convincing picture of a sound which is not loudest at its source. Consideration of these two erroneous views lends support to my claim that where the sound is *heard from* is an essential component in the notion of a source of sound. I therefore repeat myself: we cannot ignore the question of what we are aware of when we locate sounds, for it is what we are then aware of that enables us to understand sentences like ' The sound is coming from over there.'

At this stage I am tempted to throw in the towel and give up the view that in some sense Strawson is right in arguing that the auditory world is a No-Space world. For how could a non-spatial feature of our auditory experience succeed in *giving a sense* to the phrase ' source of sound ', as opposed to providing mere *clues* to where the (independently understood) source of sound is? Perhaps one should be content with pointing out that auditory space is an impoverished sort of space, and that this impoverishment is what leads one to wish that it could be explained away altogether. It is impoverished space because I cannot draw a picture of the pattern of sounds I hear, I can only plot their direction. Sounds lack spatial dimensions; one can speak of stereophonic apparatus producing a ' wall ' of sound, but this means that the various sounds it produces seem to come from different directions, not that any particular sound can be regarded as extended. In this defeatist mood I should say to the philosopher who is dissatisfied with the scientific explanation of sound location: ' You are wrong to think there is any further question unanswered. You should stop asking how it is that we tell that a sound is coming from the right, since it is clear that when you ask it you are only going to be satisfied with an answer of the form: we say that a sound is coming from the right when it has audible characteristic Q where Q is not a spatial characteristic. But there is no non-spatial characteristic of sounds on the basis of which we attribute to them spatial characteristics, any more than there are non-spatial characteristics of things seen on the basis of which we attribute to them spatial characteristics.'

Perhaps this is the right course to adopt, but I devote the rest of this paper to seeing what can be said for a third way out. We can describe the two positions which we have been considering as follows: the first position is that spatial characteristics are not intrinsic to auditory experience, but that there are intrinsic features which, by virtue of correlations with the non-auditory world, allow us to attribute spatial characteristics to sound. The second position is that there are spatial characteristics intrinsic to our auditory experience, just as there are intrinsic spatial characteristics in our visual experience. The third way out is to say that spatial characteristics are not intrinsic, but that it does not follow from this that there are *other* intrinsic but non-spatial characteristics which allow us to attribute spatial characteristics to sound.

To indicate what this third view is: I don't know *how* to tell where a sound is coming from, I just point or turn my head in the direction of the sound. If there is any answer to the question how one knows that the sound is coming from the right it is ' Because that is where I am inclined to point '. One is tempted to object that we only point in the direction of the sound because that is where we hear it comes from. The answer to this is that a thing cannot justify itself, and therefore it is not because we hear a sound coming from the right that we are inclined to point in that direction. Of course this reply presupposes that the third view about sound location is correct. Its only use is to point out that the objection begs the question against the third view.

I have to argue therefore that there is no experience of hearing where a sound comes from; nor is hearing where a sound comes from analysable into having an experience and doing something else. This is not inconsistent with the necessity of some sort of awareness: subtraction of a bogus experience leaves us plenty to be aware of—our inclination to point, for instance.

Telling by ear where the sound comes from involves the ability to do something, to point or indicate in some other way the source of sound. If a person can do this then he can hear where sounds come from; and to be able to *do* something is not to have an experience. It is claimed that an experience, or feature of experience, gives us this ability. If that were so, one could have the experience, but not the ability. So we should require some reason for saying that a person has the experience other than current manifestation of the ability. But could there be any other reason for attributing this experience to a person? Suppose that a child does not turn its head or otherwise direct its attention to the source of sound, would we say that perhaps it hears sounds as coming from various directions, though it has not yet learned how to make use of this experience? Or rather would we say that it does not hear where sounds come from at all? If we should say the latter, then there is no having the experience without the ability. Nor, presumably, could there be a having the ability without the experience. So we are to say that a person has this experience when and only when he has the ability. The alleged experience has lost the necessary logical distinctness.

It might be objected that this argument does away with absolutely all perceptual experience. For we only say that men see, hear and smell things because they use their senses to discriminate. So should we not say here too that the experience is attributed because of, and only because of, an ability, an ability to discriminate. But the argument was intended to show that there was a *difference* between telling by ear where a sound comes from, and, say, telling how loud it is. This objection is not very well founded. Certainly we say that a person, *e.g.*, sees colours, that colour is a feature of his visual experience, because he can perform feats of discrimination, but it is not true that we only attribute the experience to a person who has this ability to discriminate. We attribute the experience to a person before he is able to do anything with the experience. A child, we say, sees colours before he is able to sort things by their colour. Colour is a thing that we, as it were, ' read into ' the experience of a person before the time that he begins to exhibit any relevant discriminatory powers. On the other hand if a child shows no ability to locate sounds we do not read any spatial features into his auditory experience, even though subsequently he somehow acquires the ability. So the objection can be answered. The alleged experience of hearing where a sound comes from is more indissolubly linked with the ability to indicate the source of sound than at least some perceptual experiences are linked with the abilities which are our grounds for ascribing them.

However, the way in which the objection has to be answered indicates that the argument is not one to rely on. For until we can offer some other grounds for distinguishing the ability to locate sound from those perceptual abilities which serve as grounds for attributing perceptual experience, it remains a mystery why we do what we do, namely say that a child sees colours before it can distinguish things by their colours, whereas we do not suppose any experience which antedates that ability to locate sounds. My answer to this is that we are not attributing any experience at all when we say that a person hears where a sound comes from, so there is nothing which can antedate acquisition of the ability. But this is just what is denied by my opponent.

The first point of difference which I wish to press between the location of sound and, let us say, the ability to distinguish sounds by their pitch, is that the former cannot while the latter can be specified in purely auditory terms. A person who can distinguish sounds by their pitch and timbre can thereby distinguish flutes from trombones, which are not sounds at all, but nevertheless his ability can be characterized simply in terms of the ability to differentiate various kinds of *sound*. On the other hand description of our ability to locate sounds necessarily makes extra-auditory reference. When we locate sounds we locate them in relation to our own bodies. We move in the same space as the source of sounds: we approach them and they approach us. In other words, sounds are located in *physical* space. The conception of a purely auditory space does not seem to be an intelligible one. In contrast to this the notion of a purely *visual* space seems possible. Sounds have spatial relations to us, visual objects have spatial relations to each other. It might be objected that when I see spots before my eyes and one is to the left of the other this involves a relationship with the observer also: spot A is on *my* left and spot B is on *my* right. Yes; but this does not mean that *I* could possibly be between spot A and spot B if only the interval between them was large enough. There is a purely visual space in that there is a visual space in which we as observers do not belong. There is no auditory space in which we as observers do not belong. If I really hear sound A coming from my right, and sound B coming from my left, then I am between the sources of these sounds. We can say therefore that the location of sound necessarily makes reference to physical bodies. Now does this not suggest that there is something odd about saying that it is a feature of our auditory experience which enables us to locate sounds? We should have to say that this feature enabled us to detect a relationship between a sound and something which is not a sound, but a physical body, namely ourselves. Well, couldn't there be purely auditory features of sound which we learn to correlate with the various relationships in physical space which the source of sound can have with our bodies? The answer to this must be a challenge: say what you hear when you hear that a sound is coming from the right in such a way as to avoid making any reference to the position of your own body!

There is a second feature which seems to distinguish the ability to locate sounds from the ability to make other perceptual discriminations. Recognition plays an essential rôle in those perceptual abilities which are legitimate criteria for attributing perceptual experience. It does not play this rôle in the location of sounds. If I indicate the direction of the source of a sound I have not necessarily had to recognize anything in order to do this. On the other hand if I put this piece of coloured paper amongst a pile of similarly coloured pieces, and can go on doing the same thing, then I must have recognized the bits of paper as being the same in colour. Anything I do which is dependent on my awareness of colour is consequent upon some recognition (perhaps recognizing that two things are the same colour without recognizing what colour they are). My indicating the source of sound, on the other hand, is not a consequence of my recognizing anything.

What about pointing to a thing seen? The crucial difference is that we point to something seen with something visible, the hand, whereas we do not indicate the source of sound with something audible. When I point to a thing seen, I raise my hand (my *hand*), until in my visual field it is close to the thing at which I desire to point. I must have some knowledge of what it is for one thing to be close to another, and recognize that my hand *is close* to something. This becomes clear when we think of the sort of lessons we should have to give to a child who pointed very inaccurately. I have been discussing the paradigm of pointing to a thing seen. One can also point to a thing seen with something that is not actually at the moment visible. If I am prevented from seeing my hand, I can still point with it, though without much accuracy. This is in some ways rather like indicating the source of sound; I only wish to argue that the paradigm is dependent on recognition, and thus relevantly different from sound location.

What are the arguments for saying that sound location is not dependent on recognition? Not merely the very weak verbal one that it sounds odd to speak of recognizing where a sound comes from (does it?), but that recognition introduces the possibility of mistakes which are not found in the field of sound location. To say that a perceptual ability is recognition-dependent perhaps *is* to say that certain mistakes are possible. Mistakes due to faulty recognition are not due to faults or irregularities in the sense organ. So where a perceptual ability depends on recognition, we must be able to distinguish between errors which are, and those which are not due to sensory defects. If a child does not seem to be able to locate sounds, and, for instance, has difficulty in telling who is speaking, we should certainly say that there was something wrong with its ears. It would be difficult to understand the hypothesis that it was making some sort of mistake, there was something that it had not learned to do properly. On the other hand if it claims that a sound is quiet when it is in fact loud, this may be due to deafness, but it may just be due to the fact that it has not learned to handle the concepts ' loud ' and ' quiet '.

However it is not true that whenever a person goes wrong in locating a sound we think that there must be something wrong with his ears. (Nor, for that matter, are all perceptual errors due either to a sensory defect, or to misrecognition.) I can mislocate a sound through sheer carelessness. But it is easy enough to distinguish mistakes due to carelessness from mistakes due to misrecognition. The possibility of the former does not entail the possibility of the latter. Misrecognition comes under the general heading of faults of memory; a mistake due to carelessness does not.

Again it is an oversimplification to say that since sound location is *unlearned*, there is no question of mislocation of a sound being due to faulty learning, or faulty memory of lessons learned, and that *this* is why misrecognition finds no place here. For it seems reasonable to suppose that we might practise locating sounds, and get better, *i.e.* more precise and more reliable at it. So there could be a sort of learning and a sort of failure to retain what had been learned. But this sort of practice would be different from practising, say, aircraft recognition: it would be much more like taking exercises to improve visual acuity; and taking exercises is not the same as having lessons, even as giving oneself lessons. The topic of perceptual errors needs more thorough investigation. At present it seems reasonable to believe that recognition introduces the possibility of errors of a kind not found in sound location.

Now if we do not have to recognize anything in order to locate a sound, this tells against the thesis that there is some feature of our auditory experience which enables us to locate sounds. For the ground for speaking of features of perceptual experience at all is that they are presupposed by acts of recognition. I cannot recognize something without being sensibly aware of it.

' Certain perceptual abilities serve as criteria for attributing experiences to persons: sound location does not involve an ability of this kind. Therefore sound location does not serve as a criterion for attributing experiences.' The argument is clearly invalid; it would only be valid if perceptual abilities of this kind were the only criteria for attributing experiences. Pains are experiences, but we do not attribute them on the basis of perceptual abilities of this kind. I do not have to recognize my state in order to exhibit the sort of behaviour which serves as a criterion for attributing pain. Might not the behaviour associated with sound location be like this? Turning one's head in the direction of the sound, is, after all, not so very unlike the characteristic response to pain. They are both, for example, unlearned responses.

I indicate very briefly what I think is the feature of pain behaviour which counts, that is, the feature which makes it possible to attribute experiences on the basis of pain behaviour. Pain behaviour is not something *sui generis*; it is a species of grief or misery. If I carelessly chop a piece off my finger, my evident distress could be due to the pain, equally it could be due to the disfiguration. Hence pain behaviour is a species of grief or misery which is not directed towards a public object. On the other hand, since it is grief, it must have an object, so that we think of it as having a *private* object. Unless pain behaviour had affinities to other types of behaviour which were directed to public objects, why should we think of it as having an object at all?

The notion of perceptual experience is related in an utterly different way to the behaviour which serves as the criterion for ascribing it, so that it is understandable that it is felt to be a dubious notion. It is not that perceptual behaviour, though itself lacking a public object, has affinities to other types of behaviour directed towards public objects. If one can speak at all of perceptual behaviour as being directed towards objects, it is obviously directed towards *public* objects. It would seem entirely unnecessary to create private objects of perceptual behaviour as well; as if one were to invent a private object of grief to accompany the publicly spilt milk that is cried over. It is in virtue of some other feature that perceptual behaviour is taken as a criterion for attributing perceptual experiences. The location of sound, it is my contention, does not have this feature.

CAUSALITY, AND A METHOD OF ANALYSIS

J. M. Shorter

Introduction

THE purpose of this paper is twofold: to make a contribution to the discussion on Causality initiated by Professor Z. Vendler,[1] and to discuss a doubt which many philosophers have felt from time to time about the method of analysis used by, for example, Vendler in his article. The doubt about the method is that it leads, in some cases at least, to endless and inconclusive debate. As an illustration of such a debate I shall take the Causality issue. I shall argue that there is indeed a sort of inconclusiveness here, but that this sort of inconclusiveness is harmless. It does not indicate any inadequacy in the method being used, but something about the material being investigated. This material is in fact such that a certain sort of answer is impossible. The method, properly applied and understood, reveals this fact; which is as important a discovery about the material as any other. If, however, one starts with the assumption that this sort of answer *must* be possible, then the debate will indeed seem endless and inconclusive in cases, like the case of causality, where there is no such answer to be obtained.

What then is this assumption? It is the assumption that the use of an expression can always be grasped either in terms of the notion of a unique 'core meaning' with deviants from the core; or, where the expression is ambiguous, in terms of two or more core meanings each with its own deviants. In the latter case it is felt that, for any given particular use of that expression in a sentence which is easily understood by a speaker of the language, it must be possible to say which sense that expression has. This assumption is, I believe, false. I shall argue in particular that in a sentence like 'The explosion was the cause of the accident' there is, in the nature of the case, no answer to the question ' Is the word " explosion " being used in what Vendler calls the event-like sense or in what he calls the fact-like sense? ' A proper and

---

[1] Z. Vendler, ' Effects, Results and Consequences ', *Analytical Philosophy*, ed. R. J. Butler (Oxford, 1962), pp. 1–15; S. Bromberger, ' What are Effects? ' *op. cit.*, pp. 15–20; W. H. Dray, ' Must Effects have Causes? ' pp. 20–25; Z. Vendler, ' Reactions and Retractions,' *op, cit.*, pp. 25–31.

unprejudiced application of Vendler's method shows clearly that there is no answer to this question and why there is no answer. Provided that we see this, then we see too that we have succeeded in getting an answer to the question with which we started out, which was, to adapt Vendler's own words to this particular case: 'What is the pattern to which expressions containing the word " cause " conform? ' The pattern is precisely one that makes it impossible to say which of the two senses the word ' explosion ' here possesses. Vendler himself does not, I think, see this; nor do other practitioners of the method he uses appear to be aware of this sort of possibility. The result of such unawareness is an appearance of deadlock.[1]

The Doubt about Vendler's Method

In general the doubt against which I wish to defend Vendlerian (Austinian, &c.) analysis (when this is carried out without the mistaken preconceptions from which its practitioners commonly suffer) arises from the number and elasticity of the moves by which a theory may be defended against attack. There seem to be so many things to say to defend oneself against a prima facie counter-example to one's own theory, that very often two or three theories can be rendered immune to decisive refutation even although they are mutually incompatible. Let us then first make a list of some of the most important defensive manoeuvres.

1.   The sentence offered as a counter-example is bad or at least not very good English. Little weight, therefore, should be attached to it. For example Vendler, to rebut the view that causes are events, cites the sentence ' The cause of the pavement's rising was that the ground swelled '. In reply Professor Dray writes, ' The reply I am inclined to make to this is that, even if the latter statement is intelligible enough, it is too questionable a piece of English usage to be made the basis of such a startling philosophical claim.'[2]

2.   There is nothing wrong with this sentence as such, but it is not used in the context you suggest it would be. For example the sentence 'This statement fits the facts' might be adduced in support of the view that facts are events rather than true propositions. In reply it could be argued that such a sentence would only

[1] See note p. 145.   [2] Op. cit., p. 21.

be used where a new statement is seen to fit in with, to be compatible with, a number of other statements already accepted as true. For example, a police detective, finding that what a suspect says fits in with what he has already accepted as true, might say 'What he says seems to fit the facts ' and be inclined to believe him. On the other hand the following dialogue is quite unnatural:

Smith: It is snowing.

Jones (looking out of the window): What you say fits the facts.

3. This is an untypical deviant from the basic pattern, from the core meaning. Any natural language can be expected to contain a few such exceptions to the general rule. Such a move clearly cannot be made very often. It is usually backed up by a suggestion as to why such a deviant exists. Such suggested explanations of deviance are of a wide variety and are rarely more than plausible. For example Vendler holds that ' unexpected ' and ' violent ' are quite different categories of adjective applicable to quite different categories of noun. Where they qualify one noun on different occasions this is because the noun is ambiguous and falls into two distinct categories. As a counter-example, Bromberger cites the sentence 'A violent and unexpected explosion caused a lot of damage.'[1] This is a deviant, according to Vendler, and comes about because of the familiarity of the phrase ' unexpected violence.'[2]

4. This sentence is elliptical and can be expanded into such-and-such. For example, Vendler holds that effects and the things to which they are attributed belong to the same general category. The sentence ' The moon has an effect upon the surface of the oceans ' seems to be a clear counter-example. But, says Vendler, it is elliptical for ' The moon's attraction has an effect on the surface of the oceans.'[3]

5. This is the most important move. It is to allege an ambiguity, either in the term being discussed or in some other term.

Vendler, for example, starts his article by distinguishing three senses of verb nominalizations. This allegation of ambiguity is used to demolish a whole series of arguments designed to show that causes are events. Explosions can occur, be loud, last a certain time, and in general satisfy all the tests for being events. They can also be causes. It would seem, therefore, that causes

[1] *Op. cit.*, p. 17. [2] *Op. cit.*, p. 30. [3] *Op. cit.*, p. 6.

L

must themselves be events. To this Vendler can reply that an ambiguity in 'explosion' has been overlooked. This word has different senses in 'watched the explosion' and in 'the explosion caused the accident'.

With all the moves available including an allegation of deviance to fall back on when all else fails, it is not surprising that scepticism should sometimes be felt about the whole procedure. This scepticism is often increased rather than abated when one sees the method in operation. There turns out to be a lot of disagreement about what is good and what is bad English. The variety of explanations offered for alleged deviants renders it plausible to suppose that, with ingenuity, it should be possible to find some explanation for any alleged deviant. Moreover such explanations are often untestable in practice if not in principle. In many cases, too, allegations of ambiguity can be questioned, and seem to be made merely *ad hoc*, as a means of reserving a pet theory. Moreover one is allowed to go to great lengths here. For example Vendler admits it as a real possibility that in 'The freezing of the water caused the swelling of the ground which caused the rising of the pavement' the word 'which' should be of a different category from the phrase 'the swelling of the ground' to which it refers.[1] It often seems arbitrary whether we should choose to say that we have an ambiguity or that we have a counter-example of a philosopher's thesis. Let us alter our present example to make it a prima facie counter-example to Vendler's thesis about cause and effect. We then get: 'The freezing of the water had an important effect, namely the swelling of the ground, which in turn caused the rising of the pavement.' We can, in theory, say here either:

1. This is a genuine counter-example to Vendler's thesis about causes (that they are events).

2. This is a genuine counter-example to Vendler's thesis about effects (that they are propositional-like).

3. 'Which' has a propositional-like sense even though its antecedent is a phrase with an event-like sense. So both Vendler's theses are correct.

But can we be sure that one of these is right and the others are wrong?

[1] *Op. cit.*, pp. 28–29.

The sense of ' cause '.

Vendler's thesis about ' cause ' is both plausible and yet highly unorthodox. It seems, therefore, as likely a case as any in which the method is incapable of giving an answer. Let us then put it to the test and see if in the end it *does* fail to give us a grasp of the pattern of use exhibited by the word ' cause '. We will proceed by trying first to cast doubt on all Vendler's reasons for holding his thesis. We will then try to make a positive case for the contrary thesis. Finally we will see if we can cast doubt equally well on the reasons for holding the contrary thesis.

Vendler's case is stated succinctly thus:

> Now we are ready for the proof. As we recall, only nominaliza-
> tions in the fact-like sense can be transformed into noun clauses,
> only they can take tenses, can be subject to modalities and negation,
> and, finally, only they can keep the object in the original position.
> Now I submit the following sentences to illustrate the possibility
> of performing these moves on relevant nominalizations:
> John's having arrived caused the commotion.
> John's being able to come caused our surprise.
> John's hitting the bar-tender caused the fight.
> The cause of the fight was that John hit the bar-tender.
> I continue by pointing out that there are negative causes as
> there are negative results. We can say that John's not seeing the
> red light caused the crash, or that the signalman's failure to pull the
> switch caused the accident, and we may add that the signalman's
> failure to pull the switch was the result of his hangover. Now it
> is obvious that John's not seeing the red light or the signalman's
> failure to do something cannot be construed as events or processes.
> Accordingly, they cannot be effects or things to which effects are
> attributed either. The accident is not an effect of any failure,
> nor is a failure to do something an effect of any hangover.
> Finally, in examining adjectives that the word 'cause' can take
> we at once see that they agree with those appropriate to results, and
> differ from those we found suited to effects. Causes are never
> strong or weak, violent or mild, sudden or prolonged, dangerous or
> harmless; but they may be likely or unlikely, probable or improb-
> able, proximate or remote (and then not proximate or remote in
> a physical, but rather in a logical sense). Similarly, causes, like
> results and unlike effects, can be stated, told, learned, remembered,
> or forgotten, but not felt, watched, observed, or measured.[1]

Let us consider his evidence bit by bit:

A. ' Event-like nominalizations do not take tenses but we *can* say
" John's having arrived caused the commotion." '

[1] *Op. cit.*, p. 14.

Possible lines of rebuttal.

1. This is an unusual locution and not the best English. One cannot place much weight upon it. The usual thing to say would be ' John's arrival caused the commotion '.

2. It is elliptical for ' The realization that John had arrived caused the commotion '. It is only when some such expansion as this is possible that we use the past tense nominalization. In the present example the appropriate situation for such a nominalization would have to be something like this: John arrives, though he was not expected; the news of his arrival spreads, and as people realize that he has arrived a commotion starts. 'My having knocked the glass of the table caused it to break' *does* sound strange just because no such expansion suggests itself. Put more generally, the expansion of a sentence ' x having occurred caused the y ' is ' The state of affairs, occurrences, &c., consequent upon the x-ing caused the y '. For example, ' My having left the switch on caused the fire ' is elliptical for ' The switch's being on, and it was on because I left it on, caused the fire.' When we make the appropriate expansion in these cases, we see that the cause is always specified by a present tense nominalization.

3. The past tense here is a deviant. But we can see how it has come about. Present-tense nominalizations in causal sentences have an event-like sense. But past tense nominalizations look very like present tense ones. They, therefore, get used in causal sentences without the absurdity striking us.

B. ' Only nominalizations in the fact-like sense can be subject to modalities, and yet we can say " John's being able to come caused our surprise ".'

Rebuttal.

This is clearly elliptical for something like ' Our hearing that John was able to come caused our surprise '. It is difficult to find a plausible example where only inanimate objects are concerned. For example it is hard to see a satisfactory completion of ' The milk's ability to turn sour caused. . . . '.

C. ' Only nominalizations in the fact-like sense can be transformed into noun clauses, and yet we can transform

    (i) ' John's hitting the bar-tender caused the fight ' into

    (ii) ' The cause of the fight was that John hit the bar-tender.'

Possible replies.

1. (ii) is not the best English.

2. This is not a genuine transformation because the expression ' the cause of the fight ' is itself ambiguous, and in (ii) means ' the causal explanation of the fight '. This is shown by the possibility of transforming (ii) into

> (ii*a*) ' The causal explanation of the fight was that John hit the bar-tender.'

On the other hand

> (i*a*) ' John's hitting the bar-tender was the causal explanation of the fight '

does not strike one as a very natural sentence.

D. ' Nominalizations in the fact-like sense can take the object directly after themselves as well as after the word " of ". In the event-like sense the word " of " is necessary. For example we must say

> ' John's cooking of dinner is slow,'

but we can say either

> ' John's cooking of dinner is unlikely,'

or

> ' John's cooking dinner is unlikely ".'

In reply to this it may be pointed out that we *can* say

> ' Cooking dinner is the cause of endless trouble ' but we *cannot* say

> ' Cooking of dinner is the cause of endless trouble.'

The rules of the insertion of ' of ' are clearly complex. But enough has been said to show that it is not simply determined by whether or not the nominalizations are fact-like or event-like.

E. 'Causes are never strong or weak, violent or mild, sudden or prolonged, dangerous or harmless; but they may be likely or unlikely, probable or improbable, proximate or remote.'

Reply

It is true that you can say that something was the probable cause of the accident, or the unexpected cause of the accident. But this does not support Vendler in the least. One can also say

> (i) ' 55 was the probable age of the man,'
> (ii) ' Pink was the probable colour of the curtains,'
> (iii) ' 10 p.m. was the probable time of the accident,'

and so on. But does this show that ages, colours and times have a fact-like sense? Clearly not, as is shown by the impossibility of inferring from (iii)

'10 p.m. was probable.'

Similarly from

'John's hitting the bar-tender was the probable cause of the accident'

one cannot infer

'John's hitting the bar-tender was probable.'

It is also possible to explain why words like 'loud' and 'brief', that are used to characterize events, cannot be applied directly to the word 'cause'. When we are investigating the cause of something, we are typically interested in the production or prevention of that thing. We want to know what event caused that thing. It is quite beside the point to be given extraneous information about that event. We need to identify it, not know some of its properties. It is, therefore, quite futile to say 'The cause was loud' without saying what the cause was. A sentence of the form 'The cause of so-and-so was such-and-such' is an answer to the question 'What was the cause?' This is why it sounds odd to put *any* adjective after the words 'The cause was . . .', whether the adjective is one like probable or one like 'loud'. The same oddity is found in 'The most conspicuous occurrence immediately preceding the riot was loud.' But this sentence is quite respectable if 'a loud explosion' is substituted for 'loud'.

F. 'Causes, like results and unlike effects, can be stated, told, learned, remembered or forgotten.'

Reply

1. It is in general true that sentences of the form

'He told me (he learnt, he remembered, &c., &c.) the so-and-so of the such-and-such'

are elliptical for

'He told me (&c.) what the so-and-so of the such-and-such was.' For example, 'He learnt the date of the Battle of Hastings' means 'He learnt what the date of the Battle of Hastings was.' 'He learnt the cause of the accident' is surely no exception. It clearly means 'He learnt what the cause of the accident was'. For from

' He learnt the cause ' and ' The cause was the explosion ' it does not follow that he learnt the explosion, or even that he learnt that an explosion occurred.

2.   It is surely false that effects cannot be told, &c. What is wrong with ' He told me the effect of the news on his father '?

G.   ' Causes cannot be felt, watched, observed, or measured.'

Reply

1.   One can feel that so-and-so is the case, that the bed is hard, for example. So one would expect that causes could be felt if ' cause ' has a fact-like sense.

2.   It may be that one cannot speak of watching causes. But it is equally true that one cannot speak of believing or expecting causes. Yet what one is said to believe can be probable or improbable. We can neither believe, feel, or expect, nor watch or observe the causes of things. This fact requires special explanation whichever of the two views you like about causality.

H.   Finally, Vendler points out that we can use negative nominalizations in causal sentences, as for example in ' John's not seeing the light caused the crash '; and also similar negative phrases like ' John's failure to see the light '.

To this, too, it is possible to find a reply:

1.   The word ' failure ' is itself a nominalization from the verb ' to fail '. Like other nominalizations it appears sometimes to have a fact-like and sometimes to have an event-like sense. Sometimes it can and sometimes it cannot be replaced by a noun clause. In

(i) ' His failure to see the red light was expected '

we can substitute such a clause. But we cannot do so in

(ii) ' His failure to see the red light was followed by an accident.'

In default of knowing *in advance* the sense of ' cause ', we do not know whether to classify

(iii) ' His failure was the cause '

with (i) or with (ii). It will not do for Vendler to say, as he does,[1] that a failure is obviously not an event. The question is what batteries it enters into, and (ii) shows that it at least has affinities of an important sort with event-like nominalizations.

[1] *Ibid.*

2.   As for the phrase ' John's not seeing the light ', it is clearly clumsy and unidiomatic in the causal sentence. However it is intelligible here in so far as it is taken to mean what ' failure to see ' means, and can be dealt with in the same way as that phrase. It seems to me that the above criticism shows beyond any doubt that Vendler has not made out a case that is at all conclusively in favour of his thesis about ' cause '. Equally clearly the criticism has not established any counter-thesis about ' cause '. If we now put ourselves in Vendler's position we can easily show that the event hypothesis has not been established. It would be tedious to go through all the above arguments and show this in detail. One example will suffice, and the reader may be left to do the rest for himself. The sentence ' John's being able to come caused our surprise ' was dealt with by suggesting that it was elliptical for ' Our realization that John was able to come caused our surprise '.

It is, however, still open to Vendler to deny this. It can hardly be said to have been conclusively proved. Alternatively he can agree that it is elliptical, but point out that ' realization ' is a nominalization and contend that it here has the fact-like sense. It is very clear that a decision here can only be reached on the basis of independent reasons for thinking that cause has an event-like or a fact-like sense.

We can, I think, sum up the evidence so far presented by saying that Vendler has rather best of it. It is true that much of his evidence is quite worthless, *e.g.*, *F*. But in other cases his opponent has had to work hard to provide special explanations for what does on the face of it favour Vendler. Nevertheless these explanations are, in most cases, reasonably plausible. Nor is it surprising that Vendler should so far have had to this extent the best of the argument. For, so far, we have confined ourselves to an examination of the evidence brought by him in support of his own case. Matters will be equalized if we can find cases where it is he who has to do the explaining away. It is not hard to find such cases. Consider, for example, ' The cause of the accident was an explosion which was loud and could be heard many miles away '. The word ' which ' has here the event-like sense. It refers to ' explosion ', and so ' explosion ' too presumably has the event-like sense. Here Vendler has to produce the explanation, and we have already seen what the explanation might be.[1]

[1] *Vide supra*, p. 0.

Another type of example that presents an even greater difficulty for Vendler is the sentence which, before specifying the cause, tells you something about it. For example,

' The cause of the accident was something *Smith* did, namely . . . ' or

' The cause was something which occurred earlier in the evening, namely . . . '

In such cases you certainly cannot substitute a noun clause for ' the cause '. Indeed the case is so clearly one of an event-like sense for ' cause ' that Vendler must surely fall back on an accusation of deviance. He might say something like this. There are cases, rare ones, where we do not know what the cause was but do know that it had to do with something done by Smith. If we try to say this using the usual form of words for causal sentences we get ' The cause was that Smith did something ' or ' The cause was Smith's doing something '. But these sentences will not convey what we want to. They tend to suggest that the cause was that Smith did something, as opposed to doing nothing, that the effect would not have been brought about only if Smith had done nothing at all. But what we want to convey is that there was some specific deed of Smith and that the cause was his doing that specific deed. A convenient way of conveying this is to use ' cause ' in the event-like sense and say ' The cause was something which Smith did '. But such a use is untypical and has come about to fulfill a special and not very common need.

On the whole it seems quite clear that evidence favours the process and fact theories about equally. There is no prospect whatever of being able to decide between them. Both can accommodate the evidence but each in a different way. What one theory sees as deviant, or as something requiring special explanation, the other theory sees as the clearest example of the core meaning. So the debate is inconclusive: there is nothing to choose between the one theory or the other. But to say this, though true, is misleading. For it suggests that there is more to be discovered about the use of the word ' cause ', and that, if only we could discover it, we would be able to come to some conclusion about which of the rivals is correct. But this is surely a mistake. We have now got a pretty clear view of the concept of causality, as far as the present issue goes. Our use of ' cause ' is such that it can equally well be grasped by seeing it in accordance with the event pattern or the fact pattern. To know this is surely to know enough; to know, apart from details, all there is to know. To think otherwise is to have a preconceived idea about what our use of the word ' cause ' must be like, to assume that it can be captured only in *one* core-meaning-cum-deviant framework. But we have clearly seen that this is not in fact so: it fits two such frameworks equally well.

However in the present case there is a better way of thinking of and of grasping the pattern of usage than either of the two theories considered by Vendler. It is moreover a way of thinking that Vendler ought himself to have come to if he had applied his own method with greater care and consistency. There is a striking difference between his treatment of verb nominalizations and his treatment of causal expressions. The former, he finds, can have more than one sense. In some cases they have the fact-like sense, in others the event-like sense. The latter he assumes without question to be unambiguous, to have just one sense. Finding cases that one would naturally expect to exist on the ' fact ' hypothesis, he concludes that ' cause ' has *in general* a fact-like sense. He ignores the cases which fit easily only into the ' event ' hypothesis. By a like selection of favourable cases one could produce the illusion that nominalizations have always a fact-like (or event-like) sense. In fact causal expressions are themselves very like nominalizations. In some sentences they can and in others they cannot be replaced by noun clauses, as we have just seen. So if we are consistent we must say that causal expressions, like nominalizations, ' enter all the batteries.' They become selective only in ' specific co-occurrences ' with other words. They too have sometimes the fact-like and sometimes the event-like sense. The superiority of this way of looking at things is not that our pattern of usage can be grasped more clearly in this way than in terms of either of the rival theories. It is simply that it avoids their arbitrariness. For neither can give a reason for seeing the phenomena in accordance with its own favoured pattern, of regarding this sentence rather than that as deviant.

It might seem, too, that we have now shown in a quite straightforward way that the method Vendler uses, properly applied, does give a conclusive result. It shows that the word ' cause ' can have more than one sense. It certainly does that, but the same sort of inconclusiveness we noted before now reappears in a different guise. In a sentence like ' The explosion was the cause of the

accident ' we cannot determine the sense (fact or event) of either
' explosion ' or ' cause '. For we can replace ' the explosion ' by a
that-clause, or by ' something which occurred earlier '. We can
replace ' the cause of the accident ' by either ' loud ' or ' improbable '. But again the impossibility of coming to a conclusion here
is not a defect of the method. It is not as if in such cases the
expressions do really have a specific sense but the method does not
enable us to find out which sense. Rather the impossibility of
deciding reflects the nature of our pattern of usage. As Vendler
has said, a verb nominalization ' enters all the batteries. Only in
a specific co-occurrence with certain sets of adjectives *or* with
words like " effect ", " result ", " cause ", and so on, does a
nominalization become selective; only then does it belong to a
battery.'[1] But Vendler is mistaken in supposing that a nominalization becomes selective when it co-occurs with ' cause '. For
' cause ' itself ' enters all the batteries '. In the present example
each of the words ' cause ' and ' explosion ' requires that the other
should determine its sense. But neither can perform this service
for the other until the other has performed a like service for it.
Thus they both remain as undetermined as to sense as they were
when considered apart from a specific sentence. To realize this is
precisely to see clearly what our pattern of usage is, and it is the
merit of the sort of analysis used by Vendler that, properly applied,
it brings this out so clearly.

[1] *Op. cit.*, p. 29.

THE INTENTIONALITY OF SENSATION:
A GRAMMATICAL FEATURE[1]

G. E. M. ANSCOMBE

I

Intentional Objects

Berkeley calls "colours with their variations and different proportions of light and shade" the "proper" and also the "immediate" objects of sight.[2] The first at any rate long seemed obvious to everyone, both before Berkeley and since his time. But Berkeley's whole view is now in some disrepute. Sense-data, a thoroughly Berkeleyan conception given that name by Russell, have become objects of ridicule and contempt among many present-day philosophers.

That word "object" which comes in the phrase "object of sight" has suffered a certain reversal of meaning in the history of philosophy, and so has the connected word "subject", though the two reversals aren't historically connected. The subject used to be what the proposition, say, is about, the thing itself as it is in reality—unprocessed by being conceived, as we might say (in case there is some sort of processing there); objects on the other hand were formerly always objects *of*—. Objects of desire, objects of thought, are not objects in one common modern sense, not individual things, such as *the objects found in the accused man's pockets*.

I might illustrate the double reversal by a true sentence constructed to accord with the *old* meanings: Subjectively there must be some definite number of leaves on a spray that I see, but objectively there need not: that is, there need not be some number such that I *see* that number of leaves on the spray.

When Descartes said that the cause of an idea must have at least as much formal reality as the idea had objective reality, he meant that the cause must have at least as much to it as what the idea was of would have, if what the idea was of actually existed.

[1] Given as a Howison Lecture at the University of California in Berkeley, 1963. I should like to express my gratitude to the University of California at being appointed Howison Lecturer.
[2] Throughout this paper I use double quotes for ordinary quotations (and so singles for quotes within quotes) and singles I use as scare quotes.

The "realitas objectiva" of an idea thus meant what we should call its "content"—namely what it is of, but considered as belonging purely to the idea. "What a picture is of" can easily be seen to have two meanings: what served as a model, what the picture was taken from—and what is to be seen in the picture itself, which may not even have had an original.

Thus formerly if something was called an object that would have raised the question "object of what?" It is hardly possible to use the word "object" in this way nowadays unless it actually occurs in such a phrase as "object of desire" or "object of thought". Suppose somebody says that the object of desire, or desired object, need not exist, and so there need not be any object which one desires. He is obviously switching from one use of the word "object" to another. If, however, we speak of objects of sight, or seen objects, it will usually be assumed that "objects" has the more modern sense: these will be objects, things, entities, which one sees. Now to prevent confusion I will introduce the phrase "intentional object" to mean "object" in the older sense which still occurs in "object of desire".

"Intentional" in these contexts is often spelt with an s. This was an idea of Sir William Hamilton's; he wanted to turn the old logical word "intention" into one that looked more like "extension". I prefer to keep the older spelling with two t's. For the word is the same as the one in common use in connexion with action. The concept of intention which we use there of course occurs also in connexion with *saying*. That makes the bridge to the logician's use.

There are three salient things about intention which are relevant for my subject. First, not any true description of what you do describes it as the action you intended: only under certain of its descriptions will it be intentional. ("Do you mean to be using that pen?"—"Why, what about this pen?"—"It's Smith's pen."—"Oh Lord, no!"). Second, the descriptions under which you intend what you do can be vague, indeterminate. (You mean to put the book down on the table all right, and you do so, but you do not mean to put it down anywhere in particular on the table—though you do put it down somewhere in particular.) Third, descriptions under which you intend to do what you do may not come true, as when you make a slip of the tongue or pen. You act, but your intended act does not happen.

Intentionality, whose name is taken from intention and expresses these characteristics of the concept *intention*, is found also in connexion with many other concepts. I shall argue that among these are concepts of sensation. Like many concepts marked by intentionality, though unlike intention itself, these are expressed by verbs commonly taking direct objects. I shall speak of intentional verbs, taking intentional objects. I have mentioned the history of the word "object" to forestall any impression that "an intentional object" means "an intentional entity".

Obvious examples of intentional verbs are "to think of", "to worship", "to shoot at". (The verb "to intend" comes by metaphor from the last—"intendere arcum in", leading to "intendere animum in".) Where we have such a verb taking an object, features analogous to the three features of intentionalness in action relate to some descriptions occurring as object-phrases after the verb.

The possible non-existence of the object, which is the analogue of the possible non-occurrence of the *intended* action, is what has excited most attention about this sort of verb. "Thinking of" is a verb for which the topic of the non-existent object is full of traps and temptations; "worshipping" is less dangerous and may help us to keep our heads. Consider the expression "object of thought". If I am thinking of Winston Churchill then he is the object of my thought. This is like "What is the object of these people's worship?" Answer: "The moon." But now suppose the object of my thought is Mr. Pickwick, or a unicorn; and the object of my worship is Zeus, or unicorns. With the proper names I named no man and no god, since they name a fictitious man and a false god. Moreover Mr. Pickwick and Zeus are nothing but a fictitious man and a false god (contrast the moon, which though a false god, is a perfectly good heavenly body). All the same it is clear that "The Greeks worshipped Zeus" is true. Thus "X worshipped——" and "X thought of——" are not to be assimilated to "X bit ——." For, supposing "X" to be the name of a real person, the name of something real has to be put in the blank space in "X bit ——" if the completed sentence is to have so much as a chance of being true. Whereas in "X worshipped ——" and "X thought of ——" that is not so.

This fact is readily obscured for us because with "X thought of ——"the more frequent filling-in of the blank is a name or description of something real; for when the blank is filled this way in a true sentence, it is the real thing itself, not some intermediary, X thought of. This makes it look as if the reality of the object mattered, as it does for biting. Nevertheless, it is obvious that vacuous names can complete such sentence-frames. So perhaps they stand in such frames for something with a *sort* of reality. That is the hazy state of mind one may be in about the matter.

A not very happy move to clarify it is to say, "Well, X had his idea of Zeus, or unicorns, or Mr. Pickwick, and that gives you the object you want." This is an unhappy move on several counts. First, it makes it seem that the *idea* is what X was worshipping or thinking of. Second, the mere fact of real existence (is this now beginning to be opposed to existence of some other kind?) can't make so very much difference to the analysis of a sentence like "X thought of ——." So if the idea is to be brought in when the object doesn't exist, then equally it should be brought in when the object does exist. Yet one is thinking, surely of Winston Churchill, not of the idea of him, and just that fact started us off. When one reads Locke, one wants to protest: "The mind is not employed about ideas, but about things—unless ideas are what we happen to be thinking about." Whatever purpose is served by introducing ideas, by saying, "Well, they had an idea of Zeus," we cannot say that the idea is the object of thought, or worship. It will not be right to say X worshipped an idea. It is rather that the subject's having an idea is what is needed to give the proposition a chance of being true. This may seem helpful for "worshipping", but not for "thinking of"; "thinking of" and "having an idea of" are too similar; if the one is problematic, then so is the other.

Let us concentrate on the fact that many propositions containing intentional verbs are true, and let us not be hypnotized by the possible non-existence of the object. There are other features too: non-substitutability of different descriptions of the object, where it does exist; and possible indeterminacy of the object. In fact all three features are connected. I can think of a man without thinking of a man of any particular height; I cannot hit a man without hitting a man of some particular height, because there is no such thing as a man of no particular height. And the possibility of this indeterminacy makes it possible that when I am thinking of a particular man, not every true description of him is one under which I am thinking of him.

I will now define an intentional verb as a verb taking an intentional object; intentional objects are the sub-class of direct objects characterized by these three connected features. By this definition, "to believe" and "to intend" are not themselves intentional verbs, which may seem paradoxical. But, say, "to believe — to be a scoundrel" will accord with the definition, so that it is not so paradoxical as to leave out belief and intention altogether.

But now comes a question: ought we really to say that the intentional object is a bit of language, or may we speak as if it were what the bit of language stands for? As grammarians and linguists use the words nowadays "direct object" and "indirect object" stand for parts of sentences. So if I call intentional objects a sub-class of direct objects, that may seem already to determine that an intentional object is a bit of language.

However, the matter is not so easily settled. Of course I do not want to oppose the practice of grammarians. But it is clear that the concept of a direct object—and hence the identification of the sentence-part now called the direct object—is learned somewhat as follows: the teacher takes a sentence, say "John sent Mary a book" and says: "What did John send Mary?" Getting the answer "A book" he says: "That's the direct object." Now the question does not really suppose, and the pupil, if he goes along with the teacher, does not take it, that any particular people, of whom the sentence is true, are in question, and so we may say that when the teaching is successful the question is understood as equivalent to "What does the sentence 'John sent Mary a book' say John sent Mary?" The grammatical concept of a direct object is acquired by one who can answer any such question. The correct answer to such a question gives (in older usage) or itself is (in more recent usage) the direct object. Now suppose that someone were to ask: "What is communicated to us by the phrase that we get in a correct answer? Is the phrase being used or mentioned?" It is clear that nothing is settled about *this* question by a choice whether to say, following older usage, that the phrase *gives* the direct object or, following more modern usage, that "direct object" is a name for a sentence-part.

I propose—for a purpose which will appear—to adopt the older usage. Then the question "What is the direct object of the verb in this sentence?" is the same as "What does the sentence say John sent Mary?" and the question "What does the phrase which is the answer to that question communicate to us, *i.e.* is it being used or mentioned?" can be asked in the form "Is the direct object a bit of language or rather what the bit of language stands for?"— and *this* is now not a mere question of terminology, but a substantive-seeming question of curious perplexity. For someone pondering it may argue as follows: It won't do to say that in this example a book is the direct object. For if we say that we can be asked: "Which book?"; but the sentence isn't being considered as true, and there is no answer to the question "Which book?" except "No book"; and yet without doubt the verb has a direct object, given by the answer "A book". So it must be *wrong*, and not just a matter of terminology, to say that the grammatical phrase "direct object" stands for, not a bit of language, but rather what the bit of language stands for. And, if intentional objects are a sub-class of direct objects, the phrase "intentional object" too will stand for a bit of language rather than what the language stands for; we are evidently not going to have to plunge into the bog made by the fact that in the most important and straightforward sense the phrase giving the intentional object may stand for nothing.

But wait—in that case *must* we not say, "the phrase which *is* the intentional object" rather than "the phrase giving the intentional object"? This is indeed a difficulty. For the intentional object is told in answer to a question "What?" But the answer to "What do they worship?" cannot be that they worship a phrase any more than that they worship an idea. A similar point holds, of course, for direct (and indirect) objects in general.

It may be argued (it was argued to me by Mr. G. Harman; I am obliged to him) that this is no argument. Perhaps we cannot say "What John is said to have sent is a phrase". But then no more can we say "What John is said to have sent is a direct object"— for the sentence did not say John sent Mary a direct object.

What this shews is that there is a way of taking "The direct object is not a direct object" which makes this true; namely, by assimilating this sentence to "The direct object is not a girl". (One could imagine explaining to a child: "The girl isn't the direct object, but the *book* that John sent.")

Frege's conclusion "The concept horse is not a concept" was based on the same sort of trouble about different uses of expressions. What "cheval" stands for is a concept, and what "cheval" stands for is a horse; these premisses do not, however, yield the

M

result that if Bucephalus is a horse he is a concept. Similarly, what John is said to have sent Mary is a book, and what John is said to have sent Mary is a direct object; these premises do not yield the result that if John gave Mary a book, he gave her a direct object.

Frege eventually proposed to deal with the trouble by stipulating that such a phrase as "What 'cheval' stands for" should *only* be used predicatively. A parallel stipulation in our case: "What John is said to have sent Mary is . . . " may only be completed with such expressions as could fill the blank in "John sent Mary. . . ." ' ".

The stipulation, while harmless, would be based on failure of ear for the different use of the phrase "What John is said to have sent Mary" in the explanation "What John is said to have sent Mary is the direct object of the sentence." But an ear for a different use cannot be dispensed with, as the further course of the argument shows.

The argument began with stating reasons why a direct object can't be something that the direct-object phrase stands for. Yet one can, one correctly does, say "A book" in answer to the question "What does the sentence 'John sent Mary a book' say John sent Mary?" which asks the same thing as "What is the direct object in that sentence?" Nevertheless the way the phrase "a book" is being used is such that one can't sensibly ask "Which book?"

We must conclude of 'objects' (direct, indirect, and likewise intentional) that the object is neither the phrase nor what the phrase stands for. What then is it? The question is based on a mistake, namely that an explanatory answer running say "An intentional (direct, indirect) object is such-and-such" is possible and requisite. But this need not be so. Indeed the only reasonable candidates to be answers are the ones we have failed. But what is the actual use of the term? Given a sentence in which a verb takes an object, one procedure for replying to the question: "What is the object in this sentence?" is to recite the object phrase.

If putting the object phrase in quotes implies that the object —*i.e.* what John is said to have sent Mary, what the Greeks worshipped—is a piece of language, that is wrong; if its not being in quotes implies that something referred to by the object phrase is the object, that is wrong too. To avoid the latter suggestion one might insist on putting in quotes; to avoid the former one might want to leave them out. One is inclined to invent a special sort of quotes; but the question is how the phrase within such new quotes would function—and if we understand that, we don't need a new sign. So ends the argument.

To repeat, I am not opposing the practice of grammarians and linguists for whom the expression "direct object" is defined as an expression for a phrase; they use that as I use the expression "direct-object phrase". But, as I have argued, the question "What does the sentence say John gave?" is fundamental for understanding either "direct object" or "direct-object phrase" as I am using those expressions; and hence for understanding "direct object" when it is used for a phrase. And though the question is answered (like many questions) by uttering a phrase—in this case "a book"—the phrase has *a special use* in answer to that question "What does the sentence say John gave?" *It* can name neither a piece of language, nor anything that the piece of language names or otherwise relates to, nor indeed anything else. The interest of the question and answer is the rather special interest of getting grammatical understanding. Grammatical understanding and grammatical concepts, even the most familiar ones like sentence, verb, noun, are not so straightforward and down-to-earth a matter of plain physical realities as I believe people sometimes suppose. The concept of a noun, for example, is far less of a physical concept than that of a coin; for someone might be trained to recognize coins with fair success though he knew nothing of money, but no one could be trained to recognize nouns without a great familiarity with language; and yet the concept of a noun is not one which he will automatically have through that familiarity, as he will have that of a coin if he operates with coined money. Indeed the explanations of grammatical terms are only hints at what is really grasped from examples. Thus no one should think that by merely adopting the usage of modern grammarians, for whom the direct object is a word or words, he has avoided handling difficult concepts and remained in a plain man's world of plain things.

"The direct object is what John sent" (="what the sentence says John sent.")

"The intentional object is what X was thinking of."

These two sentences are parallel. It is for the sake of parallelism that we opted for the old-fashioned usage of "direct object". For even in that usage, no one will be tempted to think that direct objects as such are a special type of entity. Just this temptation exists very strongly for objects of thought and sensation; that is, for intentional objects, which appear as entities under the names "idea" and "impression".

It may be objected: The context "The sentence says John sent Mary ——" is itself intentional. How, then, can my considerations about direct objects throw light on intentional objects? Fully spelled out they are themselves merely examples of sentences whose objects are intentional objects. (I am indebted for this objection and the discussion of it to Professors Bernard Williams and Arthur Prior and Mr. P. T. Geach.)

The answer is that what is said in the objection is true. But these examples, where we talk about direct objects, are harmless and profitable because certain sorts of suggestion about direct objects are patent nonsense. For example no one would think that if a sentence says John sent Mary a book, what it immediately and directly says he sent her was a direct object, and only in some indirect fashion, via this immediate object, does it say he sent her a book. I want, that is, to use a comparison with patent nonsense about direct objects in order to expose as latent nonsense of just the same kind some very persuasive views about ideas and impressions. Not that ideas and impressions are to be excluded from consideration; but as they enter into epistemology they will be rightly regarded as grammatical notions, whose rôle is readily misunderstood. And "grammatical" is here being used in its ordinary sense.

We must now ask: does any phrase that gives the direct object of an intentional verb in a sentence necessarily give an intentional object? No. Consider: "These people worship Ombola; that is to say, they worship a mere hunk of wood." (Cf. "They worship sticks and stones.") Or "They worship the sun, that is, they worship what is nothing but a great mass of frightfully hot stuff." The worshippers themselves will not acknowledge the descriptions. Their idol is for them a divinised piece of wood, one that is somehow also a god; and similarly for the sun.

An intentional object is given by a word or phrase which gives a *description under which*.

It will help if we consider shooting at, aiming. A man aims at a stag; but the thing he took for a stag was his father, and he

shoots his father. A witness reports: "He aimed at his father."
Now this is ambiguous. In the sense in which, given the situation
as we have described it, this report is true, the phrase "his father"
does not give an intentional object. Let us introduce the term
"material object": "his father" gives, we shall say, the *material* object
of the verb in the sentence "He aimed at his father" in the sense in
which this was true. Not because he hit his father—he might
after all merely have gone wide of the mark. But because the
thing he took for a stag actually was his father. We can ask what he
was doing—what he was aiming at—*in that* he was aiming at a
stag: this is to ask for another description "*X*" such that in "He was
aiming at *X*" we still have an intentional object, but the description
"*X*" gives us something that exists in the situation. *E.g.* he was
aiming at that dark patch against the foliage. The dark patch against
the foliage was in fact his father's hat with his father's head in it.

Thus, the given intentional object (the stag) being non-
existent in the situation, we looked for another intentional object
until we found one that did exist. Then the phrase giving that
intentional object, and any other true description of the existent
thing in question, give the *material* object of "He aimed at. . . ."

Does this account depend on the report's being true? No; but
if the witness lies or is quite mistaken, all the same he can be
questioned about what his report meant. Does he mean the phrase
"his father" to give the intentional, or only the material, object?
If only the material object, what does he mean by "He aimed at
. . . ?" That you could see that the man was taking aim, and
where his target lay? There might not be true answers to these
questions, but the witness has got to pretend there are or be
confounded.

And now, for greater ease of expression, I will speak, as is
natural, of the material and intentional objects of aiming, of
worshipping, of thinking. This should always be interpretable in
terms of the verbs and their objects.

There need not be a material object of aiming. If a man were
totally hallucinated, and, shooting at something in his hallucinatory scene, hit his father, that would not make his father the
material object of his aiming. Similarly, if there is no description,
still giving the intentional object of worship, which describes anything actual, the worshippers, materially speaking, worship a
nothing, something that does not exist.

Not that it will then do to say "They worship nothing," but only: "What they worship is nothing." For "They worship nothing" would imply that no sentence "They worship such-and-such" will be true; and in the case supposed some such sentence is true.

Questions about the identity of an intentional object, when this cannot be reduced to the identity of a *material* object, are obviously of some interest. How do we decide that two people or peoples worship or do not worship the same god? Again, when a proper name is obscure and remote in its historical reference, like "Arthur", the question may arise whether two people are thinking of the same man—if they have different, incompatible, pictures of him.

But I perceive that my saying "when this cannot be reduced to the identity of a *material* object" may mislead: for by *material* objects I do not mean what are now called "material objects"— tables, planets, lumps of butter and so on. To give a clear instance: a debt of five dollars is not a material object in this latter sense; but given that someone had contracted such a debt, my thought "that debt of five dollars" would have as its material object something described and indicated by the phrase giving the intentional object of my thought. When it is beyond question that the phrase giving an intentional object does describe and indicate a material object in this sense, then the question as to the identity of the intentional object reduces to the question as to the identity of the material object. Are we referring to the same debt? That is, perhaps, not too difficult to establish. But when either there is no real debt or it is very obscure whether there is, the case is altered.

The fact that we can use the concept of identity in connexion with intentional objects should not lead us to think there is any sense in questions as to the kind of existence—the ontological status—of intentional objects as such. All such questions are nonsensical. Once more we can clear our heads by thinking of direct objects. The answer to "What is the direct object in 'John sent Mary a book'?" is "A book". This is the right answer as much when the sentence is false as when it is true, and also when it is only made up, as it is in this case, to illustrate a point. It is evident nonsense to ask about the mode of existence or ontological status of the direct object as such: or to ask what kind of thing *a book* is, as it is thought of in answer to the question about the direct object.

II

Sensation

In the philosophy of sense-perception there are two opposing positions. One says that what we are immediately aware of in sensation is sense-impressions, called "ideas" by Berkeley and "sense-data" by Russell. The other, taken up nowadays by "ordinary language" philosophy, says that on the contrary we at any rate *see* objects (in the *wide* modern sense which would include *e.g.* shadows) without any such intermediaries. It is usually part of this position to insist that I can't see (or, perhaps, feel, hear, taste or smell) something that is not there, any more than I can hit something that is not there: I can only *think* I see (&c.) something if it isn't there, or only in some extended usage of "see" do I see what isn't there. I shall say most about seeing, as most people do in discussing this topic. The other verbs are for good reasons (which aren't very relevant to my topic) often treated rather differently, especially by ordinary language philosophy.

I wish to say that both these positions are wrong; that both misunderstand verbs of sense perception, because these verbs are intentional or essentially have an intentional aspect. The first position misconstrues intentional objects as material objects of sensation; the other allows only *material* objects of sensation; or at any rate does not allow for a description of what is seen which is *e.g.* neutral as between its being a real spot (a stain) or an after-image, giving only the content of an experience of seeing concerning which one does not yet know whether one is seeing a real spot or an after-image. (I am obliged to Professor Frank Ebersole for telling me of an experience of his which supplied this example.)

To see the intentionality of sensation it is only necessary to look at a few examples which bring it out.

1. "When you screw up your eyes looking at a light, you see rays shooting out from it."

2. "I see the print very blurred: is it blurred, or is it my eyes?"

3. "Move these handles until you see the bird in the nest." (Squint-testing apparatus; the bird and the nest are on separate cards.)

4. "I see six buttons on that man's coat, I merely see a lot of snow flakes framed by this window-frame—no definite number."

5. ". . . a mirage. An approaching pedestrian may have no feet (they are replaced by a bit of sky)." (Example from M. Luckiesh.)

6. "With this hearing aid, when you talk I hear some screeching noises; no low tones and the consonants are very indistinct."

7. "I hear a ringing in my ears."

8. "I heard a tremendous roaring noise outside, and wondered with alarm for a moment what great machine or floodwater could be making it. And then I realized that it was only my little dog snoring close at hand." (Example from W. James.)

9. "Do you know how a taste can sometimes be quite indeterminate until you know what you are eating?"

10. "I keep on smelling the smell of burning rubber when, as I find out, there is no such thing."

Someone who wishes to say that the verbs of sense are used right in normal cases *only* with real things as objects, and even with real things correctly characterized, may say that these are exceptional uses. Either the context (eye-testing apparatus) or what is said, with the tone of voice and special emphasis appropriate to it, shews this. There was presumably a definite number of snow flakes falling so as to be seen from a certain position, and that was the number seen; only the subject did not know how many there were, was not able to tell by looking as he could tell the number of buttons on the coat. He expressed this by saying he did not *see* a definite number of snow flakes; but this is an odd use of "see", different from the more normal use we get in the following example:

11. "I saw someone in the study just now." "Nonsense! You can't have, because there isn't anyone there." "Well, I wonder what I saw, then."

Now this may be; on the other hand the oculist testing the degree of a squint does not have to teach a new use of "see" or of "I see a (picture of a) bird in a nest" before he can ask "Do you see the bird in the nest?"—the bird-picture and the nest-picture being in fact spatially separated. To call such a use "new" simply means that some difference between it and what is being called the old use strikes us as important.

There is indeed an important difference; though it is wrong to regard the uses which it marks as, so to speak, *deviant*, for our concepts of sensation are built up by our having *all* these uses. The difference we are attending to is that in these cases, object phrases are used giving objects which are, wholly or in part, merely intentional. This comes out in two features: neither possible non-existence (in the situation), nor indeterminacy, of the object is any objection to the truth of what is said.

Now 'ordinary language' views and 'sense-datum' views make the same mistake, that of failing to recognize the intentionality of sensation, though they take opposite positions in consequence. This failure comes out clearly on the part of an ordinary-language philosopher if he insists that what I say I see must really be there if I am not lying, mistaken, or using language in a "queer", extended (and therefore discountable) way.

The Berkeleyan sense-datum philosopher makes the same mistake in his insistence that *e.g.* one sees visual impressions, visual data. I would say that such a philosopher makes an incorrect inference from the truth of the grammatical statement that the intentional object, the impression, the visual object, is what you see. He takes the expression "what you see" materially. "The visual impression is what you see," which is a proposition like "The direct object is what he sent", is misconstrued so as to lead to "You see an impression", as the other never would be misconstrued so as to lead to "He sent a direct object."

This is a more interesting and permanently tempting mistake than the other, whose appeal is merely that of a common-sense revolt against a Berkeleyan type of view. But both doctrines have a great deal of point. To take the 'ordinary language' doctrine:

First, what I shall call the material use of verbs of sense exists. The material use of "see" is a use which demands a *material* object of the verb, "You can't have seen a unicorn, unicorns don't exist." "You can't have seen a lion, there wasn't any lion there to see."

These uses are quite commonplace. It is not merely that the object-phrase is taken materially—as we have seen, that may be the case with an intentional verb without reflecting on its intentionality. Here the verb "to see" is not allowed to take a *merely* intentional object; non-existence of the object (absolutely, or in the situation) is an objection to the truth of the sentence. We see the double use of the verb "see" by contrasting it with "worship". No one would ever say: "They cannot have worshipped unicorns, because there are no such things."

Second, the words giving the object of a verb of sense are necessarily most often intended as giving *material* objects of sense: for this is their primary application. To see this, consider the following. Suppose a bright red plastic toy elephant looks greyish brown to me in a certain light. Only if I do not know that the greyish brown colour is mere appearance do I say without any special context (*e.g.* that of describing impressions), or apology, or humour: "I see a greyish brown plastic toy elephant." This is because we understand the description-of-an-appearance "greyish brown" by understanding the description "greyish brown": this describes what the appearance is of. To do that, it must in the first instance be a description of such a thing as it would be true of (for the appearance is an appearance of that)—really, and not merely in appearance: this will be its primary application. But, being a description of a sensible property, it must also in its primary application enter into the object phrases for the appropriate verbs of sense, since we get to know sensible properties by the appropriate senses.

Further, we ought to say, not: "Being red is looking red in normal light to the normal-sighted," but rather "Looking red is looking as a thing that *is* red looks in normal light to the normal-sighted." For if we ought rather to say the first, then how do we understand "looking red"? Not by understanding "red" and "looking". It would have to be explained as a simple idea; and so would looking any other colour. It may be replied: These all are simple ideas; "looking yellow" and "looking red" are the *right* expressions for what you show someone when you show him yellow and red, for he will only learn "yellow" and "red" from the examples if they look yellow and look red; so it is *looking-yellow* and *looking-red* that he really gets hold of and has been introduced to, even though you *say* you are explaining "yellow" and "red". This would come to saying that in strictness "looking" should be part of every colour word in reports of perception: it will then cease to perform the actual function of the word "looking". It was plausible to say: Only if it looks red to him will he learn what is meant; but wrong to infer: What he then grasps as the correlate of the word "red" is a red look. Even granted that he knows he is to learn the name of a colour, still it invites misunderstanding to rely on something that only *looks* red to teach him the word; if he notices that it only looks red, how natural for him to suppose that "red" was the name of the colour that it actually *is*. If you tell him: "It's the colour that this 'looks'," this presupposes that "looks *C*" and "*C*" are originally, and not just subsequently, distinct: that, in short, "being red" is not after all to be explained as a certain looking-red.

Again, things do not always look the same shape, colour, size, and so on, but we commonly look at and describe them, saying, *e.g.* "It's rectangular, black and about six foot in height," without paying attention to how they look—indeed we might say that often things *look* to us, strike us, not as they look but as they are! (Conviction that *only* so is "looks" used rightly was the cause of confusion to an over-confident ordinary language philosopher on an occasion famous in Oxford: F. Cioffi brought in a glass vessel of water with a stick in it. "Do you mean to say," he asked, "that this stick does not look bent?" "No" said the other bravely: "It looks like a straight stick in water." So Cioffi took it out and it *was* bent.)

So much at least there is to be said on the side of the "ordinary language" philosopher. But, turning to the sense-impression philosophy, how much it points out and can investigate which often gets querulously dismissed by the other side! There is such a thing as simply describing impressions, simply describing the sensible appearances that present themselves to one situated thus and thus—or to *myself*.

Second, the sense-impression philosophy will be right in its way of taking the Platonic dictum: "He who sees must see something." Plato compared this to "He who thinks must think something," and has sometimes been criticized on the ground that "seeing" is a relation of a subject to an object in the modern sense of that last word, while thinking is different: that such-and-such is the case isn't a thing. But "He who sees must be seeing something" is being wrongly taken if taken as meaning: "Whenever anyone can rightly be said to see, there must be something there, which is what he sees." Taken in that sense, it is not true; to say it is true is to legislate against all except the material use of "see". The sense in which it is true is that if someone is seeing, there is some content of his visual experience. If he says he can see ("can see" is English idiom for "is seeing") we can ask him "What can you see?" He may say "I don't know." Perhaps that means that he doesn't know what the material object of his seeing is; perhaps simply that he is at a loss to make out *what* what he (in any sense) sees *looks like*. But then we can say: well, at any rate, describe what colours, what variation of light and dark you see. He may say: "It's frightfully difficult, it all changes so fast, so many colours shifting all the time, I can't describe it, it doesn't stay long enough" —and that's a description. But he cannot say: "How do you mean, what I see? I only said I could see, I didn't say I could see something—there's no need of a *'what'* that I see." That would be unintelligible.

This brings out the third point in favour of the sense-impression philosophy, which offers it some support even in its strict Berkeleyan form. The minimum description that must be possible if someone can see, will be of colours with their variations of light and darkness. One cannot say "Colour, light and dark? No question of any such things," in response to a *present* enquiry about what one sees.

That is to say, it is so with us. Perhaps we could imagine people whose language has no colour vocabulary, though they are sighted, *i.e.* they use eyes and need light to get about successfully, &c. A man of such a people, taught to read by sight, learns names of letters, could read out words which were black on white, but could not understand the words "black" and "white". We'd say we do not know 'how he tells' the words, the shapes. But is that to say anything but that for us appeal to colours is used in an account of how we tell shapes? Whereas perhaps for him there is in this sense no such thing as a 'how he tells' —any more than there is for us with the colours themselves. We don't ask for a 'how we tell' it's red, as we ask for a 'how we tell' it's the word "red", and accept as part of the answer "by seeing these shapes, *i.e.* colour patches of these shapes." We may wonder "How could there be such recognition of a thing like the pattern of a word— *unmediated* recognition? How could it but be mediated by perception of colour?" (One of the origins of the notion of simple ideas, elements.) But though in this case we have an account of the perception of the pattern as mediated by the perception of colour, think of our recognition of human expressions. We feel that this is the *kind* of thing to be mediated, but fail in our attempts to describe the elements and their arrangements, seeing which we recognize a cheerful or ironical expression. But, one may say, optically speaking he must be being affected by light of the wavelengths belonging to the different colours. Yes—but does that show that, so to speak, the content of a colour concept is pushed into him, so that all he has to do is utter it in a name, whose use he will later make to fit with other people's in its range of application? I believe this is thought. (Cf. Quine about "square" and each man's retinal projection of a square tile, *Word and Object*, p. 7.) Formulated, this loses its plausibility. For one thing, the optical process does not exhibit anything to the man in whom it takes place. For another, no concept is simply given; every one involves a complicated technique of application of the word for it, which could not just be presented by an experience-content. The fact that there is no 'how we tell' about colour-recognition does not mean that training in practices—most strikingly the practices comprising that technique of application—is not as necessary for the acquisition of colour concepts as those of substances or square roots.

Pursuant to this false conception of the primitively given, Berkeley—and Russell—thought that all else in description of the seen, all besides the arrangement of colour patches in the visual field, was inference and construction. This is not acceptable. There are impressions of distance and size, for example, independent of assumptions about what a thing is. One may be utterly perplexed what a thing is just because one is seeing it as at a different distance from the right one, and hence as the wrong size. Or vice versa. I once opened my eyes and saw the black striking surface of a match-box which was standing on one end; the other sides of the box were not visible. This was a few inches from my eye and I gazed at it in astonishment wondering what it could be. Asked to describe the impression as I remember it, I say: "Something black and rectangular, on end, some feet away, and some feet high." I took it for three or four feet distant, and it looked, if anything, like a thick post, but I knew there could be no such thing in my bedroom. Or I have taken a small black prayer book for a great family Bible sort of volume, judging that it lay on a footrest some feet away instead of a nearby ledge nearer eye-level. These were not judgments of distance based on identifications of things—the supposition of what thing it might be was based on an impression of size which went with a false impression of distance.

Departing, then, from Berkeley, we can note that descriptions of visual impressions can be very rich and various. There can be impressions of depth and distance and relative positions and size; of kinds of things and kinds of stuff and texture and even temperature; of facial expression and emotion and mood and thought and character; of action and movement (in the *stationary* impression) and life and death. Even within the compass of the description "colours with their variations of light and shade" there are diverse kinds of impression.

It remains to sort out the relations between the intentional and material objects of sensation; as I have done most of the time, I will concentrate on seeing.

While there must be an intentional object of seeing, there need not always be a material object. That is to say "X saw A" where "saw" is used materially, implies some proposition "X saw——" where "saw" is used intentionally; but the converse does not hold. This leads to the feeling that the intentional use is somehow prior to the material use. The feeling seems to run contrary to the recognition of, the feeling, that for descriptions of objects of sight the material application is the prior one. Both feelings are—legitimately—satisfied by allowing that an intentional object is necessarily involved in seeing, while granting that this does not confer epistemological priority on purely intentional sentences, which indeed, in a host of the most ordinary cases of reported seeing, are never formulated or considered.

John Austin, who opposed the view that there are two senses of "see" according as the seeing has to be veridical or not, remarked casually that there were perhaps two senses of "object of sight". I think it was in this connexion that he contrasted "Today I saw a man born in Jerusalem" and "Today I saw a man shaved in Oxford"—both said in Oxford. At any rate, one says, you didn't *see* him born today; perhaps you did see someone being shaved. So the one description, while true of what you saw, in a sense does not give what you saw. A description which is true of a material object of the verb "to see", but which states something that absolutely or in the circumstances 'you can't have *seen*', necessarily gives *only* a material object of seeing.

In speaking of the material object of aiming, I said that if a man aimed at that dark parch against the foliage, and that patch was his father's hat with his father's head in it, then his father was a material object of his aim; but if he aimed at some patch in a totally hallucinatory scene, and hit his father, you could not say that.

Now if we try to apply this explanation to the case of seeing we run into difficulties which reflect back on the case of aiming. But in the case considered the material object of aiming was arguably an *intentional* object of seeing. For what else—it might be asked—is a dark patch against the foliage?

This may seem to plunge us into confusion. For surely what is *only* an intentional object of seeing can't be a material object of aiming? Then when does a description give a material object of sight? One kind of case we have seen: when a description is true of what is seen, but does *not* give an intentional object. "I see a man whose great uncle died in a lunatic asylum"—the relative clause gives an absolutely non-intentional description. "I see a girl who has a mole between her shoulder-blades"—in the circumstances it gives a non-intentional description. For she is facing me, &c. "You can't have *seen* that," one says.

But why? If I can't see that, why can I see Professor Price's tomato? It has a backside that I don't see. Mr. Thompson Clarke draws our attention to the fact that a view of a tomato and a half-tomato may be exactly the same. That is so; but it is not like the fact that a view of someone with and without a mole between his shoulder blades may be exactly the same. If you look at a tomato and take only a single view, you *must* see what *might* be only a half tomato: that is what seeing a tomato is. Whereas there is a view of the mole; and no front view *is* a view of a mole between the shoulder blades. Such a mole does not stamp the front view as may approaching death or a load of troubles, and so there is no impression of it—just as there is no "born in Jerusalem" look about a man.

But a material object of seeing is not necessarily given by a description of what is before my eyes when they are open and I am seeing; if I am totally hallucinated, then in no sense do I see what is before my eyes. Thus it is essential to a material object of seeing that it is given by a description which is true of *what is seen*; and we have to enquire into the significance here of this phrase "*what is seen*".

The problem is this: there is a material object of ϕ-ing if there is a phrase giving an intentional object of ϕ-ing which is also a description of what exists in a suitable relation to the ϕ-er. Now this can't be a description of what exists merely by describing the intentional object of some *other* act (he aims at the dark patch that he sees); if simply describing an intentional object of ϕ-ing will not—as of course it will not—guarantee that we have described a material object of ϕ-ing, then how can it give a material object of some other verb, ψ-ing?

All would be plain sailing if we could say: we have a material object of sight only if *some* intentional description is also true of what really—physically—exists. And perhaps we can say that the dark patch against the foliage is not merely an intentional object of seeing; there really is a dark object or a region of darkness there.

But this is not always the case when we see. Suppose I have defective sight: all I see is a shiny blur over there. That blur, we say, is my watch. We therefore say I see my watch, though very indistinctly; and I want to say that my watch is the material object of seeing. But I may not be able to see it as a watch; all I see is a shiny blur. But the description "a shiny blur" is not true of anything that physically exists in the context. Supposing the father had a dark hat on, it would follow that, to mention the puzzle that perplexed Moore for so long, the dark patch against the foliage was *part of the surface of a material object* (*modern sense*); but certainly 'a blur' is no part of the surface of my watch. But it may be I have no other description of what I see than "a shiny blur over there". So is there any intentional description which is also a description of a material object of sight?

Yes; for even if my watch is not a blur, it is a shiny thing and it is over there. Suppose I had said: I see a roughly triangular red blur here, and some causal connexion via the visual centres in the brain could have been discovered between that and the presence of my watch over there—would it have been right to say: "What I am seeing is my watch"? I believe not.

An interesting case is that of *muscae volitantes*, as they are called. You go to the doctor and you say: "I wonder if there is

something wrong with my eyes or my brain? I see"—or perhaps
you say "I *seem* to see"—"floating specks before my eyes". The
doctor says: "That's not very serious. They're there all right" (or:
"You see them all right")—"they are just the floating debris in the
fluids of the eye. You are a bit tired and so your brain doesn't
knock them out, that's all." The things he says you see are not
out there where you say you see them—*that* part of your intentional description is not true of anything relevant; but he does not
say that what you are seeing is that debris *only* because the debris
is the cause. There really are floating specks. If they caused you
to see a little red devil or figure of eight, we should not say you
saw them. It may be possible to think of cases where there is
nothing in the intentional object that suggests a description of
what is materially being seen. I doubt whether this could be so
except in cases of very confused perception—how could a very
definite intentional description be connected with a quite different
material object of seeing? In such cases, if we are in doubt, we
resort to moving the supposed material object to see if the blurred,
not colour-true, and misplaced image of it moves.

When you said: "I see"—believing that the objects were quite
illusory—you *intended* your description purely as an intentional
one; you were giving the words "floating specks" a secondary
application. It came as a surprise to you that you would have had
the right to intend the words materially. In the well-known case
of H. H. Price's mescaline illusion, when without any derangement
of his judgment he was able to describe what he saw—a great pile
of leaves on his counterpane, which he knew not to be there—we
again have a secondary application: the words "a pile of leaves"
were intended *only* as a description of an impression.

It is important to notice that very often there is no answer
to the question whether people intend the word "see" in its *material*
use or not: that is, whether they are so using the word "see" that
they would have to take it back supposing that what they said they
saw was not there. If they were mis-seeing something that was
there, they would usually want to correct themselves, finding
out 'what they really saw'. But what if the seeing were
hallucinatory?

The question would be: Supposing that turned out to be the
case, would you claim that you mean "see" in such a way that all
you have to do is alter your intentions for the description of the

N

object, from intending it in its *primary* application as a description of the *material* object of sight to intending it in a *secondary* application as a description of a mere *impression?*

Faced with such a question, we have in general the right to reject it, saying like Tommy Traddles: But it isn't so, you know, so we won't suppose it if you don't mind. And even if we have not this right, we generally entertain no such supposition and *therefore* are unprepared with an answer. We need not have determinately meant the word "see" one way or the other.

We may make a similar point about 'phantom limb'. I take the part of the body where pain is felt to be the object of a transitive verb-like expression "to feel pain in——". Then when there is *e.g.* no foot, but *X* not knowing this, says he feels pain in his foot, he may say he was wrong ("I did not see a lion there, for there was no lion") or he may alter his understanding of the phrase "my foot" so that it becomes a purely intentional object of the verb-like expression. But it need not be determined in advance, in the normal case of feeling pain, whether one so intends the expression "I feel pain in——" as to withdraw it, or merely alters one's intentions for the description of the place of the pain, if one should learn that the place was missing.

MESSRS. GOODMAN, GREEN AND GRUE[1]

R. J. Butler

In *Fact, Fiction and Forecast* Professor Nelson Goodman advances an interesting problem about our willingness to ' project ' a predicate like ' green '.[2] There is no mystery in the fact that since all observed emeralds have been remarked to be green, we opt for all emeralds being green without exception. But there is a little mystery, for Goodman, in the preferential treatment accorded to ' green '. Suppose that time t is in the future, and that there is a predicate ' grue ' which ' applies to all things examined before t just in case they are green but to other things just in case they are blue '.[3] ' Grue ' would generally, I think, be called a *mixed* predicate, since its definiens contains two other predicates which fall under the same determinable of being coloured, and it would generally, I think, be called a *temporal* predicate since its definiens contains reference to a date. But whatever its characteristics as a predicate, Goodman is impressed by the fact that there is now precisely the same inductive support for all emeralds being grue as there is for all emeralds being green. And moreover, at any moment before t the inductive support for the one hypothesis appears to be as strong as the inductive support for the other. Yet because these hypotheses yield incompatible predictions beyond t, it is of paramount import that only the one predicate be projected from observed to unobserved cases. The Riddle of Goodman is not why we ought to project the one rather than the other—there is no *ought* about it[4]—but rather why we do project the one rather than the other.

Carnap's answer to the Riddle is that no temporal and perhaps no mixed predicates are projectable within the inductive sciences.[5] Purely qualitative predicates are legitimate candidates for pro-

---

[1] Professor C. G. Hempel's generous comments on an earlier draft of this paper have enabled me to tighten the argument considerably. This does not imply agreement upon major issues.

[2] N. Goodman, *Fact, Fiction and Forecast* (London, 1954), ch. III, pp. 63–86.

[3] *Ibid.*, p. 74.

[4] S. F. Barker and P. Achinstein, ' On the New Riddle of Induction ', *The Philosophical Review*, LXIX (1960), p. 511.

[5] R. Carnap, ' On the Application of Inductive Logic ', *Philosophy and Phenomenological Research*, VIII (1947), pp. 146–147.

jection, but about all others Carnap has qualms. I think that most of us, including Goodman, share in the qualms of Carnap, and feel that there is something very strange in the notion of projecting, within the inductive sciences, what we would ordinarily recognize as either a mixed or a temporal predicate. Hunches and qualms are by no means identical with bias and prejudice, and since philosophy is largely a matter of having insights and of being able to justify some of them, hunches and qualms are entitled to their day in court.

It is unfortunate, therefore, that in the present case we are confronted with a conflict of qualms, for the Riddle of Goodman arises from (I do not say derives from) consideration of Hempel's First Paradox. This paradox concerns two simple assumptions about the nature of confirmation and a few principles of logic, any of which we would feel queasy about giving up.[1] The first assumption is that any statement is confirmed by any of its logical consequences. Thus a universal statement is confirmed by any of its existential instantiations. And the second assumption is that any statement confirms any logical consequence of any statement confirmed by it. That is to say, if an existential statement confirms a universal statement, then it also confirms the conjunction of that statement with some other. Thus if we take any two statements S_1 and S_2, *no matter how unrelated they may be*, then by virtue of the first assumption S_1 confirms $S_1.S_2$, since S_1 is a logical consequence of $S_1.S_2$, and by virtue of the second assumption S_1 confirms S_2, since S_1 confirms $S_1.S_2$ which, in turn, logically implies S_2. Now let S_1 be the assertion that all emeralds examined prior to t are green, and let S_2 be the prediction that all emeralds examined from t onwards will be blue. Then the conjunction $S_1.S_2$ is remarkably like the claim that all emeralds when examined are grue. By virtue of the first assumption S_1 confirms $S_1.S_2$, and by virtue of the second assumption S_1 confirms S_2. But equally S_2 could be the statement that from t onwards all emeralds examined will be green. The extent of my claim so far is that Goodman's Riddle can be set up in a manner akin to Hempel's First Paradox: whether it is a special case of that paradox is a matter up for consideration.

One thing we can be sure of is that Goodman would not set up his Riddle in a manner akin to Hempel's First Paradox. In

[1] Cp. Goodman, *op. cit.*, p. 69 ff.

fact he explicitly rejects the first assumption, which permits heterogeneous couplings: it just is not the case that whatever confirms S_1 confirms $S_1.S_2$ no matter how unrelated S_1 and S_2 may be. For this reason he asserts that ' while the statements that confirm a general hypothesis are consequents of it, not all of its consequences confirm it '.[1] Goodman's point is purely negative: in the case of a heterogeneous couplings like ' 8497 is a prime number and the other side of the moon is flat and Elizabeth the First was crowned on a Tuesday ' the ' establishment of one component endows the whole statement with no credibility that is transmitted to other component statements '.[2] Goodman accepts the formal restriction that a hypothesis is confirmed only by those of its consequences that can be deduced from it by instantiation, but he believes in addition that the ' confirmation of a hypothesis by an instance depends rather heavily upon features of the hypothesis other than its syntactical form '.[3] Extra-logical considerations, that is to say, enter into the nature of confirmation itself. It is in this context that ' grue ' is swept on to the stage: Goodman's question is to find other than logical criteria for eliminating the hypothesis that all emeralds are grue.

My purpose in this paper is to discover whether Goodman has touched upon extra-logical considerations, or whether, in setting up his Riddle he has tacitly reintroduced something akin to Hempel's First Paradox, with a qualification about heterogeneous couplings. In order to set up the Riddle in his way at all, Goodman must be permitted to introduce ' grue ' as a predicate on a par with ' green '. ' Grue,' it is claimed, is a predicate which can be a value of any variable which can have ' green ' as a value. In presenting the Riddle Goodman uses no more than the rule that an evidence statement of the form

$$Pa, Pb, Pc \ldots . Pk$$

confirms the corresponding generalization

$$(x)Px,$$

the difficulty arising from substituting first ' green ' and then ' grue ' for P.[4]

Goodman's answer to the Riddle is that we consult not merely the record of what has been observed, but also the record of past projections. ' Green ' has ' the more impressive biography,' it is

---

[1] *Ibid.*, p. 70.   [2] *Ibid.*   [3] *Ibid.*, p. 73.   [4] *Ibid.*, pp. 74–75.

'a veteran of earlier and many more projections', it is, in a word, 'entrenched',[1]—not merely because it has been successfully projected in the past, but also because it belongs to a family of similarly projected predicates in terms of which other predicates co-existensive with this one can be constructed. It is for these reasons that we regard the projection of 'green' as legitimate, and refuse to project 'grue'. Compared to 'green', 'grue' is a bastard. And therefore it is disinherited, and cut off without a penny. But just as laws of legitimacy vary from one country to another, so vary the rules of projection as between languages. In an answer to Carnap which has a touch of brilliance, Goodman argues in effect that the line of succession might have passed through 'grue' and 'bleen' instead of through 'green' and 'blue', 'bleen' applying to all things examined before t just in case they are blue but to other things just in case they are green. And furthermore, it is claimed that the two lines of succession are entirely symmetrical, for just as in the green-blue language 'grue' applies to all things examined before t just in case they are green but to other things just in case they are blue, so in the grue-bleen language 'green' applies to all things examined before t just in case they are grue but to other things just in case they are bleen.

If the two lines of succession are entirely symmetrical then it follows immediately that our acceptance of one rather than the other is governed by extra-logical considerations: and what else could be relevant except considerations concerning the past history of the language? If this be so, which predicates are regarded as mixed and which as temporal would seem to be no more than a matter of family entrenchment. And this, if correct, smudges the time-honoured qualitative-non-qualitative dichotomy, for we are left without means of segregating purely qualitative predicates from those containing reference to spatio-temporal position. Goodman is maintaining that no matter what predicates are taken as non-positional, a language can be devised in which they are positional, and vice versa. At the very least Goodman will be thought to have shown that complications concerning other dates are irrelevant to the predicate calculus.

There is a rising tide of popularity for the view that what is projected in a language is merely a matter of history. 'Grue' is defined in *our* language in terms of green and blue and a date; but

[1] *Ibid.*, p. 95.

it is a temporal predicate *for us*, it is claimed, only on account of our record of past projections. In similar vein Quine argues that ' the linguist . . . imposes his object-positing ontology without special warrant '.[1] In a curious way, we are being made to feel prisoners of our own conceptual framework, as if a ' conceptual framework ' were something which could imprison one's thought.

How much does Goodman's claim involve? I doubt if he is committed, as his critics contend, to the view ' that the predicate " grue " is for the speaker of the grue-bleen language a non-temporal predicate, in that such a speaker does not need to ascertain the date of an object before being able to tell whether the object is grue or not '.[2] It is thought that Goodman must assume this, for otherwise the grue-bleen language would not be symmetrical with the green-blue language. For Goodman, however, looking at clocks and calendars is quite incidental to logical considerations. He can look at the symmetry of his definitions: there is no need to look elsewhere. ' I simply do not know,' he writes, ' how to tell whether a predicate is qualitative or positional, except perhaps by completely begging the question at issue and asking whether the predicate is " well-behaved "—that is, whether simple syntactical universal hypotheses applying to it are lawlike '.[3] To say that on Goodman's account the predicate ' grue ' is non-temporal for Mr. Grue (a speaker of the grue-bleen language) is to presume that Mr. Grue can make the very distinction which, it is being claimed, cannot be made. Thus once again Goodman is in position to fend the attack with a counter-thrust, even although one may *feel* that his opponent's lance was well-placed.

If 'grue ' is to be declared illegitimate on the basis of extra-logical considerations, then that fact alone would signify a most important advance in inductive theory, even if the extra-logical considerations in question proved to be evasive. But even when Professor Goodman has by definitions attempted to show that Mr. Grue is, after all, only the mirror-image of Mr. Green, two nagging hunches remain: the first, that Mr. Grue is really an impostor, who only looks like Mr. Green when wearing the appropriate disguise; the second, that Mr. Grue is a charlatan

[1] W. V. Quine, ' Speaking of Objects ', *Proceedings and Addresses of the American Philosophical Association*, XXXI (1957–58), p. 5.

[2] S. F. Barker and P. Achinstein, *op. cit.*, p. 513.

[3] *Op. cit.*, p. 79.

whose language is without relevance to inductive theory. ' Grue,' we are told, applies to all things examined before *t* just in case they are green but to other things just in case they are blue. On this definition anything examined before *t* and found to be green is grue, and furthermore is grue forever thereafter, no matter what colours it may later have, because it was then examined and found to be green; and any other thing examined at or after *t* and found to be blue is grue, no matter what colours it may previously have had. Something is grue, on this definition, just in case one conjunct of the formula is true: there is no need to look at the other conjunct, since it applies to *other* things. There need be no identity at all between things that are grue before *t* and things that are grue at or after *t*. All that is necessary in order for there to be grue things at any particular time is that there be green things if that time is prior to *t* and blue things if that time is not prior to *t*. Since the conjuncts are completely irrelevant to each other the definition might just as well be stated disjunctively, and this is precisely how some critics of Professor Goodman have stated it: something is grue at a given time ' if and only if either the thing is then green and the time is prior to time *t*, or the thing is then blue and the time is not prior to *t*.'[1] It is interesting that Professor Goodman has permitted this disjunctive formulation. However else the two formulae may differ they have in common this very important fact, that provided at any time one conjunct-or-disjunct is confirmed then the truth of the other is completely irrelevant. It therefore cannot serve as the handmaid of prediction.

Clearly this is not how Professor Goodman wants his definition to be interpreted when talking about induction, for according to the definition, he says, ' the prediction that all emeralds subsequently examined will be green and the prediction that all will be grue are alike confirmed by evidence statements describing the same observations '.[2] ' The two incompatible predictions . . . are equally well confirmed according to our present definition '.[3] It is most important to observe, however, that predictions are formally licensed by those recalcitrant propositions, subjunctive conditionals. If I am able to say ' If this emerald were examined

[1] S. F. Barker and P. Achinstein, *op. cit.*, p. 511.
[2] *Op. cit.*, p. 75.
[3] *Ibid.*

at t it would be found to be grue ' then, and only then, am I able to say predictively, ' This emerald will be grue at t '. And if the prediction is later confirmed, its confirmation licenses equally recalcitrant counterfactual conditionals of the form, ' If this emerald had been examined prior to t, it would have been found to be green '. There is no prediction which is not thus related to subjunctive and counterfactual conditionals. And furthermore, there is another family of counterfactuals licensed by any subjunctive conditional which licenses a prediction, for if I am able to say ' If any emerald were examined at t it would be found to be grue ' then I am also able to say ' If this only were an emerald it would be found to be grue at t '.

It is very obvious that the definition of ' grue ', in its disjunctive form, does not permit any of these conditionals, because there is no guarantee that the it referred to in the two disjuncts is the same it; and in the conjunctive form the reference to *other* things makes it perfectly explicit that the same x's are not being referred to. No matter how much evidence were collected, therefore, no predictions would be licensed in accordance with the definition of ' grue ', not even incompatible ones.

Proprietors of formulae seldom sanction tinkerings. Nevertheless, I intend to tinker a little with the conjunctive formulation, enough to open the door to the recalcitrant conditionals. When the definitions are thus made relevant to the problem of induction it will become apparent that they cease to be strictly symmetrical, and further that Hempel's First Paradox, complete with heterogeneous couplings, is astonishingly to the point. The alteration I propose to make is just a teeny-weeny one: I am going to replace *other things* in the second conjunct by *things examined at or after t*, so that the predicate ' grue ' now applies to all things examined before t just in case they are green and to things examined at or after t just in case they are blue. Conjunctive force is hereby restored to the conjunctive formulation, for the conjuncts are no longer completely irrelevant to each other. It is no longer the case that the conjunction is true just in case one of its conjuncts is true, which was an odd kind of conjunction anyhow.

With this alteration Mr. Grue may happen the day after t to consult his calendar and remark that emeralds are *still* grue, just as under different circumstances Mr. Green may consult his calendar and remark that emeralds are *still* green. What is odd about ' grue ' is not simply that it encases a date, because any apparently purely qualitative predicate is co-extensive with another encasing a date. For example, let us introduce the predicate ' greten ' which applies to all things examined before t just in case they are green and to all things examined at or after t just in case they are green. Once again Goodman can say, if he likes, ' I simply do not know how to tell if a predicate is qualitative or positional. . . .' Lack of symmetry in Goodman's argument arises not because ' grue ' as an English word contains a temporal reference, but rather because of the kind of temporal reference which ' grue ' contains.

Surely Mr. Grue would have to admit that at t all of those things which are still grue will have undergone a change. If he were to dispute the fact it could be proved to him, because at t the change will be measurable. Prior to t grue things emit light-waves of certain wave-lengths, whereas thereafter they will emit light-waves of quite a different range. Now it is perfectly true that Goodman might play a game of grue with our descriptions of the light-waves. He might take our numerical descriptions of units of measurement and insist, for example, that x measures ' thrive ' thousand angströms at time n just in case it measures three thousand angströms and n is prior to t or five thousand and n is not prior to t. He might even play a game of grue with what is to count as a unit of measurement. But somewhere or other there has to be an end to this kind of thing, and I suggest that the end is right there, with the notion of length itself. If the definitions were symmetrical, then perhaps the game could be extended indefinitely with regard to determinants, but there must be some agreement upon determinables in order for the game to proceed at all.

Even if Mr. Grue had no interest in angströms, and could offer no scientific account of what had happened, he would surely *know* after t that there had been a change among those things that were *still* grue, and that t marked an important date in the history of his people, the Day of the Shifting of Colours.

' Grue,' then, has an odd claim to distinction, for it is a predicate which encases a date that marks a change: but what kind of change does grue mark? One will not be able to observe the process of a green thing becoming grue on the Day of the Shifting of Colours. It will be the kind of thing that is all over in a flash, a moment so short that no one will be able to observe the change in process. This assumption is necessary, because by definition there can be no moment at which there is any doubt concerning the colour of the thing in question. Could it be a moment without duration, a change without process, so that the impossibility of observing it is not physical, but logical? But I submit that a change without process is as eerie as a process without change.

Since Heisenberg we have become familiar with the claim that there might be a change without process, but even when familiar with the theory we still have qualms about the change in question. The hunch is well founded, for after the quantum jump we lack criteria of identity for establishing that the new arrival is the same old electron previously tracked. Perhaps it *is* new: we simply do not know, nor can we know. Nor is it important for theories of quanta that we should know: a one-to-one correlation is sufficient. In contrast I am in no doubt that although you have changed since I last saw you, you are the same philosopher with whom I previously battled. Yours is not a change without process, and the all-important criteria of identity are not lacking. Whenever something undergoes a discernible change, it can be said that had *it* been examined at an earlier stage, *it* would have been found to be different. This counterfactual, we have seen, is not permitted by the original definition. Unless altered in the manner recommended, Mr. Grue surveying his emeralds at or after *t* is in the same boat as a quantam physicist scruting his quanta.

This throws doubt upon whether Mr. Grue, surveying emeralds at *t*, would be in a position to admit that there had been a change, for *what* would have changed? Professor Goodman is confronting us with a problem concerning the identity of the things about which we make predictions, and not merely with a problem of identifying predicates. For he says, ' It is clear that if we simply choose an appropriate predicate, then on the basis of these same observations we shall have equal confirmation, by our definition, for any prediction whatever about other emeralds—or indeed about anything else '.[1] ' For instance,' he says in a footnote appended to this sentence, ' we shall have equal confirmation by our present definition for the prediction that roses subsequently examined will be blue. Let " emerose " apply just to emeralds examined before time *t*, and to roses examined later. Then all emeroses so far examined are grue, and this confirms the

[1] *Ibid.*

hypothesis that all emeroses are grue and hence the prediction that roses subsequently examined will be grue. The problem raised by such antecedents has been little noticed, but is no easier to meet than that raised by similarly perverse consequents.'[1] We might well raise our eyebrows at the manner in which the distinction between a thing and its qualities is being smudged. But this is not peculiar to the new Riddle of Induction: it characerizes a logical tradition subscribed to by Goodman, with roots in Russell's Theory of Descriptions. What is important is that although Goodman appreciates that his Riddle carries over from the identification of predicates to the identity of things, he appears not to see that for this precise reason his definition, as originally given, has nothing to do with predicting. His remarks at least suggest, however, that the logical outcome of the argument that Mr. Grue's definitions of both things and qualities are symmetrical with Mr. Green's is that there is no guarantee that one's language is not entirely private, since in anybody's language time t may be any moment whatsoever.

Mr. Grue will obviously want to ' go public '. I can conceive of no attempt he might make to escape from his solitude which would not lead him to reinstate the adverb ' still ' along with the recalcitrant conditionals. Two alternatives are open to Goodman. Either he must prohibit such adverbs as ' still ' from associating with perverse predicates, thereby sentencing Mr. Grue (along with the rest of us) to solitary confinement, or he must grant permission to such adverbs to associate freely and thereby try to keep ' grue ' and ' green ' side by side in the social register. The latter attempt is foredoomed from the beginning. It is impossible to admit the possibility of things *still* grue at t without admitting that they will then have undergone a change. This has the consequence that Mr. Grue's colour-words are not in fact symmetrical with Mr. Green's. That there had been a change of the kind in question would be something inferred after the event. This particular change has been built into the meaning of ' grue '.

Let us look at the definitions in the light of the Day of the Shifting of Colours and observe the asymmetry. Whenever the time t is linked with a change of the kind in question, that fact will be marked by an asterisk. Mr. Green applies ' grue ' to all things examined before t^* just in case they are grue, but to other things examined at or after t^* just in case they are green. In

[1] *Ibid.*, pp. 85–86.

contrast, Mr. Grue applies ' green ' to all things examined before t just in case they are grue but to things examined at or after t just in case they are bleen. The t which enters into Mr. Grue's defini- tion of ' green ' does not mark a change of the kind in question, because green things do not change at time t; but nevertheless time t must in this instance be made to coincide with t^*, because time t^* enters into Mr. Grue's definitions of ' grue ' and ' bleen ' which are used, as above, in his definition of ' green '. Mr. Grue applies ' grue ' to all things examined before t^* just in case they are grue but to things examined at or after t^* just in case they are grue. Compare this to Mr. Green's ' green ', which is indefinable. This lack of symmetry is systematic, in a manner which enables Mr. Green to make some distinctions not available to Mr. Grue. Let us coin two words encasing a date which just happens to coincide with the Day of the Shifting of Colours. They are ' greten ' and ' grute '. For Mr. Green, ' greten ' applies to all things examined prior to t just in case they are green but to things examined at or after t just in case they are green. It is clear that Mr. Green can draw a distinction between ' greten ' and ' green '. But this distinction is not available to Mr. Grue, for in both cases he applies the word to all things examined prior to t just in case they are grue but to other things examined at or after t just in case they are bleen. And furthermore, as we have seen, the ominous asterisk reappears in the definitions of ' grue ' and ' bleen '. In contrast, both gentlemen can distinguish 'grute' from 'grue', it being the case that ' grute ' encases two dates which just happen to coincide. We might tabulate the initial distinctions as follows:[1]

1. *Mr. Green's ' grue ':* ' x is grue at n '. $\equiv$. (x is green at $n \equiv n > t^*$) $\underset{.}{\vee}$ (x is blue at $n \equiv n \leqslant t^*$)

2. *Mr. Grue's ' green ':* ' x is green at n '. $\equiv$. (x is grue at $n \equiv n > t$) $\underset{.}{\vee}$ (x is bleen at $n \equiv n \leqslant t$)

3. *Mr. Grue's ' grue ':* ' x is grue at n '. $\equiv$. (x is grue at $n \equiv n > t^*$) $\underset{.}{\vee}$ (x is grue at $n \equiv n \leqslant t^*$)

4. *Mr. Green's ' green ':* Indefinable.

5. *Mr. Green's 'greten':* ' x is greten at n '. $\equiv$. (x is green at $n \equiv n > t$) $\underset{.}{\vee}$ (x is green at $n \equiv n \leqslant t$)

6. *Mr. Grue's 'greten ':* ' x is greten at n '. $\equiv$. (x is grue at $n \equiv n > t$) $\underset{.}{\vee}$ (x is bleen at $n \equiv n \leqslant t$)

[1] In these definitions ' > ' means ' before ', and ' $\leqslant$ ' means ' at or after '. ' $\underset{.}{\vee}$ ' is the the non-exclusive disjunction placed over the conjunctive sign to dramatize the dilemma, discussed above, concerning whether Goodman's definitions are disjunctive or conjunctive.

It will be observed that 1 is not symmetrical with 2. Nor, for a different reason, is 3 symmetrical with 4. Because Mr. Grue makes no distinction at all between 2 and 6, one might expect 3, if not symmetrical with 4, to be symmetrical with 5. In fact it is Mr. Grue's ' grute ' which appears to match 5—until we remember that ' grute ' is parasitic upon ' grue '.

Any predicate which has built into it the notion of a change is of a very different kind from one which has not been so contrived. I share Goodman's qualms in admitting as temporal *any* predicate which encases a date, for no matter what date ' greten ' encases, Mr. Green will not fall into error on that account. ' Greten ' is co-existent with his ' green ', but the line of succession does not pass through such a word, because there is no reason for entrenching it in preference to its cousin of purer stock. On the other hand, I have no hesitation at all in admitting as temporal a predicate like ' grue ' which encases a date that marks a change. It is precisely on this account that Mr. Grue's definitions are not symmetrical with Mr. Green's, for in Mr. Grue's tongue the date encased in his definition of ' green ' marks the change associated with his ' grue ', whereas in Mr. Green's tongue the change associated with ' grue ' does not in the least infect his ' green '. Nor does it infect his ' greten ', which may perchance mention precisely the same date without marking the associated change. This absence of symmetry between the two languages arises from the fact that knowing what it is like for there to have been such a change is a built-in feature of Mr. Grue's colour-words, whereas Mr. Green's language is free from such architecture, except when he is trying to cope with Mr. Grue.

The Riddle of Goodman therefore rests on a mistake, but so far I have pointed to the mistake without tracing it to its source. To claim that all emeralds are green is to advance a single hypothesis. Such inductive support as it has involves an inference of classical type, from observed members of a class to other members of the same class. The case is very different with the claim that all emeralds are grue, for this claim couples two hypotheses, not one. The first, that all emeralds prior to *t* are green, shares in all the inductive support that is forthcoming for all emeralds being green. The second, that at time *t* some things, including all emeralds, will change from green to blue, has only indirect inductive support. If there were no change at all in the world, this hypothesis would have no support whatsoever. Because there is change in the world, it has some indirect support. But it has no direct inductive support: there is no evidence that the predicated change will occur at t. Thus if my tinkering with ' grue ' in order to make it relevant to induction be approved, Goodman's New Riddle becomes a species of Hempel's First Paradox, for what we now have in the assertion that all emeralds are grue are two statements —let us call them S_1 and S_2. It will be noted that $S_1.S_2$ is a heterogeneous coupling. The attempt to transfer inductive support from 'All emeralds are green ' to 'All emeralds are grue' was ill-conceived, for the latter hypothesis involves an inference from observed members of one class, the class of things green prior to t, to unobserved members of quite another class, the class of things that are blue and not prior to t. This inference can be made good only by producing direct inductive support for the concealed hypothesis, that at t some things, including all emeralds, will change from green to blue. Without such support, there is no assurance that ' grue ' is a class-concept at all. In passing over the concealed hypothesis a fundamental principle has been dishonoured: that all strictly inductive inferences[1] proceed from observed members of a class to at least one other member of the same class. Doubtless Goodman would maintain that his purpose in presenting the New Riddle was to draw attention to vagaries concerning the notion of a class-concept. But there are enough problems surrounding the notion of class without our imagining that perverse predicates like ' grue ' pose more[2].

[1] It remains a moot point whether the class of strictly inductive inferences has members.

[2] Professor Hilary Putnam has objected that in fact Mr. Grue's definitions are symmetrical with Mr. Green's provided that an ' adequate ' distinction is made between a formal language containing such definitions and matters of fact. Since a formal language, it is alleged, conveys no information about the world, the distinction between t and t^* cannot be made, and therefore asymmetry cannot be established on its basis.

But what is the status of t in the definition of ' grue '? If the definition is relevant to the problem of induction, t must be such that it can be given a value (say, January 1, 2000 A.D.). But 'January 1, 2000 A.D.' contains not a little information about the world, as is inevitable since any dating system contains reference to some arbitrarily chosen historical event. If ' January 1, 2000 A.D. ' can be substituted for t, then by what fiat am I prevented from mentioning any other day identifiable by reference to an historical event (such as ' the Day of the Shifting of Colours ')?